What College Students Think

by

ROSE K. GOLDSEN
Cornell University

MORRIS ROSENBERG
National Institute of Mental Health

ROBIN M. WILLIAMS, JR.
Cornell University

EDWARD A. SUCHMAN
New York City Department of Health

D. VAN NOSTRAND COMPANY, INC.

PRINCETON, NEW JERSEY

TORONTO   LONDON

NEW YORK

D. VAN NOSTRAND COMPANY, INC.
120 Alexander St., Princeton, New Jersey (*Principal office*)
24 West 40 St., New York 18, New York

D. VAN NOSTRAND COMPANY, LTD.
358, Kensington High Street, London, W.14, England

D. VAN NOSTRAND COMPANY (Canada), LTD.
25 Hollinger Road, Toronto 16, Canada

First Published April 1960
Reprinted May 1960

Foreword

IT HAS ALWAYS been fascinating to try to visualize how people in other countries, at other times, or from different social groups have felt and looked at the world. Books on the "spirit of the Renaissance" or "patterns of culture," or "Middletown," which do this for us, have become classics just because they have served this end. Most western languages have developed special terms for the phenomenon that such works try to capture. The French talk of mentality and the Germans of world image; in this country the words "value system" convey the same idea. Writers who try to capture the spirit of a social group in this sense rely on many sources: literary and artistic products, private letters, reports of travelers on customs and institutions. All these are drawn upon. Craftsmen from many fields make their contributions: historians, anthropologists, novelists, and others.

In recent years a new skill has been developed which adds substance to our knowledge of various sectors of the social systems. It is the interpretation of quantitative social research. Obviously, the systematic collections of interviews and observations—the tools of the discipline—cannot be extended into the past. At the moment, therefore, its main contribution is to tell us about the ways of thought of specific groups here and abroad. In the long run, however, this newcomer will bring about a rather revolutionary change in at least two respects. The future historian will not be dependent on materials that have just accidentally survived; we can now better select what is likely to be relevant information.

iii

And, in addition, we can lay the groundwork for a much more detailed and differentiated analysis. There was undoubtedly not just one medieval mind. Social strata probably differed in their outlooks much more then than they do today, yet we are restricted in our knowledge to a very small slice of medieval society. As a matter of fact, we need not go that far back to make this point. When, fifty years after the French Revolution, Tocqueville described the pre-revolutionary society, he stated that nothing could really be said about the peasants because there were no traces of their way of life and their political outlook. Contemporary social research guarantees that such obliteration will not occur again.

The present book is an outstanding example of this new intellectual development. It describes the "mental world" of American college students and the reader should take it up with two goals in mind—for the sake of the findings and to get acquainted with this rather new way of understanding our contemporary scene. The purpose of this introduction is mainly to help in the appreciation of such analysis.

Some of the results reported here are surprising. When American students think about their future jobs they are not nearly as concerned with economic security as is generally assumed. In view of the fact that most of the interviews in this study were done at rather sophisticated colleges, the number of respondents who profess traditional religious beliefs may also come as a surprise to some. Going beyond such straightforward accounts, some simple comparisons open unexpected vistas. Students who belong to fraternities engage a great deal in conventional dating activities patterned around dances, parties, and maybe some drinking. But they really would like to know their partners better, engage in serious talk, or participate more in the cultural life of their communities. Mutual social pressure deteriorates their leisure time activities below their own level of aspiration. Inversely the lack of social controls shows in the larger colleges where cheating at examinations is more prevalent.

The reader's interest in many of the results will depend upon how well he is acquainted with and how much concerned with the various problem areas investigated; for the student of politics the data on sex attitudes might be more unexpected. The vocational counselor will find the details on occupational values practically useful. He may be interested to find that students in the Ivy league colleges are less interested in vocational training than are the students in other schools. The list of contents should be used as a guide for emphasis. But let no one say *after* he has read table and text that he knew it all before. This is a well known fallacy which can easily be checked by the following example. In Chapter 8 the authors discuss the students' quest for certainty and one of their questionnaire items asks whether it is important to know one's plans for the future in advance. How is this related to the students' religiousness? They might be religious because they have a fear of uncertainties, so a positive correlation might be expected. But it could also be that religion gives one a feeling of safety and so reduces anxiety regarding the future. Both outcomes would be plausible, but only one could be the more prevailing one. Table 8-7 shows that the desire for a clearly outlined future is markedly more frequent among religious students.

One other do-it-yourself exercise can be suggested. Many tables —some of them in the appendix—tell how the students in eleven different colleges responded to the questions asked. The reader might pick a college that he thinks he knows well and collate from all the tables its specific profile. He will be pleased to see some of his impressions reflected in some of the figures, and that will give him confidence in other more unexpected findings. Those who choose to do a profile of Harvard, Yale, or Cornell will probably be surprised to learn that the students think too much emphasis is put on athletics.

Not all of the findings are immediately understandable. Take as an example Table 4-1. The students were asked how many dates they had and also at what age they intended to get married. There is a high correlation between those two pieces of information to the effect that those who have many dates intend to get married much earlier. But what is the mechanism behind these findings? Is it that the students who want to get married early date a lot of partners in order to reach their goal better? Or is it that dating success with the other sex makes one optimistic about his marital future? Or is it some basic need that accounts for both the frequency of dating and the plan for an early marriage? The information the authors have collected doesn't provide a full explanation of this unexpected result, yet the very questions which are raised are of importance and will undoubtedly form the starting point for subsequent studies more specifically designed to provide the interpretation.

How does such an interpretation proceed? Before pointing to a few examples, a general observation should be made. We are properly proud of the high literacy in this country. But does it keep pace with what is really needed? The country has become so large and modern life so complex that many things can only be grasped in statistical terms. In certain areas that has become accepted. We no longer talk just about bad times. We have learned to watch the cost-of-living index. But in matters of personal relations and beliefs we still are resistant to accept and understand the language of quantification. And yet how can we trace the effect of family background on students' beliefs or discover the characteristic attitudes of career-minded girls without using more subtle forms of tabulations and without introducing indices by which to distinguish types of students.

Take as a simple example the role of fraternities which is examined in Chapter 3. More fraternity members, as compared with the independent students, engage in extracurricular activities and claim that they are having a good time. But such things cost money and fraternity students come from more well to do family backgrounds. How do we separate the role of this background from that of the fraternity itself? The reader is earnestly urged to look at Table 3-3, and make sure that he sees all the implications. By comparing two columns, line by line, he can compare the activities of fraternity students and those of their independent peers on the same income level. By looking down the two columns he can see how strong the influence of family income is in both groups. In many cases, by comparing the trends in the two groups, he can see that the fraternities tend to equalize the style of life among their members; money makes a somewhat smaller difference among them. Just for the record let us add that fraternity students also have a less good scholastic record.

Statistical literacy even among well educated people is not yet well developed. So long as our high school curriculum does not train younger people in this new language, so long as our discussion magazines make it a point of honor for the essayist to avoid facts and figures, we cannot expect that one book will make much of a difference. But I attach special hope to this one book. The interpretations are so skillful and the language so clear that it might by these virtues recruit some converts to the language of social research.

Let us look at still another aspect of this problem—the use of indices combining a multiplicity of information into one concept. Take as a typical example what the authors call the faith-in-human-nature-index. Each student was asked questions such as these: Can people be trusted? Are people likely to come to each other's help in an emergency? and so on. (For details see Appendix 17.) No single item of this kind would be very revealing. But taking a number of them as indicators the respondents can be classified according to the frequency with which their answers express a fundamental belief in the possibility of personal decency and cooperation. This attitude shows a surprising number of relations to other topics. Students who have little faith in human nature are much more convinced that war is inevitable. They support federal restrictive legislation against deviant opinions and thus violate a basic tenet of American political tradition. And they have little confidence in the efficacy of the individual citizen's participation in the political life of the country. Here the idea of trust put into quantitative form accounts for a large number of broad attitudes on public affairs.

Another index which plays a similar central role is a measure of the students' religiousness, covering their beliefs as well as their actual practices (p. 159). Such a classification does not, of course, reflect all the nuances of one's religious experiences. And yet it is useful as a means of helping to document the important fact that more religious students are more inclined to restrict the freedom of others' opinion. This correlation between religiousness and intolerance becomes understandable in Chapter 8 where faith in human nature and the quest for certainty are drawn upon for clarification. This intricate piece of analysis is probably the most important and instructive sequence in the book and will surely lead to many a discussion and reinterpretation.

Enough has been said to locate the present publication in the contemporary intellectual scene. What remains is to comment briefly on the position taken by writers who have expressed views greatly opposed to those which I share with the authors of this book.

Two distinguished scholars have recently made themselves spokesmen against empirical social research. One is Pitirim A. Sorokin, who was himself a pioneer in the use of quantitative procedures in sociology. When, in his writings of a quarter-century ago, he characterized the prevailing temper of various cultural periods, he used counts of books, paintings, and buildings as evidence. He now objects that we often count the verbal responses of people, given in the course of interviews or of observed conversations.* He feels we are "in the blind alley of hearsay stuff" (p. 297). But isn't it rather that a book like the present one adds new types of material to what was available before? One need only imagine that some questionnaires would be found buried in a cave under an 8th century Arab University to sense how this would have enriched many a Sorokin book. He seems to feel that what people say is uninteresting, that only what they do matters. Yet in his book on *Fads and Foibles in Modern Sociology* he is continuously interested in opinions expressed by others. Of course, words and acts sometimes diverge. But such discrepancies happen more rarely than he implies and are themselves of very great interest. In our urbanized and democratic society, words and expressed opinions become ever more important.

Sorokin is especially worried about "quantophrenia," the use of quantitative methods such as those used by my colleagues here. Now the reader will notice how carefully they weigh their evidence and how often they check various results against each other. Such conservatism is a matter of course in the research fraternity. And yet Sorokin—using intelligence tests as an example—inveighs

---

* *Fads and Foibles in Modern Sociology* (Chicago: Henry Regrery Co., 1956).

against the "conceited belief in infallibility" which he imputes to the empirically-minded sociologist. I don't know where he found this conceit, but I do know where he finds the evidence that tests are not infallible. He takes it from numerous papers written by the psychometricians themselves in which they point out the shortcomings of their methods and report their efforts to improve them. Sorokin reviews this literature in two sections devoted to "inductive deflation of tests" (p. 70 and pp. 91 ff), without noticing that he thus defeats his own argument on the blindness of the technicians.

Probably Sorokin's extreme criticism results from impatience with the slow progress of a field to which he contributed so much. But what of another adversary—the historian, Jacques Barzun? Can his attitude be the consequence of concern over what an eminent literary critic has described as the effective sociological analysis of problems that were once reserved for the novel and the humanities. Barzun has written a book on some contemporary cultural problems.* I strongly agree with much of what he says, and I can testify that he backs up with wise action his ideas about education and other matters of the mind. But when he talks about what he amusingly calls the "misbehavioral sciences," his usual incisiveness is missing. He too comments on the use of tests; here is one of his remarks: (p. 139)

> No other practice explains as fully the intellectual defects of our students up to and through graduate school than their ingrained association of knowledge and thoughts with the scratching down of checkmarks on dotted lines.

I don't want to debate here with an educational leader of Barzun's eminence the merits of various educational practices. But as a historian he well knows how difficult it is to trace the causes of a complex condition in society. A most exacting investigation would be required to attribute so great a role to the use of certain kinds of tests. If Barzun were to undertake to explain why German-English relations deteriorated before the first World War, he would with his usual skill work through the full range of a

---

* *The House of Intellect* (New York: Harper Bros., 1959).

responsible inquiry. But because he does not like quantitative
tests he makes up his mind without such investigation. It might be
suggested that the careless use of historical explanations is another serious defect in American education that has to be rem-
edied by injecting a good dose of the methodological precautions
of social scientists. Perhaps the study of books such as this one
will provide some of the intellectual discipline which the latin
grammar was supposed to give in the old days.

The gap between the two worlds occasionally becomes quite
distressing. Barzun disapproves of "pseudoscientific language in
the psychosocial sciences" and quotes as an example the title of a
paper, "Hostile Drive, Conflict, and the Recall of Hostile Material." The psychologist will easily recognize the intellectual tradition from which this paper comes; he might even guess the design
of the study. (He cannot do more because the historian does not
give the source for this special piece of evidence.) But what matters
here is a lengthy footnote by Barzun (p. 228). He first points out
that hostile drives can be of different kinds—sudden, or brooded
over, and so on. He ends with these words:

> And how is hostile drive measured—by intensity or by effect,
> both necessarily expressed in words and defying the touch of
> number.

Now a historian cannot be expected to know the extensive literature on measurement in general and on the measurement of drives
in particular. But the quoted sentence in itself can be taken in
only one way. It is an introspective statement to the effect that
Barzun's personal definition of "drive" does not jibe with what he
feels when he uses the metaphor "touch of number." The readers
of this book will encounter careful efforts to put the touch of
numbers to such "intangibles" as alienation, career orientation,
and other notions mentioned before. The terms are of course only
tags directing attention to the purpose for which indicators were
selected and combined into indices. What needs to be judged are
the ensuing classifications, the way they enter into findings and
the interpretation to which they lead. If this publication gives the
general reader a better understanding of the merits and limita-

tions of such procedures, it will bring fresh air into the house of intellect.

For the sake of completeness I have to mention one more recent critic who seems to promote a kind of sophisticated commercialism. C. Wright Mills has objected to detailed studies of specific problems as exemplified by this book. His starting point is the fact that modern man is troubled.* Someone must give the answers to all the problems we face. The sociologist is the one who should do it, with the help of a distinct quality, sociological imagination, "that journalists and scholars, artists and publics, scientists and editors are coming to expect" (p. 5). But, alas, today's sociologists are "failing to meet the cultural expectations, that are coming to be demanded of them" (p. 14). We sociologists would all like to have and to satisfy such a distinguished clientele. (Incidentally, one cannot "demand expectations"; presumably, expectations are held and answers are demanded.) But how to do it? Unfortunately, Mills does not give very definite advice. He asks that sociologists have concern for the "human variety" and he is confident that "when we understand social structures and structural changes as they bear upon more intimate scenes and experiences, we are able to understand the causes of individual conduct and feelings . . ." (p. 162). Kings who have wanted the philosopher's stone or immediate cures for currently incurable diseases have usually advanced charlatanism not knowledge.

What is needed is sober and competent inquiry into particular problems of importance. *What College Students Think* is a fine example of such an effort.

PAUL F. LAZARSFELD

New York, N. Y.
February, 1960

---

* *The Sociological Imagination* (New York: Oxford University Press, 1959).

Preface

THE PRESENT VOLUME reports some of the more general findings
of a research program conducted by the Cornell Values Study.*
This research has relied heavily on the cooperation, support, and
good will of many persons and groups. We are glad to have the
opportunity to acknowledge here our indebtedness to them.

The Carnegie Corporation of New York provided most of the
funds for the research. Mr. John Gardner, of the Corporation,
was particularly helpful in the early stages of planning the study.

A group of social scientists from the Cornell faculty participated
in a seminar which examined some of the knotty theoretical and
philosophical problems in the methodology of studies in the sociology of knowledge and research on values. These meetings were in-
valuable for research planning. Participants in the seminar were:
Urie Bronfrenbrenner, Stuart Brown, Leonard S. Cottrell, Mario
Einaudi, Alexander Leighton, Robert MacLeod, Morris Opler,
Edwin Reubens, Gregory Vlastos, and Asahel Woodruff.

Colleagues who aided in administering the questionnaire at the
participating universities were S. F. Camilleri, Dwight Chapman,
Walter Crockett, Donald N. Elliott, Albert H. Hastorf, Wayne
Holtzman, David C. McClelland, Daniel O. Price, William S.
Robinson, Peter Rossi, Fred L. Strodtbeck, Preston Valien, and
Martha Williamson.

Much of the job of processing the data and aiding in compiling
the statistical materials was handled in successive stages by Jessie

---

* Other publications and research reports of the project are listed in Appendix 24.

L. Cohen, Suzanne Guimaraes, Sonya Yuspeh, and Montserrat Zayas. Their effort was beyond the call of duty, their contribution inestimable.

And finally, the students: captive audience in the classroom, subjects and respondents in the laboratory and in the field, we wish to register our thanks to them. Particular acknowledgments are due to the many who helped us with the leg work and acted as resource persons in the earlier stages of the research. We have space to mention only some of them by name: Roger Baldwin, Jr., Allan Danzig, James Gibbs, Harley Frank, Roger Kallen, Gerald Klerman, Pauline Mahar, John Marcham, Norman Pava, Charles Perry, Roger Peranio, Nicholas Wood. To the many more who are unnamed, and to all our anonymous respondents we are none the less grateful.

From its inception in 1950, the study has been under the joint direction of Robin M. Williams, Jr., Edward A. Suchman and Rose K. Goldsen. Morris Rosenberg joined the group in 1951.

We hope that the present volume will convey a feeling for the climate of opinion characteristic of some important American college campuses in the fifties, and of its significance. Yet we are keenly aware that the usefulness of this sort of research lies as much in the kinds of questions it raises as in the partial answers it provides. We need sharper concept formation, keener measures and, above all, continuing studies through time of many more campuses and of widely differing populations. It is our wish that the research we report here will stimulate such efforts in the social sciences and in education.

Rose K. Goldsen

Ithaca, New York
February, 1960

Contents

List of Tables

Introduction

THIS BOOK REPORTS what college students have told us about the way they see the world they live in, what they want out of it, and why. We wish to convey to you the flavor of what they said: how they live, what they think of some of our major social institutions, their beliefs about love and work, war and peace.

How the Story Develops

Because they are college students, we begin by analyzing their ideas on the aims of higher education. What kind of education do they think they want? What aspects of their university training do they consider deserving of their kudos or their criticisms? How do their ideas on these subjects change as they pass through school? Why do some students seem to value broad academic educational aims while others stress the vocational training or the social skills they think the colleges ought to provide? Why do certain subgroups on the campus seem to be successfully insulated against change?

Next we examine the kinds of careers the students choose, analyzing some of the motivations behind these choices, and discussing what they have told us about the meaning they expect their work to have for them. We show some of the rewards and satisfactions they anticipate from their occupational lives. We explain the kinds of images each profession calls up in their minds and illustrate how, in choosing a field, they try to strike a balance between their own estimates of their interests, values, and capabilities, and the demands and rewards they feel each kind of career might entail. We speculate about some of the implications their approach to work may have for the level of professionalization in the different occupations. The first part of Chapter 2 tells about the men; the second part about the women. The perennial problem of the working wife and mother, particularly important to college-trained women, is touched upon here.

In Chapters 3 and 4 we break the pace to give you a glimpse at some of the principal aspects of social organization on the campuses. For the college student's significant world centers as much about fraternity life and extra-curricular activities, drinking, dating, and "having a good time," as it does about getting an academic education and preparing for a career.

Chapter 3 discusses the function of fraternities in the campus social structure, and shows how they set the pace for a distinctive style of life on many of our campuses. *Men and Women* is the title of Chapter 4, and it reports what the students told us about dating and love, marriage and the family. What are the characteristics of "an ideal mate?" How many children make up an ideal family? What about sex-relations?

The second section of the book looks at somewhat broader problems: broader in the sense that the issues analyzed in these chapters are urgent for most of us, on or off the campus, and regardless of our age. Chapters 5 and 6 analyze what the students say they believe about some important issues of national politics, economic philosophy, democratic government, war and peace.

Chapter 5 tells about political apathy and economic conservatism. Few students become deeply moved by anything political, or develop strong enough feelings about political occurrences to "get worked up" over them. They are in no way rebellious; they are for the most part conservative—a mood which became reinforced during the period covered by this research, and particularly reinforced for those participating in special social subsystems such as the fraternity. Yet we find their conservatism to be a rather differentiated brand; for, characteristic of many students, conservative or otherwise, is a certain readiness to acknowledge the legitimacy of humanitarian and welfare measures usually associated with liberalism.

Chapter 6 indicates that American college students declare their allegiance to traditional democratic rights. Their testimony on the kinds of rights they feel an ideal democracy would grant its citizens indicates this. Yet, the analysis finds a certain gap between some of the ideals they express and some of the political attitudes they report at the same time. These attitudes are traced back to their philosophical roots in fundamental assumptions about the nature of human nature, as the students see it.

Such assumptions are engaged, too, in their approaches to ways to prevent war, which are also analyzed in Chapter VI. The students support measures which range from the highly idealistic to the highly forceful; but those who are cynical about human nature tend to support the forceful measures, while those who are more optimistic about mankind look to the idealistic.

When we trace the way these opinions develop and change, it is evident that the dominant mood is disenchantment. The students we studied became disillusioned with *all* measures for preventing war, except two: strong leadership, and "understanding on the part of every citizen for all peoples at home and abroad."

Chapters 7 and 8 analyze what the students told us about some of the elements of their religious and ethical beliefs. They are, they say, virtually all believers. Yet we find no support for any contention that the campuses are seeing a revival of religion. On the contrary, we find a relative absence of commitment and identification with religion. In religion, as in politics, the students "play it cool." The content of their beliefs is decidedly away from orthodoxy; as we analyze their testimony, it would appear that individualistic and relativistic approaches to religion are characteristic. Most students are agreed on the importance of religious values which appear to represent some least common denominator of personal religious and ethical belief. Yet when we trace some of the links between religious belief and social attitudes, we find certain patterns of thought which suggest that religious belief, for many students, seems to be engaged in the service of their psychological quest for certainty—a quest which is also linked to rigidities and intolerances in secular matters.

We say a great deal in this book about the "values" of the students, and it is necessary to explain what we mean by that term. Sometimes we mean a goal or an end; then we report what they say they are striving for, what they consider ideal. Sometimes we mean an evaluation, a judgment; then we report what the students say they consider important or unimportant, good or bad, desirable or undesirable, worthy or unworthy. Sometimes we mean their underlying assumptions about human relations; and sometimes we mean their ideology.

There is method in this apparent eclecticism; for we consider "value" in at least two senses. In the first sense, we view a value as that which is considered desirable, satisfying, good, or worthy—in short, the thing which is valued. It is in this sense, perhaps, that values can be most easily observed and measured.

In the second sense, we consider "value" to be not the referent, but the standard by which an object is determined to be desirable, good, or worthy. It is in this latter sense of the criteria which justify or legitimize the desirable that values are perhaps more difficult to observe. They can often be only inferred in order to account for the links which are found to exist among numerous values-as-referents. They are often implicitly imbedded in stated assumptions, judgments, and ideologies.

This is, in fact, one of the main points of the final chapter. For in Chapter 9 we depart from the tables and the measures and the proofs and the definitions to engage in this sort of conceptual specification. In that chapter, too, we launch some speculations about what the implications of this analysis may mean for American society. We do this humbly, for we are well aware that the expertness lent us by this research ends with the college students and that they are *not* "American society." Yet we do it with a certain degree of assurance, too. For these young people, after all, make up one important segment of the country; and their values and beliefs are determined *by* American culture—and determining *for* it. We have, moreover, every reason to believe that the *patterns* of traits, beliefs, attitudes, and values which we trace here among college students, are likely to prevail as well among much wider sectors of American society.

Sampling and Level of Proof

This leads to a very important question which belongs with technical matters of sampling, but which we shall touch upon briefly here. Just what is the level of our proof? Just whom do the students in this study represent? Just how did we decide what questions were important to ask?

Our proofs are based mainly on statistical correlations; for the data we collected were gathered by means of questionnaires which the students read and filled out themselves. And figures are by far the simplest and most succinct way to summarize the distribution of opinion on the variety of subjects we covered, and for the many students who cooperated in the research. As important as the figures themselves, of course, is the range of topics and the kinds of choices which the questionnaire offered. It was developed only after we had conducted many long and intensive personal interviews with the students; only after our staff had spent many long months getting to know them, joining them in their everyday activities, participating in their clubs and organizations, visiting their rooms, apartments, dorms, fraternities and sororities, their coffee and coke rendezvous. And bars. The questionnaires, we believe, fix in a manner which allows statistical summary, the sorts of subjects which the students, themselves, had spontaneously brought up when they talked with us and with each other. That is why we feel that the questions we chose to ask give some idea of the issues which are salient in the college students' world. We must add, in all frankness, that they undoubtedly reveal a good deal about us, too, since these are the things that sprang to our notice, these are the things we cared to find answers to.

We said our aim is to convey "the flavor" of the students' world. We try to do this in a variety of ways. Sometimes we simply report the kinds of things students said to us in conversation or in informal interviews. Sometimes we present frequency distributions showing the consensus at each of the eleven universities that participated in the research. In this case we base our evidence on

randomly chosen cross-sections of the male students at each one—
a total of 4,585 cases.* Sometimes we try to approximate the flavor
of student opinion across the nation. In that case, we base our
estimates on the reports of 2,975 students—cases chosen from
among the total number interviewed in such a way that each participating university contributes only its fair share to make up a 6
per cent sample of all eleven student bodies.

This is certainly not a national sample. We expressly chose universities as far removed from each other geographically and socio-
logically as Cornell, California, and Wesleyan; Texas and Harvard; Yale and North Carolina; Dartmouth and Wayne; Fisk and
Michigan. And we selected these particular campuses precisely because they are an adequate selection of the most influential *types*
of universities in this country, not the most representative. Responses of this cross-section give some idea of the probable range
of college student opinion in important types of universities in
the nation. Thus, the distributions we report here constitute a
sort of bench mark against which equivalent distributions of
opinion on any other type of campus can be measured.

At all universities except our home campus, Cornell, we had
sampled only the men—a decision which was dictated simply by
technical reasons. But we did want to have the feminine point of
view which our own coeds were gracious enough to provide. When
we tell you how the men say they feel *about* women, or about
questions *involving* women, we usually rely on our national study.
But when we tell you what the women, themselves, said, we are
talking about the Cornell coeds.

Sometimes the development of opinion as the students go
through their college years is traced. This sort of change-analysis is
again based on the responses of Cornell students. When we first
got the idea for this research in 1950, we tried it out on a cross-
section of our own students. In 1952, when we branched out and
repeated the study across the nation, we selected for re-study as
juniors and seniors many of the same Cornellians who had participated in the earlier study as freshmen and sophomores. This is

---

* This is the total number of men. If the distribution includes the random sample
of Cornell women, the total number is 4,830. See below.

the group we call the "panel," and it is by comparing changes in their outlook between these two points in time that we can tell you something about how the students' ways of looking at things may have altered during these college years.

Certain of the detailed questions asked in the earlier pilot study were later dropped from the nationwide research. Some of the questions about love and marriage and family size, for example, were not repeated. A few of the more complicated questions on government and politics were also dropped. When more current information is simply not on record, our analysis returns to this earlier phase of the study.

A comment is in order here about the nature of our evidence. Even if all students who cooperated in this survey provided the information we requested with the best faith in the world, it is nevertheless true that many of the values, beliefs, opinions, and attitudes discussed in this book are complex, difficult to pin down, often based on elusive feelings which may not even be accessible to consciousness. The question so often asked of survey analysis— "But do they *really* say what they think?"—is based, in part, on awareness of this complexity.

This question is not relevant for the present analysis. We report what the students say they think and believe, and analyze its significance. This is public testimony, enabling us to sketch the profile the college students turn to the world, so to speak. That profile shows what values, beliefs, norms, and standards the students accept as legitimate. These declarations of legitimacy constitute an important set of social facts. They are an important social product and are at the same time analyzable as possible determinants and modifiers of future cultural trends. For they point to areas of the culture which are relatively resistant or relatively vulnerable to social change, and suggest the possible direction of such change.

We must add a final word about measurement. Often there exist no absolute limits to the kinds of concepts we discuss: sociability, religiousness, career-mindedness, liberalism, conservatism. Our figures do not measure the way a ruler does (against an absolute standard defined arbitrarily as an inch, a foot, a yard). They do not measure the way a batting average does (against an absolute standard of 1,000 times out of 1,000). Our figures give relative measures. They can tell only which students are "more so" and which turn out to be "less so." The limits of such measures are unknown, set by the particular phrasing of a question and the distribution of responses within this particular population. The reader of this book—indeed the reader of any report which summarizes statistically testimony about values, attitudes, states of mind—should steel himself against considering these measures as absolute. For there is an important difference between the precision with which one may interpret *the fact* that 3 per cent of the students said they were under 18 years old and the precision with which one may interpret *the fact* that 15 per cent scored in the highest position on a measure of something we call faith-in-human-nature. The limits of age in years may be defined, and the sense in which these students respond to the term, "age," varies but negligibly. But the limits of "high" or "low" faith in human nature cannot easily be stated; and the sense in which people might respond to any indicator of the concept undoubtedly varies considerably.*

Thus, validation of these relative measures lies principally in the internal consistency of the analysis itself. They may be considered valid to the extent that they lead to detection of patterns which make sociological sense. For, while it is perfectly true that any single individual may report a tangled multiplicity of beliefs, and may often assert opinions, attitudes, and values which seem contradictory or even diametrically opposed to each other, it is the scientist's article of faith that these tangles do not occur at random. His conceptual tools tell him where to seek the order in these tangles. His technical tools are suitable only insofar as they aid this search for order.

We express the regularities which we find in terms of the odds that conceptually related traits will cluster together. However, the long shots are always with us, reminding us that the human creature remains complex, whimsical, and often—happily—defiant of classification.

---

* See Appendix 17 which discusses the technique of scale-analysis, a device which reduces such response-variability.

1

The Students Look At College Education

TODAY AS NEVER BEFORE students are flocking to the college campuses. Classrooms are bulging, living facilities are severely taxed, qualified teaching personnel are in short supply, and the competition for college space is the keenest in history. A college degree is no longer the privilege of a limited elite; in the United States higher education is rapidly becoming mass education.

The widening base of who is being educated raises important questions about assumptions that underlie fundamental policies of higher education. We wish to examine some of these assumptions among the student population. What do college students, themselves, feel and think about the kind of educational fare they are entitled to? How do they react to what they are getting? The students, after all, are the material the colleges have to work with. How, then, do the students approach the college experience? What does it mean to them?

"THE COLLEGES ARE DOING A GOOD JOB"

For context we begin with something as general as the students' frame of mind. It is decidedly approving. College students feel that college education is important, useful, and of good calibre. Their morale is high. They *like* going to college. They say their colleges and universities are *doing a good job*. They say that what

1

they, themselves, are doing on the campuses is *worthwhile and important*. In fact, we found only three topics in our entire study on which students showed such close agreement: that love is important in marriage; that religious freedom is essential in a democracy; and that the opportunity to go to college is important and meaningful.

Almost every student in our samples said "having the opportunity to go to college is very important to me." The vast majority say that "the colleges are doing a good job"; that "most of what I am learning in college is very worthwhile." Most students say that their own university is adequately meeting their educational standards. They feel that college education equips them for life outside the campus. They deny that their colleges are behind the times. Indeed, as many as 37 per cent have no misgivings about agreeing to the extreme view that "America has the best system of college education in the world."

When we asked the students to evaluate the university's role in educating for values, quite apart from the communication of subject matter, again their reactions showed high approval. The vast majority deny that they have found college to be in any way a disillusioning experience; only a handful say they have lost respect for college education. Nor does any substantial percentage agree with the kinds of criticisms sometimes voiced—that American colleges and college teachers place insufficient emphasis on teaching religious values or American ideals and values.

It is not solely that the students approve of their college education in general; they express feelings of loyalty to their own campuses and many even tend to personify their schools. They do not see an impersonal institution with a strictly educational function. They see a group that has "its own personality, something over and above the individual members in it." Indeed, when we asked these students to check any of eight different groups which they felt had this quality, "your college" led the list. More than family, more than church or religion, more than nation, the students feel that their college possesses this special quality of *personality* rather than *impersonality*.

Yet their overwhelming approval and strong identification by no means precludes certain serious criticisms of specific aspects of university life. The most widespread criticisms, however, are directed *not* toward the nature of the educational experience itself, but rather toward certain administrative policies which suggest tendencies toward an impersonal mass-approach to education. Many of the students we polled said they felt that charges of "production-line teaching methods" are justified; that teachers are underpaid; that few or none of the professors take a personal interest in their students; that the colleges overemphasize athletics perhaps at the expense of academic interests.

The liberal or conservative atmosphere of the university is somewhat less likely to be a target for criticism. Yet it would distort the picture to gloss over the subgroups who criticize the colleges for racial or religious discrimination in admissions policy; who say that there is suppression of academic freedom, and that college teachers "are afraid to say what they really believe these days." (The distribution of opinion evaluating these aspects of the colleges and universities is shown in detail in Appendix 1. Ivy League colleges and the Northeastern men's colleges are least critical; the large Southern universities and Fisk seem to be more issue-conscious. But overall approval, campus to campus, is marked.)

The students' overwhelming approval of many aspects of college education then, does not indicate an unquestioning acceptance of anything and everything about college or university life. Their enthusiastic general evaluation does not prevent many of them from being critical of certain characteristics and practices that they say diminish the value of the educational experience and make the colleges fall short in certain important respects. Nor does it mean that their opinions can be viewed as competent evaluation of the sort of educational experience they are having. The point is that their morale is high, their spirit is good, their frame of mind is receptive. This is what is significant in the general agreement that "the colleges are doing a good job."

THE GOALS OF COLLEGE EDUCATION

"Doing a good job"—about what? What precisely are the tasks the university is expected to perform?

Most students feel that the university has not one job to do, but many, diverging principally in the relative emphasis they declare that each of these jobs deserves.

Well, first and foremost, you have to prepare yourself for your career, your specialty. You can't have a real career without college, that's the first thing they ask you. But you should learn more than just your own field. Education in general, culture. You have to learn about ideas. You have to learn to think critically. Not to accept things blindly. Another thing, when you come to college you meet many different kinds of people. One of the most important things is to learn how to get along with them.

I think it's important to broaden yourself culturally, to learn how to think. Of course it's important to prepare yourself for a job. But even an engineer has to write reports. And he should also know about citizenship and world problems. That's just as important as knowing how to build a bridge.

For me the most important thing about college is that I hope to prepare myself for marriage. I plan to marry as soon as I graduate. But I'll have to work, too, until my husband is settled, and I'll want to work after the children are old enough, so I definitely want to finish and get my degree. It will help me get a job, yes. But I think the things I learn here—not only in classes but also in hash sessions—will help me to do my main job which is to be a wife and mother.

Too many people seem to forget that in college you should be learning not only knowledge, but also how to live a full and meaningful life. There's more to life than your career. In college you should have an opportunity to clarify your ideas about morals and ethics, what you think is right and wrong. Important and unimportant in the "big" sense of the word.

Most of the students we talked to showed this tendency to list not one value of the college experience, but several, and to arrange them in a hierarchic order of importance. We tried to capture this multi-faceted approach in the questionnaire, which asked for the same sort of hierarchic ranking. Here is the question we asked.

College students have different ideas about the main purpose of a college education. Some of their ideas are listed below. As you read this list, consider what educational goals you think the IDEAL college or university OUGHT TO EMPHASIZE.

The students were then instructed to indicate whether they considered each goal to be of high, medium, or low importance, and to indicate the rank order of each "highly important" one. The distribution of responses made by cross-section of students across the nation is given in Table 1-1.

The most generally accepted opinion is that college ought to provide "a basic general education and appreciation of ideas." Since this approach to college education is intrinsic in academic educational tradition, we shall, for the sake of brevity, refer to this alternative as an indicator of an academic set of educational values. This approach is emphasized by a substantial majority of the students: 74 per cent rate it highly important.

The view that college ought to "develop your ability to get along with all kinds of people" focuses upon the importance of social and interpersonal skills. For this reason we refer to this alternative as an indicator of "interpersonal" educational values. The interpersonal emphasis in higher education appears to be about as widespread as the academic: 72 per cent said they considered it highly important.

The opinion that college ought to provide "vocational training . . . skills and techniques directly applicable to your career," stresses the value of college as a means to a given end. Again, for the sake of brevity, we refer to this alternative as an indicator of instrumental educational values, an approach which is considered highly important by 60 per cent of the students.

Student opinion seems to focus mainly on these three approaches to higher education. It is equally important, however, to observe that large proportions say that the other goals of college education are also weighty. Fifty per cent stress the university's role in training for citizenship; 45 per cent rate the moral functions of university training as highly important. There are the less popular goals of education, but they are still emphasized by many of the students. Only the family-training role of the university is likely to be rejected by considerable numbers.

The climate of opinion varies in certain characteristic ways, campus to campus. For example, students at the Eastern men's colleges with a relatively long tradition behind them (Harvard, Yale, Wesleyan, Dartmouth) are least likely to stress vocational education and most likely to emphasize "basic general education and appreciation of ideas." At Wesleyan—a denominational campus—they are more likely to stress "moral capacities, ethical standards and values." There seems to be a certain tendency for opinions to be tailored, as it were, to the distinctive environment of each individual campus. (Appendix 2 shows these responses for each campus.)

But the students evaluate an "ideal" college education by applying several sets of standards simultaneously. All these standards may genuinely be considered "highly" important. What do they say they feel deserves higher education's principal emphasis?

We can approximate an answer to this question by looking at the first column of Table 1-1, which shows which educational goals were ranked as *the* single most important aim of an ideal university. The majority of students stress either a "basic general education and appreciation of ideas," or "vocational skills and techniques directly applicable to your career."—Thirty-five per cent and 36 per cent, respectively, select these as "the single most important" aim of an ideal university. Still the proportion who place primary emphasis on the interpersonal approach to higher education is substantial enough (17 per cent) to preclude the possibility of misunderstanding, or the whimsical entry of a checkmark.[1] The other aims of education we have been discussing turn out to be clearly secondary. But "getting along with people"—as many observers of American culture have remarked and deplored —is certainly considered a legitimate purpose of higher education by a discernible subgroup of the students.

But this generalization turns out to be an accurate description principally of the beginning students. Academic educational values, more than any of the others we are discussing, are the ones whose claim to legitimacy seems to become reinforced on the campuses we studied, as the students mature.

As the students pass through their colleges, certain of the educa-

---

[1] For some remarks on the interpretation of frequency distributions of questionnaire responses, see Introduction.

TABLE 1-1. IMPORTANCE OF VARIOUS EDUCATIONAL GOALS
(Eleven universities: Total = 2975) *

. . . CONSIDER WHAT EDUCATIONAL GOALS YOU THINK THE IDEAL COLLEGE OR UNIVERSITY OUGHT TO EMPHASIZE	PERCENTAGES OF STUDENTS RANKING EACH GOAL AS:			
	Highly Important			
	First	*Other High*	*Medium*	*Low*
Provide a basic general education and appreciation of ideas	35	39	24	3
Develop your ability to get along with different kinds of people	17	55	26	3
Provide vocational training, develop skills and techniques directly applicable to your career	36	24	31	9
Develop your knowledge and interest in community and world problems	3	47	44	6
Help develop your moral capacities, ethical standards and values	8	37	40	15
Prepare you for a happy marriage and family life	1	21	42	36

* Percentages in this and subsequent tables may add to 99 or 101 due to rounding of decimal places. Note that per cents in this table are to be added horizontally.

tional values they profess shift position in the hierarchy of all educational values considered important. Thus, just as the climate of opinion on the most desirable educational goals varies from campus to campus, it varies as well from college class to college class. Upperclassmen, for example, almost unanimously place primary emphasis on academic or vocational education: the interpersonal approach drops to a position of secondary importance. Seniors may still view the opportunity to develop skills in interpersonal relations as perhaps a fortunate by-product of the college years, but the proportion who consider this approach important enough to deserve principal attention declines in the final year of college. It is mainly in the earlier years that such an approach has primary value for any significant proportion of the college students.

The changing climate of opinion year by year is apparent in another important sense. In the freshmen and sophomore classes, the opinion that vocational education should be the most important aim of college education takes precedence over all others. Among juniors, emphasis on vocational education or general education as principal aims of education is about equally balanced. But in the senior year, the point of view that college ought to provide chiefly a "basic education and appreciation of ideas" is far more prevalent than any other.

None of the other educational goals we studied shifts its relative rank in the hierarchy of educational values characteristic of each college class. For example, the university's role in educating students for enlightened citizenship appeals to relatively more upperclassmen than underclassmen, but it still remains a secondary educational value. Training for moral and ethical values, and preparing for family life likewise remain secondary educational values, and do not vary in their relative appeal for one class rather than another. (Details on these relationships can be seen in Appendix 3, which compares the relative importance of each of these educational goals among first, second, third, and fourth year students.)

It may, of course, be unjustified to infer from this that as the students go through college, more of them learn to value the broad, general educational approach which we have called academic, and fewer learn to value the instrumental approaches, particularly the interpersonal one. It is always possible that this sort of year-by-year comparison of college classes could have nothing at all to do with learning. This would be so, for example, if the students who were juniors and seniors when we polled them, had initially started college emphasizing the very aims of education that they reported in this study. Then the only "effect" that the college years could be credited with would be to have reinforced— or at least not to have tampered with—the original ideas with which they had set out.

This possibility was investigated, not at every university, but among the Cornell students in our sample. On this campus there were 944 students who had filled out our questionnaire twice: once in 1950 when they were underclassmen, and again in 1952 when they were upperclassmen. This group we call the "panel." [2]

---

[2] For details on the panel, see Introduction.

When we compared the way the students in this panel reported their educational values in 1952 with what they had said on the same subject as freshmen and sophomores two years earlier, the inferences based on the simple year-by-year comparison of classes were borne out. Many of these students, at the close of their college careers, had come to arrange their educational values in a hierarchy that differed from the one with which they had started out. Their values did indeed develop and change as they were going through college, and in the directions already suggested.[3]

We illustrate this development of opinion in two ways. First we shall simply compare the relative emphasis students gave to each educational goal in their early college years, with the relative emphasis they gave to these goals when they were finishing school. If proportionately more students upgraded the importance of an educational goal, we can say that the college years encouraged them to value that goal. If proportionately more students downgraded the importance of a goal, we can say that the college years discouraged a tendency to value it. We can say the goals that students felt deserved no more and no less emphasis at the close of their college years than they had originally allotted them were relatively unaffected during college.

Table 1-2 traces the movement of opinion in this manner. Roughly half the panel members changed their minds about the relative value of the academic, the instrumental, and the interpersonal educational goals, while the other half kept their original opinions. In contrast, the proportions of students who changed their minds about the value of educating for "community and world problems," or "moral capacities, ethical standards and values," or "a happy marriage and family life," are considerably smaller. When it comes to these secondary educational goals, the majority of the students leave the campus having found no reason to change their minds about their secondary importance. But

---

3 In the absence of equivalent information for a control group of young people who were not in college, it cannot be established that such changes were indeed an *effect* of college rather than of, say, maturation. This is why, in the text, we talk about changes "during the college years." Quite frankly, we feel that the inference would be supported if such comparative data were available.

(Cornell Panel)

OPINION IN 1950 COMPARED WITH OPINION IN 1952	Basic General Education (Academic)	Vocational Training (Instrumental)	Get Along with People (Interpersonal)	World Problems	Ethical Standards	Happy Marriage
CONSIDER WHAT EDUCATIONAL GOALS YOU THINK THE IDEAL COLLEGE OR UNIVERSITY OUGHT TO EMPHASIZE . . . (Percentage choosing each goal)						
(Men: Total = 683)						
No change (1950 and 1952 responses are identical)	47	49	55	61	63	78
Changed relative emphasis between 1950 and 1952						
Increased importance	34	17	20	22	24	10
Decreased importance	19	33	25	16	12	13
(Women: Total = 261)						
No change	53	51	53	64	58	65
Changed relative emphasis between 1950 and 1952						
Increased importance	28	20	21	18	21	16
Decreased importance	20	29	26	18	21	18
(Engineering school only: Total = 263)						
No change	45	51	55	62	66	82
Changed relative emphasis between 1950 and 1952						
Increased importance	36	16	18	22	23	7
Decreased importance	19	33	27	16	11	11
(Arts college men only: Total = 210)						
No change	49	49	54	60	59	79
Changed relative emphasis between 1950 and 1952						
Increased importance	33	21	18	25	26	7
Decreased importance	18	2o	28	15	15	14

many more students seem to have encountered reason to revise their original estimates of the emphasis that the three principal educational goals deserve.

And this is the way this revision seems to occur. The value of an academic approach to college education is most likely to become enhanced. The percentage of students in the panel who learned to attach more importance to "a basic general education and appreciation of ideas" exceeds the percentage upgrading any of the other educational goals.

The reverse trend occurs in the case of the instrumental and the interpersonal approaches to college education, which tend to lose adherents. The proportions of students in the panel who learned to attach less emphasis to vocational education, or to "getting along with all kinds of people," exceed the proportions downgrading any of the other educational aims (Table 1-2). This generalization is reinforced, incidentally, by the observation that the same trends occur not only in Cornell's College of Arts and Sciences, where emphasis on a basic general education is prevalent; the pattern appears as well in the College of Engineering, where emphasis on general education is less widespread, and where the majority of students stress vocational training in college over all other educational aims.

This relatively simple analysis of the general direction of opinion changes, however, tells only part of the story. Analysis of the details of these shifts illustrates somewhat more sharply that the legitimacy of the broad general approach to education tends to be reinforced and enhanced during the college years (Table 1-3).

In the first place, the belief that it is most important for college to "provide a basic general education and appreciation of ideas," is the most stable point of view. Sixty-one per cent of the men and 63 per cent of the women who entered college emphasizing this approach to education above all others, persisted in declaring that it deserved principal emphasis. Somewhat smaller proportions (51 per cent of the men and 52 per cent of the women) maintained their initial emphasis on vocational education. Among the few who initially emphasized any of the other goals of college education as "most important," only a small minority maintained this point of view.

In the second place, the academic approach to higher education is more likely than any of the others to attract the changers. That is, students who initially said that some other approach to college education was most important, but who changed their minds during their college careers, were more likely to have been won over to "a basic general education and appreciation of ideas" rather than to any other educational approach.

TABLE 1-3. MOVEMENT OF OPINION ON EDUCATIONAL GOALS CONSIDERED
MOST IMPORTANT
(Cornell Panel)

OPINION IN 1950 COMPARED WITH OPINION IN 1952	RESPONSES IN 1950			
	Basic General Education (Academic)	*Vocational Training (Instrumental)*	*Get Along with People (Interpersonal)*	*All Other Educational Goals*
	(Percentage ranking each goal "most important")			
	Men			
Total * =	(213)	(283)	(126)	(56)
No change (Considered "most important" in 1950 and also in 1952)	61	51	35	22
Shifted "Most important" educational goal to:				
Basic general education	—	25	38	42
Vocational training	16	—	19	16
Get along with people	12	14	—	9
All other	11	10	8	11
	Women			
Total ** =	(93)	(78)	(53)	(35)
No change	63	52	39	23
Shifted "Most important" educational goal to:				
Basic general education	—	24	27	48
Vocational training	15	—	17	17
Get along with people	13	16	—	9
All other	9	8	17	3

* Excludes 5 men who did not indicate "most important" educational goal.
** Excludes 2 women who did not indicate "most important" educational goal.

In short, while it is true that the campuses offer a wide range of possible educational values for the American college student, it is also true that something occurs during the college years that encourages and reinforces an academic point of view and that is less nurturing of the vocational approach to education. For students who enter college believing that higher education should provide primarily "a basic education and appreciation of ideas" are least likely to change their minds. Students who do change their minds, are more likely to swing over to this set of values than to any of the others.

The college years, moreover, sharply undermine any tendency to assert that non-academic educational goals are of principal importance. Few students enter college believing that the college's role in educating for citizenship, moral standards and values, or marriage and family life supersedes in importance its obligation to provide a basic education or to prepare for a specific career; and even these few quickly learn to change their emphasis. Considerably more students, however, enter college believing that the primary aim of college ought to be to develop their interpersonal skills. By the time they become upperclassmen, however, most of them have learned to replace these social goals with academic ones.

The opinion that certain educational aims are more important than others is, of course, not purely idiosyncratic. It is linked to a variety of societal factors, and reflects many more general social tendencies, individual interests, and orientations.

SELECTIVE FUNCTION OF VALUES

Real concern and often indignation at the extent to which the values of American mass culture have permeated the campuses have led many educators and intellectuals to overlook an important sociological point in their often very perceptive criticisms of higher education today. American colleges and universities are a part of an international institution of higher education with a long history of academic and scholarly traditions. These traditions are incorporated explicitly as norms on many campuses, and are transmitted as such to the students. It may be perfectly true, as many critics declare, that the growing mass treatment of education in the United States weakens these norms. It may still be true that other, non-academic norms, even counter-norms, are also present. Emphasis in this country on the market value of a college education, tendencies to look with scorn upon "the eggheads," and other indications of anti-intellectual themes certainly permeate vast sectors of American colleges and universities just as they permeate vast sectors of American society.

And yet, the academic, scholastic, and humanistic values of university education are still present and apparent on the campuses, *and their legitimacy is clear-cut.* As the students pass through four years of college life, they are not likely to be immune to the impact of these values. Certainly not all students are. To make the statement by no means denies the alternative; many students go through college with a banalized and instrumental notion of what higher education means and never even become aware of alternative interpretations.

Why? Large subgroups of students are insulated against education—and against education *about* education—by their personal traits which can act as blinders; or by the special nature of certain social subsystems in which they participate on the campus and off. Let us examine some of these "insulators."

The students' social origins can have such an effect. For each of the educational outlooks we have been discussing—the academic, the instrumental, and the interpersonal—tends to be characteristic of a particular social class. We have reason to suspect that they may be class-linked, since the point of view at Ivy League campuses and at the small Eastern men's colleges, which recruit students from higher social class levels, favored a general basic education. It is mainly at the state universities and at Fisk (where proportionately more students identify themselves as "working class" in origin) that the vocational approach to education was distinctly prevalent (Appendix 2).

Further evidence of the link between educational outlook and class background appears in Table 1-4. Students who identify themselves as "upper class" are most likely to value a broad, general approach to education. To many of these young people college means training for a particular style of life—reminiscent of an earlier day when the colleges explicitly provided a community of gentlemen with the background appropriate to their station in life. That this stress on the value of a general education, quite apart from any instrumental goal it may serve, is still more characteristic of students who say they come from upper class homes may indicate the compatability of this approach to education with a whole set of upper class social values.

On the other hand, a disproportionate number of students who emphasize the practical, instrumental value of higher education cluster in the group who say their origins are "working class." It is to them, particularly, that college education tends to be appealing as a means to an end rather than as a cultural end in itself. Perhaps they view it as a vehicle that will enable them to surpass the income and prestige positions they feel their families now have in the social structure. Their stress on the vocational function of col-

TABLE 1-4. CLASS IDENTIFICATION AND PRINCIPAL GOAL OF
COLLEGE EDUCATION
(Eleven universities)

CONSIDER WHAT EDUCATIONAL GOALS YOU THINK THE IDEAL COLLEGE OR UNIVERSITY OUGHT TO EMPHASIZE . . .	IN WHICH OF THESE FOUR GROUPS DO YOU CONSIDER YOUR FAMILY TO BE?		
	Upper Class	*Middle Class*	*"Working Class," "Lower Class"*
Total * =	(384)	(1895)	(661)
	(Percentage ** ranking each goal as "highly important")		
Provide vocational training	49	58	68
Develop your ability to get along with different kinds of people	71	70	72
Provide a basic general education	76	72	67
Develop your knowledge and interest in community and world problems	56	50	47
Help develop your moral capacities	48	45	44
Prepare you for a happy marriage and family life	20	20	24

* Omits 35 students who did not answer question.
** Percentages should not be cumulated owing to multiple responses.

lege education may indicate the compatibility of this educational approach with a whole set of working class social values.

But the vocational approach to education is the one that the college years, it will be recalled, do not encourage. This suggests that at least some of the values that students learn to abandon—or at least that do not develop as they go through school—are the ones characteristic of a lower position in the class structure. In a sense, then, college socialization acts as a great leveler; it levels *away* from working class values.

This need not mean, of course, that students are consciously motivated to adopt or abandon their educational values by deliberately estimating how well they fit in with a particular class outlook. On the contrary, it is more likely that college students who come from working class families have already begun to accept certain general orientations characteristic of social classes higher than theirs on the status scale of American society; and their college experience reinforces and accelerates these middle- or upper-class orientations.

A second "insulator" against academic norms is imbedded in certain values which the students imply are important to them when they tell us something about their broad, general orientations to life. The discussion below illustrates this point by examining the relation between two of the educational goals we have been discussing and two of these general orientations: other-directedness and success-orientation.

OTHER-DIRECTEDNESS

The term "other-directed" was used by David Riesman to describe the personality of someone who is motivated principally by the desire for social acceptance and approval, who takes his cues for conduct mainly from the social group.[4] Of course, we all want approval in some degree; and we all, as members of a social group, receive and respond to cues from our society. But the other-directed personality-type does so *more* than others; social acceptance is *more important* to him than it is to others; and he lacks the

_____

4 David Riesman, in collaboration with Reuel Denney and Nathan Glazer, *The Lonely Crowd* (New Haven: Yale University Press, 1950).

alternative inner resources that would enable him to fix his own course of behavior.

The visitor to an American college campus is struck by this quality of other-directedness; sociability and "groupiness" seem to permeate the atmosphere. The lone student is the rare bird—usually the isolate, the misfit. The general pattern is for these young people to range about the university in groups, to sip their coffees or cokes together, to enter or leave classes and to loll on benches or on the grass in pairs, triads, little clusters characterized by outgoing, casual, easy camaraderie.

In their interviews, the students told us how much importance they attached to feeling accepted by a group, making friends, having "a pleasant personality," and to being well liked by others.

> Well, one of the things you want is to be accepted; to be well liked by all different kinds of people.

> I value the ability to get along with other people. Not in a passive sense, but so that they really like you, really enjoy your company, really accept you in the group.

> It isn't that you want to be popular, although that is nice too. It's that you want people to appreciate you and to accept you in the group.

> If you have a good personality, you are interesting, and people will seek you out. In this way, they accept you and this is often more important than a lot of other things.

> If you take two people, and each of them has the same background, each is equally competent, then I think that the one with the good personality will get along better in the group than the one who is not well liked.

> You want to develop your personality so that you can make friends. Really make friends, easily and with real pleasure.

Students on all the campuses we studied emphasized the importance of these traits.

The responses in Table 1-5 formed a scale-pattern which provided a more stable measure of the quality of other-directedness than would have been provided by answers to a single question.[5]

---

5 When a population answers any single question on a questionnaire, there is obviously the possibility that any one individual may have had some special idiosyncratic

TABLE 1-5. INDICATIONS OF OTHER-DIRECTEDNESS

Question	Response	Percentage Giving Indicated Response
(Eleven universities: Total = 2975)		
How important is it to you, for you to be well-liked by different kinds of people?	Very important	37
	Fairly important	47
	Fairly unimportant	13
	Very unimportant	3
What two qualities on this list do you think really get a young person ahead the fastest today? *	Having a pleasant personality	57
	Hard work	62
	Brains	31
	Knowing the right people	32
	Good luck	5
	Being a good politician	5
(Cornell 1952: Total = 1571)		
If you had your choice, which of the following would you most like to be?	Independent	24
	Successful	36
	Well liked	39
Would you say you are the sort of person who finds it easier or harder to make friends than most people?	Easier	39
	About the same	49
	Harder	12

* Percentages should not be cumulated owing to multiple responses.

Each of these responses indicates a different aspect of the quality: an expressed *need* to be liked; an expressed *wish* to be well liked, and a sort of over-all emphasis on the *importance* of "personality" —a term which can be translated, in the lexicon of student vocabulary, as that indefinable quality which has as an inevitable consequence that "people like you," "people take to you," "people seek your company," "people find you interesting."

meaning in mind when he gave that response. In order to reduce the chance of error stemming from such special meanings, the analyst of questionnaire data tries to cumulate responses to several questions, all of which bear on the same subject matter.

One technique for making such cumulative measures and for verifying that these several answers indeed refer to the same subject matter (or variable) is the so-called Guttman scaling technique. The two-item index referred to here is not a scale but an index which arranges the population in a scale pattern. Appendix 6 discusses some problems of scaling, and also presents a brief bibliography for the interested reader.

Notice that this measure deals only with the students' reports about their *feelings.* It does not include, for example, testimony about their participation in the social and group life of the campus. Such participation, while highly correlated with this measure of other-directedness, is not considered as a defining characteristic of the quality.[6]

Now, it is among students who characterize their general approach to life as "other-directed" that the appeal of the interpersonal educational approach is particularly strong. Among the variety of culturally approved choices, these young people have chosen to value highly that educational emphasis that fits best with their generally other-directed view of life.

Yet we know that socialization during the college years weakens the appeal of learning to "get along with different kinds of people" as an aim of college education. But Table 1-6 shows not all types of students are equally ready to give up its claim to legitimacy. Relatively fewer "other-directed" students turn up in the groups that have been weaned away from the interpersonal approach to education, or who never valued it highly. In contrast, those whose general orientation to life was rated as "other-directed" are disproportionately represented in the subgroups who maintained or adopted interpersonal educational values. Their general orientation seems to have insulated them against the influences that have impelled other students to abandon this point of view.

THE IMPORTANCE OF SUCCESS

Riesman, who coined the term "other-directed," points out that this type of personality is widespread in the United States. Other observers have been equally struck by a different theme of American culture: the wish for success, success for its own sake, quite aside from any specific antecedent.

This theme of success and the importance of financial rewards are taken up more fully in Chapter 2, where the students' occupa-

---

[6] For example, 80 per cent of the students rated as highly other-directed by this index report that they participate in at least two extracurricular activities, while only 50 per cent of those rated as least other-directed report equivalent participation. And the decline is regular for each of the intermediate positions.

TABLE 1-6. OTHER-DIRECTEDNESS IS LINKED TO CHOICE AND ADOPTION OF INTERPERSONAL EDUCATIONAL VALUES; SUCCESS-ORIENTATION IS LINKED TO INSTRUMENTAL EDUCATIONAL GOALS

(Cornell Panel: Men only)

CONSIDER WHAT EDUCATIONAL GOALS YOU THINK THE IDEAL UNIVERSITY OUGHT TO EMPHASIZE . . . (COMPARISON OF ORIGINAL OPINION WITH OPINION AS UPPERCLASSMEN)	INDEX OF OTHER-DIRECTEDNESS *			INDEX OF SUCCESS-ORIENTATION **		
	High (4;5)	Medium (3)	Low (1,2)	High	Medium	Low
	(In per cents)			(In per cents)		
Originally "first"						
remained "first"	43	30	26	57	46	47
dropped to "high"	51	62	45	25	28	20
dropped to "medium" or "low"	6	9	29	18	26	33
Total	(31)	(44)	(51)	(83)	(112)	(88)
Originally "high"						
raised to "first"	19	12	16	28	24	20
remained "high"	64	65	52	33	33	27
dropped to "medium" or "low"	17	23	32	40	43	53
Total	(135)	(113)	(130)	(43)	(66)	(85)
Originally "medium" or "low"						
raised to "first"	10	6	1	22	13	6
raised to "high"	43	50	29	33	30	21
remained "medium" or "low"	47	44	70	45	57	73
Total	(49)	(50)	(80)	(45)	(72)	(89)

* Highest score on the scale of other-directedness was assigned according to the indicated responses to the following questions:
How important is it for you to be well liked by different kinds of people? (Very important).
Which two qualities on this list do you really think get a young person ahead the fastest today: (Having a pleasant personality).
If you had your choice, which of the following would you most like to be? (Well-liked).

** Index composed of these answers to the following two questions:
How important to you, personally, is it to get ahead in life? (Very important).
If you had your choice, which of the following would you most like to be? (Successful).

tional values are analyzed. Although we shall see there that this goal has been somewhat tarnished for this college generation, many college students are still by no means immune to its appeal. We asked: "How important to you, personally, is it to get ahead in life?" They responded:

> (Eleven universities: Total = 2975)
> Very important   59%
> Fairly important   34
> Unimportant   6
> Very unimportant   1

Notice, too, on page 18, Table 1-5 that over a third of the Cornell students chose "successful" as a quality they considered preferable to being "independent" or "well liked."

Responses to these two questions were combined in a measure of "success orientation." These questions were chosen for the measure since they deal directly with testimony on the importance of seeking success in the abstract, without pinning the students down by asking them to specify *success in what*.

Table 1-6 shows the affinity between the assertion that success is an important general goal in life and the tendency to value highly an instrumental approach to education. For the students rated as "most success-oriented" are more likely to maintain an initially high opinion of the value of vocational education in college, or else to learn to value it highly as they go through school. Students rated as "least success-oriented" show, in contrast, a greater tendency to stick to an initially low evaluation of vocational aims, or else to learn to attach little importance to these aims as they move from underclassmen to upperclassmen. Again it is clear that the general approach to life characteristic of the first group has made them less ready to abandon vocational education's claim to be considered a legitimate educational value.

SELECTIVE POWER OF VALUES AS STANDARDS

These simple examples illustrate the selective power of values, in the sense of the standards by which judgments about worth are made. When the students first come to the campus, many of them have already decided what they want of higher education: general education, vocational training, and interpersonal skills. But they expect higher education to help them develop in other ways, as well: to build up their knowledge and interest in community and world problems, for example; to develop their moral capacities and ethical standards; to prepare them in some way for a happy marriage and family life.

As they go through college, however, students learn to accept the legitimacy of those aims of education which are imbedded as norms in the academic institution. They learn to take a more specialized view of what the principal "jobs" of a university ought to be. Non curricular aims come to be valued less; broad, general aims which stress ideas and concepts come to be valued more than vocational and technical skills.

But these changes in emphasis do not occur at equal rates among all groups of students. Even in the ostensibly specific area of education, students apply standards of judgment which are compatible with the values of their social class and the social subsystems in which they circulate; and with their broad and general orientations to life. These factors can and do act as "insulators" slowing up or halting the general tendency among students to develop in college the educational values which reflect academic traditions and norms.

2

Choosing A Career*

THE MEANING OF WORK

DURING THE COLLEGE YEARS most students decide upon the kind of work in which they will spend their lives. Just what do work and career mean to them?

Most students expect their work to provide a major source of satisfaction, second only to the satisfaction they expect to get from family relations. We asked: "What three things or activities in your life do you expect to give you the most satisfaction?" The three activities chosen were then ranked in order of importance. Here is the distribution of responses made by the students in the colleges we studied.[1] (Table 2-1)

American students, it is clear, are primarily family-centered: for them career takes second place. But they see work and career to mean much more than a way to earn a living, much more than a necessary evil that cannot be avoided. Almost all the students expect that their work will provide perhaps not *the* major source of satisfaction in their lives, but certainly a very important source of satisfaction.[2]

---

* This chapter contains a revision and reanalysis of a more detailed study of the relationship between values and choice of a career, which appears in a separate volume, Morris Rosenberg, *et al, Occupations and Values* (Glencoe, Ill.; Free Press, 1958).

1 See page 49 for discussion of responses among the women.

2 Variations among students at the several universities in this regard are very slight. See Appendix 4 for an inter-university comparison.

TABLE 2-1. IMPORTANCE OF CAREER COMPARED WITH OTHER BASIC
LIFE SATISFACTIONS *

(Eleven universities: Total = 2975)

WHAT THREE THINGS OR ACTIVITIES IN YOUR LIFE DO YOU EXPECT TO GIVE YOU THE MOST SATISFACTION?	PERCENTAGE ** WHO RANK EACH SATISFACTION AS:			PERCENTAGE WHO REJECT EACH SATISFACTION
	First in Importance	*Second*	*Third*	
Career or occupation	28	47	14	11
Family relationships	55	27	7	11
Leisure time recreational activities	5	10	42	43
Religious beliefs or activities	4	4	9	83
Participation as a citizen in the affairs of your community	1	3	13	83
Participation in activities directed toward national or international betterment	1	3	8	88

* See Appendix Table 4 for inter-university comparison.
** Percentages are to be added horizontally.

This quality of commitment is particularly characteristic of the students who have chosen, at least tentatively, to go into the arts, "glamor" occupations, and the professions. Those who have elected to enter business fields and farming are least likely to express this sense of dedication to their careers. (Table 2-2)

OCCUPATIONAL VALUES

When students say that they expect their careers to provide a major source of satisfaction in their lives, just what kinds of satisfactions do they have in mind? Many commentators on the American scene feel that the principal satisfactions, particularly among white-collar and professional workers, have to do with "success," measured usually in the concrete terms of income, status, and power. This "cash-register mentality" motivates one writer to describe the career-choice of college students as follows:

> College students wondering whether to major in history or English literature are often dissuaded by the question: What can

TABLE 2-2. CAREER AS MAJOR LIFE-SATISFACTION AMONG STUDENTS WHO
WOULD LIKE TO ENTER DIFFERENT OCCUPATIONS
(Eleven universities)

BUSINESS OR PROFESSION CHOSEN	PERCENTAGE OF THOSE WHO SELECTED "CAREER OR PROFESSION" AS THE MOST IMPORTANT SOURCE OF SATISFACTION WHO WOULD LIKE TO GO INTO EACH BUSINESS OR PROFESSION	Total *
Teaching	38	(265)
Artistic and related fields	37	(131)
Advertising, public relations, journalism	37	(93)
Medicine	35	(410)
Law	31	(202)
Architecture	30	(54)
Natural Science	26	(212)
Engineering	26	(416)
Business, real estate, finance	25	(387)
Food, restaurant, hotel	24	(25)
Farming	23	(66)
Personnel	23	(84)
Sales, promotion	18	(98)
Don't know	19	(350)

* Excludes 182 students who could not be classified on both variables, as well as those occupations chosen by too few students to warrant comparison.

you do with it when you get out? Does anyone want to write? It makes sense only if he aims at the jackpot. Would he enjoy teaching? There's more money in advertising. Careers, and indeed life experiences, are selected not on the basis of their personal satisfactions or social usefulness, but strictly in cash-register terms.[3]

Actually, we find that this "What's in it for me?" attitude is certainly not the factor that is the principal determinant of career selection. Here are the kinds of comments the students make:

I expect to go into farming. I love outdoor work, and I am happiest when I can work with my hands, fix things. I couldn't stand being indoors, having to follow a schedule all the time. That's more important to me than all the money in the world.

[3] Leo Gurko, *Heroes, Highbrows and the Popular Mind* (New York: Bobbs-Merrill, 1953), pp. 69-70. See also C. Wright Mills, *White Collar* (New York: Oxford University Press, 1951) for a discussion of the importance of money, status, and power in the meaning of work.

> I'm not sure what profession I'll follow, but I know one thing: it will be working with people—helping them. I think I have the knack of getting them to confide in me, and in that way I think I could be of help. That's more important to me than getting ahead or making a lot of money.

> Whatever kind of a job I finally end up in, I'm sure I won't stick to it unless I have an opportunity to express myself. I just don't want to follow someone else's ideas, or pace. I feel it's most important to do something creative—something that comes from you, in a special way, something original. That's more important to me than money or the acclaim.

This does not mean, of course, that the students hate money or success. There were not many who were as assured as this student, but certainly some of them shared his dream.

> My idea is to get as much preparation as I can in school, and as much experience as I can outside of school, because I plan to make a pile. It seems to me there's plenty of opportunity for a man with a good idea, and good training to promote a fortune for himself if he's not afraid to take a risk. I admit it: I want to make money and have the kind of reputation and social position that goes with it, that will make people look up to me. The kind of life I want to lead costs money and I plan to make it.

We have already reported (see page 18, Table 1-5) the climate of opinion on the campuses regarding the importance of "getting ahead" and of "being successful." But we asked, too, much more specifically, for the relative emphasis each student placed on a long list of possible satisfactions that work and career might conceivably offer.

At each campus we asked: "Consider to what extent a job or career would have to satisfy each of the following requirements before you could consider it ideal." Again the instructions were to rank each requirement as highly important, medium in importance, or "of little or no importance, irrelevant or even distasteful." Students were then told to indicate the rank order of all requirements chosen as highly important.

The students say they view work as a very important and meaningful way of satisfying not simply—not even primarily—a wish for success, but a wide range of other values. Self-fulfillment, security, and interpersonal satisfactions are the most widespread appeals: 78 per cent of the students chose "an opportunity to use my special abilities or aptitudes" as a highly important consideration in choosing a career; and 48 per cent chose "permit me to be creative and original." These responses emphasize the wish to use one's innate or acquired potentialities in work.

Security, too, looms as an occupational gratification that the students say they value. Three out of five (61 per cent) checked "enable me to look forward to a stable, secure future."

In addition, the students stress the importance of interpersonal

TABLE 2-3. IMPORTANCE OF VARIOUS OCCUPATIONAL REQUIREMENTS *
(Eleven universities: Total = 2975)

CONSIDER TO WHAT EXTENT A JOB OR CAREER WOULD HAVE TO SATISFY EACH OF THESE REQUIREMENTS . . .	PERCENTAGE ** OF STUDENTS RANKING EACH GOAL AS:			
	Highly Important	*Other*		
	First	*High*	*Medium*	*Low*
Provide an opportunity to use my special abilities	27	51	20	2
Enable me to look forward to a stable, secure future	24	37	31	8
Permit me to be creative and original	10	38	39	13
Give me an opportunity to be helpful to others	10	33	44	13
Provide me with a chance to earn a good deal of money	10	29	48	13
Give me an opportunity to work with people rather than things	7	37	36	20
Give me a chance to exercise leadership	4	28	53	15
Leave me relatively free of supervision by others	3	35	48	14
Give me social status and prestige	2	24	53	21
Provide me with adventure	1	15	40	44

* See Table 2-9 for distribution of responses to this question made by the Cornell women.
** Percentages should be added horizontally.

satisfactions: 44 per cent chose "give me an opportunity to work with people rather than things," and 43 per cent chose "give me an opportunity to be helpful to others" as among the most appealing considerations in a career.

Although few students say that money, status, prestige, and leadership are irrelevant or unimportant job considerations, still only a minority gave top priority to these values. Thirty-nine per cent checked "provide me with a chance to earn a great deal of money," 32 per cent chose "a chance to exercise leadership," and 26 per cent selected "social status and prestige" as highly important considerations in evaluating a job or career.

PSYCHOLOGICAL DISTANCE AMONG
OCCUPATIONAL VALUES

Since students evaluate an "ideal" occupation by applying several standards simultaneously, it seems reasonable to ask whether these standards tend to arrange themselves in any sort of pattern or hierarchy. One way to approach this question is to determine what has been called the "psychological distance," among the several occupational values we have been discussing.

The notion of psychological distance really formalizes something that many of us have noted intuitively in everyday life. Here is a simple example. Students of radio listening have found that tastes in music do not occur at random but form a distinctly overlapping pattern: people who listen to classical music are also likely to listen to semi-classical music; those who listen to semi-classical music are likely to listen to popular music; those who like popular music listen to hillbilly songs. But those who like classical music are very *un*likely to listen to hillbilly songs; those who like semi-classical music are somewhat less unlikely to do so; and so on.[4] In other words hillbilly music is psychologically most distant from classical music.

The same kind of regularly overlapping tastes occurs when it

---

4 Paul F. Lazarsfeld and Patricia L. Kendall, *Radio Listening in America* (New York: Prentice Hall, 1948), pp. 32-33 and Hans Zeisel, *Say It With Figures* (New York: Harpers, 1947), pp. 27-29.

comes to reading habits.[5] It probably occurs as well in food tastes, clothing styles, and the like.

We studied the several occupational requirements the students stressed from this point of view, ordering them in such a way that one could see clearly which were likely to be valued simultaneously and which were, so to speak, mutually antipathetic.

They turned out to be arranged in this sequence:

1. Permit me to be creative and original.
2. Use my special abilities and aptitudes.
3. Permit me to be helpful to others.
4. Work with people rather than things.
5. Give me status and prestige.
6. Chance to earn a good deal of money.
7. Stable, secure future.[6]

This means that the career gratifications that appear close to each other on this list are likely to be highly valued at the same time by the same person. Those that are far from each other on the list are unlikely to be valued at the same time by the same individual. That is, creativity, originality, and a chance to exploit one's special abilities and aptitudes are the kinds of demands that are psychologically compatible with each other. The common thread running through these values seems to be the emphasis on *self-expression*.

The demand that one's work provide a chance to be helpful to others and to work with people represents another cluster of psychologically compatible values. The common thread here is the orientation to *people*.

This arrangement is analogous to the links in a chain. The first two sets of values form the first set of links and are labelled "Goal values" because the stress here is placed on the satisfactions one expects to get *from* the work. In contrast, the next set of links in

---

5 Babette Kass, "Overlapping Magazine Reading," in *Communications Research 1948-49*, eds. Paul F. Lazarsfeld and Frank Stanton (New York: Harpers, 1949), pp. 130-151.

6 Appendix 5 shows the coefficients of association. The choices "freedom from supervision," "opportunity for leadership," and "chance for adventure" showed no consistent pattern and have therefore been omitted from the computations.

the chain might be called "Reward values." Status, prestige, and wealth valued as a consequence of one's work are a cluster of psychologically compatible demands that focus on the *rewards* one expects to get out of working. In the same way emphasis on a stable, secure future stresses work as a means to an end rather than as an end in itself.

These "links," by the way, are not equidistant from each other. The widest gap is between the goal values and the reward values. That is, the "people-centered" values are more compatible with self-expression values and less compatible with status values in spite of the fact that they appear adjacent to each other on the list.

There is an impressive similarity in the occupational values stressed by college students throughout the country. Aside from a few slight "irregularities," students everywhere seem to see eye to eye about what constitutes an ideal job. Students at Dartmouth, Texas, and North Carolina emphasize creativity somewhat less frequently than do those at other campuses; Harvard men report considerably less concern about security; Fisk students considerably more concern about finding the kind of work that will permit them "to be helpful to others." But by and large, the figures show substantial agreement (See Appendix 6).

MONEY, SECURITY, CREATIVITY

Traditionally, it has been considered part of the American value system for young men to aspire to monetary success. Various qualities were considered essential to attain this goal—among others, vision, daring, initiative, a willingness to take risks. During the course of the depression of the 1930's, however, a counter-ideology became prominent: the value of security. Under the stress of economic anxiety, many people gave up their interest in striving after the big money and concentrated their attention on getting nice, steady, secure jobs.

This conflict of values is said by many to be evident now on the college campuses. Presumably the students have given up the dream of rapid advancement and financial success in order to settle for security and stability.

In one respect our study supports this point of view. We have already shown that the students who say they value success in the sense of money, status, and leadership are decidedly in the minority; those who say they value stability and security are relatively more numerous.

In another sense, however, our study casts serious doubt on the certainty with which these claims can be made. We have already shown how students declare that other occupational values are much more important for them than either of the "reward values." Now we report still another piece of evidence that suggests they may not necessarily be unambiguously eager to trade monetary advancement for a secure job. We had asked:

> Here are three different types of jobs. If you had your choice, which would you pick? (Eleven universities: Total = 2,975)
>
> A job which pays quite a low income, but which you were sure of keeping.
> A job which pays quite a good income, but which you have a 50-50 chance of losing.
> A job which pays an extremely good income if you make the grade, but in which you lose everything if you don't make it.

Only nine per cent selected the first alternative. The second alternative (the moderate risk) was selected by 41 per cent, and the last alternative (the risk-everything approach) was selected by the greatest proportion, 48 per cent. Two per cent of the students did not answer the question.

Answers to a question of this type must not be thought to predict what the students would do if confronted by the actual situation. It may be that the risk-everything approach they express here indicates a fond wish or their self-confidence—the conviction, for example, that of course they would "make the grade." Perhaps they are too young and too inexperienced to feel the impact of the full meaning of the words, "lose everything."

But even if we cannot say what they might do if the chips were down, the fact remains that the greatest proportion of students, for whatever reasons, finds the "risk-everything" approach most appealing. A somewhat smaller proportion expresses a willingness to take a moderate risk, and only a negligible proportion considers it legitimate to take no risk at all.

Finally, we found that as these students went through college the appeal of the security which a job or career might offer became weaker, not stronger, while the appeal of "money" remained constant. For example, when the students in the Cornell panel were freshmen and sophomores, almost two-thirds (63 per cent) said it was highly important for an ideal job to provide "a stable, secure future." Much smaller proportions (46 per cent) placed equivalent emphasis on the opportunity to be "creative and original," and 33 per cent emphasized "opportunity to earn a great deal of money." By the time these young people had become juniors or seniors, however, the identical proportion still emphasized "money," but relative emphasis on the first two career values had reversed. As juniors and seniors substantially fewer students stressed the need for security in a career (46 per cent), and this proportion was exceeded by the proportion stressing the value of creativity (52 per cent).

The important finding in this regard, however, is not so much that certain subgroups of students are willing to testify that they value a job principally for the money and security it provides. It is more significant that these values belong together in a common approach that declares it legitimate to value work for the extrinsic rewards it offers; that these reward values are psychologically compatible with each other, psychologically incompatible with the self-expression values. True, students who say they emphasize creativity and want to exploit their own special aptitudes in their work life are relatively more numerous than those who say they value money and security. But—and it is this we wish to emphasize —they seem, either by necessity or by inclination, to feel that this choice is to be made, in American society, *at the expense* of the reward values. Conversely, those who stress the importance of money and security seem to feel that in our culture, achieving them means giving up any emphasis on the creative work values.

The point is underlined in Table 2-4. Those who report that an essential aim in their scheme of things is "to get ahead in life" are quite likely to declare, at the same time, that an ideal job would have to provide them principally with money, status, prestige, *and* security. The opinion that creativity in one's work is equally to be valued turns up relatively rarely in this achievement-oriented group. In contrast, students who say they do not necessarily consider it so important to get ahead in life tend to attach a high value to creativity in a career. Among them the legitimacy of money, status, prestige and security, as career values of importance, is stressed relatively infrequently. The first group—the achievement-oriented—have either eschewed or never developed dedication to the occupational value of creativity. The second group, their counterparts, have either eschewed or never developed dedication to the reward values in occupational life.

TABLE 2-4. ACHIEVEMENT-ORIENTED STUDENTS STRESS REWARD VALUES IN OCCUPATIONAL LIFE AND MINIMIZE CREATIVITY

(Eleven universities)

CONSIDER TO WHAT EXTENT A JOB OR CAREER WOULD HAVE TO SATISFY EACH OF THESE REQUIREMENTS . . .	HOW IMPORTANT TO YOU, PERSONALLY, IS IT TO GET AHEAD IN LIFE?		
	Very Important	*Fairly Important*	*Not Very Important Very Unimportant*
Total =	(1732)	(1018)	(197)
	(Percentage * of students ranking each occupational goal as "highly important")		
Enable me to look forward to a stable, secure future	67	56	29
Provide me with a chance to earn a good deal of money	49	28	11
Give me social status and prestige	33	18	7
Permit me to be creative and original	46	49	63

* Omits 28 students who did not answer question. Percentages should not be cumulated owing to multiple responses.

HOW MUCH MONEY?

The majority of the students who stress the more qualitative values of work, may seem to have abandoned the value of high income, but this does not mean that they have little interest in how much money they will earn. On the contrary, they have high hopes about their earning power. They appear to take it for granted that when they enter the labor market they will command good incomes. It is not that they expect their earnings to reach a high ceiling; it is, rather, that they fully expect to find "the floor" is not very low. The nation's prosperity and their own optimism relieve them of any worries about having to settle for a pittance.

We asked the students to indicate how much money they expected to earn ten years after entering their chosen field of work.

TABLE 2-5. EXPECTED EARNINGS OF COLLEGE STUDENTS
(Eleven universities: Total = 2975)

ABOUT HOW MUCH MONEY DO YOU EXPECT TO EARN TEN YEARS AFTER YOU ENTER THE BUSINESS OR PROFESSION YOU EXPECT TO GO INTO?	PERCENTAGE SELECTING INDICATED INCOME RANGE
less than $3,000	*
$3,000- 4,999	5
$5,000- 7,499	23
$7,500- 9,999	18
$10,000-19,999	35
$20,000-29,999	6
$30,000 or more	4
Don't know or no answer	10

* Less than one per cent.

Only five per cent of the students we studied said they expected to earn less than $5,000 a year, although the median yearly income for *all men college graduates* in 1948-49 was reported to be about $4,700.[7] That means that 50 per cent of the men graduates actually earned less than that amount and 50 per cent earned more. In contrast, 85 per cent of our students expect to be earning more than this national median ten years after their graduation. The median expected earnings of our group come to a little over $7,500. Of course, the Havemann and West figures on which we base the comparison were collected in 1948 and 1949, while our figures were collected in 1952. Still, whatever economic changes occurred during these intervening years cannot account for the

[7] The figure is $4,689. See Ernest Havemann and Patricia Salter West, *They Went to College* (New York: Harcourt, Brace and Co., 1952), p. 26. The analyses of these writers are based on study of a nationwide sample of 9,483 college graduates.

vast difference between the expectations reported by these younger students and the reality of the older college man's reported earning power.

With this kind of optimistic approach to their earning ability, the students can afford, so to speak, to feel they can take a risk. In no case will they be left high and dry. In today's bull market for college graduates they are probably relieved of any pressing need to make a choice between money and security; they feel that they can well expect to find a career providing reasonably adequate proportions of both. And our earlier analysis of the psychological distance between occupational values indicated that the person who wants one of these values is likely to want both.

RECRUITMENT ON THE CAMPUSES [8]

The students' optimism about earnings and job possibilities is certainly not unrealistic: college graduates are very much in demand today. Hiring procedures are quite unlike the hiring procedures of the past. Many companies no longer wait for the college graduate to come knocking at their doors to ask for a job. They send special recruiters to the campuses to look over each graduating class. Indeed, around graduation time the campuses turn into recruiting grounds where personnel people from large companies and organizations set up temporary headquarters to interview and sign up likely looking graduates.

The college placement officer, too, has changed. He is now a very active and often a very harassed link between the company representative and the student aspirant. It is he who provides the temporary cubicle on the campus where competing personnel officers set up shop. It is he who collects the data on students for the use of the recruiters, who keeps in touch with faculty members, who arranges luncheons between them and recruiters, who handles voluminous correspondence and innumerable telephone calls, who consults with company men on the over-all problems and policies of placement, and who handles the sometimes over-

---

[8] See Herrymon Maurer, "Twenty Minutes to a Career" (*Fortune Magazine,* March 1956) for an interesting summary of industry recruiting practices and personnel policies.

whelming logistic problems involved in scheduling the interviews and keeping things moving.

The seniors, as potential graduates, are the "bodies" to be interviewed and, hopefully, delivered. But there will also be a smattering of younger students filing in and out of the cubicles. Many companies are eager to find suitable underclassmen for temporary summer jobs, to create a reservoir of possible full-time workers against the day when they will ultimately graduate.

When the season is on, hundreds of young men and women are summoned to be looked over, and are kept moving in more or less orderly procession through the temporary compartments that house the recruiters. The students are spaced at roughly twenty-minute intervals, and in these twenty minutes the company representative does some fast talking. He tries to strike a happy medium between being persuasive and also being selective. He spends a good deal of the time outlining the appeals of the jobs he has to offer and the promise of his company. At the same time, he is busy trying to size up the student and decide whether he is "appropriate material." We are told that often these interviews may become simply high-pressure monologues by the recruiter, but the rule of thumb in this kind of work is to try to avoid overselling the company and to find out as much as possible about what the student has to offer.

The student, in his turn, tries to learn as much as he can about what the company has to offer. He will ask as many questions as he can muster. Usually his main concern is how his own special training and interests can fit into the needs of the company and what he can expect from the future.

Thus, he is very much concerned about training programs. Both the student and the company, each equally aware that a newly-turned-out college graduate is not yet a fully marketable commodity in business or industry, count on training programs to finish the job. These programs have been developed to a fine point by many concerns in order to tailor the college graduate to the special needs of the role for which he is being considered. The potential recruit, in turn, realizes that such training will enable him to learn enough specialized skills, for example, to be able to advance himself in the company structure, and—he hopes—in his field or discipline, as well. He knows that a good training program can increase his worth by several thousand dollars a year in the close or distant future.

While earnings are important to the neophyte, he tends to be less interested in starting salary than in the possibility of salary increases, incentive payments, and the chances for reaching a reasonable maximum in what he considers a reasonable time. He asks about housing facilities and the type of community life he can expect. And recently, the recruiters tell us, students are asking more and more questions about bonus payments and retirement programs.

In some cases this brief interview terminates in a concrete job offer. More often the company representative invites promising candidates to visit the plant for additional interviews—expenses usually paid. And the students, themselves, usually prefer to delay their decisions until they have looked over several possibilities.

Most technical students, including virtually all engineering students, are hired by recruiting today. But the practice is also becoming more prevalent for business administration and liberal arts students. The technical and engineering students, however, are at a decided advantage. In the first place, they are more in demand. In the second place, the companies are more concerned about showing how special talents and particular interests can be matched with the job. For example, the recruiter is likely to outline the precise relation between special fields of college study and the particular operations of his company.

The student who has taken general courses in business or in the liberal arts has a promising outlook too. He may find that he is less likely to be recruited, that the inducements held out to him are less dazzling, that the recruiting interview may be less painstaking, and perhaps that the interviewer is less concerned about showing how the job can match the man and vice versa. Still, he has the consolation of knowing that if he finds the right spot he can advance rapidly, and, if he has the talent, the training, and the luck, he can eventually count on top-paying jobs in management.

The increasing need for technically trained personnel in business and industry plus the delayed effect of the low birth-rate during the depression (which lowered the supply of college students currently graduating today), have combined to force industry to scramble for the college graduate "trainees." The system of recruiting is one indication of this scramble; it is one way of competing on the spot for the limited supply of graduates. As long as the demand for college graduates continues to exceed the supply, the recruiter in his temporary cubicle will probably come to be associated, at least in the college towns, with the first robins as a sign of spring.

THE NEW MIDDLE-CLASS

If the large corporations recruit the students for salaried jobs, what has happened to the old middle-class ideal of the independent entrepreneur making his way alone by his competence, his diligence, and his frugal accumulation of capital? To take the Cornell men as an example, only one-fifth had said they realistically expected to enter one of the traditional middle-class occupations as entrepreneurs (business, farming, law, medicine, etc.). Most expected to be salaried professionals—teachers, government workers, managers, technicians, scientists—selling nothing but their skills and services to large organizations.

This does not mean that the old middle-class ideal has faded from the picture completely. For example, when these students were asked: "If you could have your own choice in the matter, what kind of firm or outfit would you like best to work in after you finish your schooling?", 28 per cent said, "own business or own farm," and 21 per cent said "own professional office." Slightly less than half, therefore, said they would prefer to be individual entrepreneurs.[9] But when we asked, "Now aside from your own preference in the matter, what kind of firm do you think you are *realistically* most likely to end up working in?", only 13 per cent said "own business or own farm," and another 13 per cent said "own professional office." Many students seem to wish to establish their own enterprises, but they expect to work for someone else.

---

9 The equivalent proportions among all the students at the eleven universities we studied were 20 and 26 per cent.

There may be a relatively large discrepancy between aspirations and expectations as far as the type of firm or outfit one will work in is concerned. But this is much less true when we consider the choice of specific occupations: for 69 per cent of all the students we studied said that they "realistically" expected to go into the occupation that they wanted to enter. Only 12 per cent felt that they would have to make a compromise here. The remaining 19 per cent felt that they could make no estimate on this count.

RELUCTANT RECRUITS

For which occupations was this sort of compromising most prevalent? The index of "reluctant recruits" to each profession in Table 2-6 gives some suggestions.

It is "business" which appears to draw considerably larger proportions of reluctant recruits than any other field; although jour-

TABLE 2-6. INDEX OF "RELUCTANT RECRUITS" IN SELECTED OCCUPATIONS *
(Eleven universities)

Expected Occupation	*Index* *	*Total Realistically Expecting to Enter Occupation* **
Business	.30	(360)
Journalism	.23	(31)
Teaching	.20	(250)
Sales, Promotion	.18	(96)
Personnel	.16	(75)
Artistic and related fields	.16	(74)
Real Estate—Finance	.15	(62)
Law	.14	(182)
Advertising, Public Relations	.12	(41)
Farming	.11	(54)
Natural Science	.10	(189)
Engineering	.10	(399)
Food, restaurant—Hotel Administration	.09	(22)
Architecture	.04	(49)
Medicine	.03	(354)

* This index was constructed by simply dividing the number entering each field only as a compromise (that is, they would "most like" to go into a different occupation) by the total number who expect to enter that field.

** Omits 574 who did not know what occupation they would go into, 144 who mentioned professions classified as "other," and 19 who did not answer the question.

nalism, "artistic and related fields," and personnel also seem to have been selected as second choice by high proportions of the students. There are probably many young people who go into these fields as the commercial equivalent of the creative arts they may be drawn toward. Teaching, too, draws a high proportion of students who view the profession as a compromise; perhaps they feel they would prefer to spend their full time on research or in the creative arts, but that these aims are unrealistic.

At the other end of the list, the occupation drawing the smallest number of reluctant recruits is medicine. Indeed, examining the occupations appearing at the lower end of the table reveals something again about professionalism—or perhaps we should say pre-professionalism, considering that students are still aspirants and not yet practitioners in these fields. We know that the professions recruit students who are already committed to the idea of a career. Now we see that, by and large, careers in the established professions attract the lowest proportion of reluctant recruits.

Some noticeable exceptions to this generalization deserve special attention. Farming may not be a profession; but few students who enter this field do so with backward glances. The same is true of hotel work.

This differential distribution of the reluctant recruits in a given field of work may well be felt in the level of professionalism of that field. Professional work demands dedication and identification with one's work as well as mastery of a body of knowledge. The fields that recruit students who enter them in a spirit of compromise are probably handicapped in developing the kind of *esprit de corps* characteristic of fields that attract less reluctant neophytes. These nuances of feeling might contribute to the varied levels of professionalism in certain occupations.

Another possible deterrent to development of this *esprit de corps* is the inconstancy of the neophyte's identification with his chosen field. Since many of the undergraduates we are discussing are still shopping around for a career, they change their minds more than once as they go through school. Some may have "busted out" of the curriculum necessary to prepare for the field they had at first counted on entering. Others may have concluded that their earlier choice was misguided. Perhaps the work was not what they had thought; the courses may have turned out to be too hard or too easy, uninteresting, or too time-consuming. Still others may have newly learned about a field of work they had never before been aware of, and been won over to it.

Because of this traffic toward and away from the various occupations the students declare for, each field of work must count on a certain number of inconstant students. Advertising, government service, public relations, journalism, business, and personnel work characteristically attract many of these "shoppers." An upperclassman who says he is thinking of one of these careers is quite likely to have made this selection only after having initially considered a totally different field as a freshman or sophomore. Conversely, an underclassman who says he plans to enter one of these occupations is quite likely to have given up the idea by the time he is a junior or senior. As a result, many a senior who says he plans a career in one of these fields has been identifying himself with that field for less than the full four years of his college work.

In contrast, seniors who say they plan to go into engineering, medicine, architecture, law, or teaching are likely to have had these plans since the very beginning of their college careers. These curricula may often lose students; indeed, their defectors become the very "shoppers" who turn to the other fields. But a senior who says he plans to enter one of these occupations is most likely to have maintained his identification with the same profession steadfastly, for the full four years of his college work. (Appendix 7 presents an "index of inconstancy" for each profession chosen by the students in the panel.)

Note that the fields in which career-shoppers are few, are principally the established professions which require intensive specialized training beginning even at the undergraduate level. On the psychological side, this sort of early and constant specialization can build up the feelings of involvement, investment, and identification that tend to anchor the student to his field. His regular interaction with other people who are likewise becoming specialists reinforces this process. In sociological terms, one would predict that the student who has selected one of these fields and stayed with it throughout his college career has been more successfully socialized to the values, standards, and subculture of his profession than has his counterpart who has shopped around for a career during his early college years. The young man in his fourth year of engineering school, for example, who suddenly develops a strong interest in philosophy would thus be much more reluctant to abandon his original interest than a senior who has concentrated his work in the humanities with a major, say, in English literature. There is so much technical specialization which he would find not transferable to other fields, that his sense of waste would probably be strong. In addition, the advanced engineering student already "feels like" an engineer, already has a sense of loyalty to the profession and feels anchored to it.

OCCUPATIONAL IMAGES

Just how do the students decide which occupations to turn to? One important factor of this intricate process of occupational selection is "occupational image."

Students tend to have a discernible idea of the distinctive demands and rewards characteristic of each occupational field. In selecting their careers, they try to pick a field of work that, as they see it, provides the kinds of rewards and makes the sorts of demands that they consider compatible with their own values.

Here are some examples of this matching process. We have shown that there are, by and large, three major approaches to the values that work is expected to satisfy: the "instrumental" or "reward values" (those having to do with money, status, prestige and security); and the "goal values" (those having to do with self-expression), and the "interpersonal values," (those having to do with people).

The occupations students select are listed in Table 2-7 in the order of their appeal to students who stress the value of "money" in their work. Of course, we are dealing with young people who have not yet entered these occupations. Although we already know that many of them will change their minds even before they finish college, this tabulation tells us a great deal about the public image among college students of the major rewards to be derived from these occupations. Again, it is clear that the "professions" differ from the nonprofessional occupations in this important respect: students who turn to the professional fields tend to reject the re-

TABLE 2-7. VALUES STRESSED BY STUDENTS EXPECTING TO ENTER CERTAIN OCCUPATIONS

(Eleven universities)

WHAT BUSINESS OR PROFESSION DO YOU REALISTICALLY THINK YOU ARE MOST LIKELY TO GO INTO?	CONSIDER TO WHAT EXTENT A JOB OR CAREER WOULD HAVE TO SATISFY EACH OF THESE REQUIREMENTS ...

(Percentage in each profession who rate as highly important a "chance to earn a great deal of money.")

	Money	*Total* *
Food, restaurant, hotel	77	(22)
Business, real estate, finance	58	(422)
Sales, promotion	54	(96)
Advertising, public relations, journalism	56	(72)
Law	50	(182)
Art and related professions	49	(74)
Personnel	41	(75)
Engineering	38	(399)
Medicine	33	(354)
Farming	31	(54)
Architecture	31	(49)
Natural science	30	(189)
Teaching	17	(250)

(Percentage in each profession who select "creativity" as highly important)

	Creative and Original	
Artistic and related fields	81	(74)
Architecture	86	(49)
Advertising, public relations, journalism	83	(72)
Natural science	64	(189)
Teaching	59	(250)
Engineering	52	(399)
Law	43	(182)
Farming	48	(54)
Medicine	34	(354)
Personnel	41	(75)
Business, real estate, finance	36	(422)
Sales, promotion	36	(96)
Food, restaurant, hotel	45	(22)

TABLE 2-7—*Continued*

WHAT BUSINESS OR PROFESSION DO YOU REALISTICALLY THINK YOU ARE MOST LIKELY TO GO INTO?	CONSIDER TO WHAT EXTENT A JOB OR CAREER WOULD HAVE TO SATISFY EACH OF THESE REQUIREMENTS . . .	
(Percentage in each profession who rate as highly important an "opportunity to be helpful to others")		
	Helpful to Others	*Total* *
Personnel	75	(75)
Food, restaurant, hotel	65	(22)
Medicine	53	(354)
Teaching	47	(250)
Architecture	29	(49)
Law	45	(182)
Sales, promotion	45	(96)
Advertising, public relations, journalism	31	(72)
Business, real estate, finance	30	(422)
Art and related fields	28	(74)
Engineering	28	(399)
Natural science	30	(189)
Farming	22	(54)

* Omits 574 who did not know what occupation they would go into, 144 in "other professions," and 19 who did not answer the question.

ward values in work; those who turn to the world of business emphasize these values.

The next tabulation re-ranks the various occupations in terms of the proportions of aspirants who emphasize the self-expression value of "creativity" as a principal reward in one's work.

Notice that it is not only the artistically related fields (art, architecture, and journalism) which attract high proportions of students who stress self-expression and creativity. The natural sciences and teaching are close to the top of the list, as well.

The "interpersonal" value complex attracts students who plan to enter personnel, hotel work, medicine, and teaching. It is quite obvious that their occupational values and the nature of the work are meaningfully related, for each of these occupations involves working in close interpersonal contact with others.

There is undoubtedly an important element of reality in these occupational images. In our society a businessman has a greater

chance of earning money than does a teacher, a social worker can
expect greater opportunities for contact with people than a research chemist, and an artist has more opportunity for creative
self-expression than an accountant. We have purposely chosen extreme cases for the sake of contrast, and even they can only be
expressed as probabilities. One might also have added that a hotel
manager often has greater opportunities than a school principal
to satisfy his interest in people; that the opportunity for creative
self-expression in executive work may often be as vast and as chal-
lenging for a businessman as the production of a painting or a
poster is for an artist. In no case in American society are the rewards and demands of the many occupations exclusive to one field
of work.

There must also be, then, a highly projective quality about
these occupational images. That is, aspirants stress in the occupation of their choice the kinds of rewards and demands that they
wish for—the ones that they feel they require. This would
mean that a certain selective recruitment occurs. If students
choose occupations they *feel* are compatible with certain values
and if they differ in what they consider to be the most important
values in work, it follows that each occupation will tend to recruit
neophytes with distinctive values, with characteristic ideas about
the meaning of their work.

This leads to a third thread in our speculation. To what extent
do these occupational images and the selective recruitment of neophytes bring about a self-fulfilling prophecy? To what extent
do people now engaged in the various occupational fields of American society actually see different values in the meaning of their
work? Are there important value differences in the rewards and
demands which motivate a man or a woman to spend the greater
part of his working life "grubbing for a living" or "fulfilling himself" in his chosen life work; running the "rat race" or feeling
gratified that he is contributing his bit to the gross national product? The expectation that one's chosen career will gratify certain
values may create the conditions that can transform the wish into
the reality. What we have called "occupational images" may start
out as fictions, with little basis in a student's actual experience

with the reality of life in these professions. Fiction or no, however, these images can have real consequences for the values "really" predominant in each profession, if they serve to funnel into each field neophytes whose occupational values correspond to the values they *think* characterize the career they have selected.

Of Women and Careers [10]

So far we have been discussing occupational values and occupational choice among men. Things are different for the women; for in almost every aspect of occupational values and occupational choice, men and women tend to differ sharply. To some extent these differences can be explained in terms of the physical requirements of the occupation, but such considerations are relatively minor in the middle-class professional and white-collar occupations chiefly selected by college students. In these fields the characteristic occupational values expressed by the women are much more likely to echo the ways in which American society defines the place of men and women in the occupational structure.

In the first place, a career plays a more important part in the total life plans of a man than of a woman. For men it is a life-work; for women it is more often an interlude. (Fifty-two per cent of the women said they did not expect to be working ten years after graduation, whereas all the men expected to be occupationally active.)

The pattern is for the girls to plan for a career, to work at it before marriage, to continue working after marriage until the birth of the first child, to interrupt professional life while the children are young, and perhaps to resume occupational life after the children have reached a certain age.

> I'm pinned now and we'll be married after we graduate. I hope to get a job teaching while my husband does his graduate work. Then as soon as we're settled, I hope we'll have a family. We'll want at least three children. Then I expect I'll go back to teach-

---

10 The data in this chapter which refer to the opinions of women students, apply to the Cornell girls only, since the Cornell sample was the only one in which women students were questioned. (See Introduction.)

ing, but I wouldn't leave the children until they are out of high
school.

> Every woman should have a career. She should have a chance to
> express herself, to make her own way and to find out what she likes
> and where her talents lie. But she shouldn't work while the chil-
> dren are little. They should be raised by a full-time mother until
> they are at least six and ready for school. If she wants to work
> again part-time when they are in school, why I think that's OK.
> But not full-time until they are ready to start high school. Say
> 14 or so.

A traditional middle-class idea that a woman's only career
should be her family is rejected by almost all the students. Instead,
they are neither unequivocally for nor unequivocally against the
idea of women having careers. The attitude seems to be, "It's okay
providing . . ." Providing she is not married, or providing she has
no children, or providing her children are "old enough"—a notion
about which there is a wide range of opinion. Let the women
have careers, indeed encourage them, but be sure it does not inter-
fere with her main job of bearing and rearing children.

It is at this point, incidentally, that opinions of men and women
often diverge: 41 per cent of the men approve of women working
only if they have no children and an additional nine per cent
disapprove under any circumstances. The corresponding figures
for women are only 26 per cent and one per cent. Indeed, many of
our findings about the students' picture of marriage and family
life suggest that the American college woman sees herself leading
the life of an active and very busy person—perhaps busier and
more active than the men would have her be. Table 2-8 shows
that the women are more likely than the men to accept the idea
of combining career and family life. In Chapter 4 (page 93) it is
clear that the women prefer larger families than the men do—another example, perhaps, of their greater readiness to take on
family responsibilities.

Yet, for most of the women, family life decidedly takes precedence over working at a career. Our data indicate that just about
every college girl wants to marry and have children, and that she
fully expects to do so (see Chapter 4). Most of them see no essen-

TABLE 2-8. WOMEN ARE MORE LIKELY THAN MEN TO APPROVE OF
COMBINING CAREER AND FAMILY LIFE
(Cornell 1950)

WHICH OF THE FOLLOWING STATE-MENTS CONCERNING WOMEN WORKING DO YOU COME CLOSEST TO AGREEING WITH? Total =	*All Students* (2758)	*Men* (2008)	*Women* (750)
	(Percentage giving indicated response)		
In general, I don't approve of women having careers	7	9	1
I approve of a woman having a career if she wants one, providing she is not married	19	22	9
I approve of a married woman having a career if she wants one, providing she has no children	19	19	17
I approve of a married woman having a career if she wants one, providing her children are older than:	28	25	37
Infancy to pre school (up to 5 years)	2	1	3
Grade school (6-10 years)	4	4	6
Junior High (11-14 years)	3	3	3
High School (15-17 years)	8	7	10
18 or older	9	9	12
No answer for age	2	1	3
I approve of a married woman having a career if she wants one, regardless of the age of her children	24	22	29
Don't know or no answer	4	3	6

tial conflict between family life and a career—the sort of career, that is, that they consider "suitable" for a woman.

For the women, after all, approach the idea of work outside the home quite differently from the way the men do. Table 2-2 showed that 28 per cent of the men at all the colleges we polled expected their most important satisfactions in life to come from their professional activities. The corresponding figure for the Cornell women was six per cent. Moreover, only eleven per cent of all the men did not expect their careers to represent one of the major sources of satisfaction in their lives. The corresponding figure for the Cornell women was 31 per cent.

THE WOMEN'S OCCUPATIONS

The occupations women choose to go into are quite different from those chosen by the men. They overwhelmingly select the traditional "women's occupations." Of all the men we polled, about half desired to enter engineering, medicine, business or law; but less than one-tenth of the women chose any of these occupations. Conversely, 37 per cent of the women we polled selected teaching, social work, secretarial work, art or journalism and drama compared with about one-seventh of the men (Appendix 8).

As a result, the women are much more likely than the men to expect to be salaried employees, usually for some humanitarian, educational, nonprofit organization. Compared with the men, only a small minority of women say they expect to achieve occupational independence in the sense of becoming independent entrepreneurs or professionals. And this suits them. Although 49 per cent of all the Cornell men preferred independent business or professional enterprises, the corresponding figure for women was 17 per cent.

This may in part be their acknowledgment of the harsh reality that women are still not entirely accepted in certain occupations, but our data show that it is very likely to be expressed as a matter of taste on the part of the women. For the values that women seek to gratify in their occupational life are quite different from those that appeal to the men. Relatively speaking, the women stress the value of working with people; and they are much less likely to emphasize the reward values of occupational life.[11]

Women in American society, more than men, think of themselves as sensitive to the nuances of interpersonal relations; they are more interested in being socially useful, in dealing with people and touching their lives in a direct and personal way. If they enter "appropriate" occupations, it is not only because these are the ones accessible to women, but also because they are the occupations that the women feel will permit them to put to good use their special talents for interpersonal relations and interest in people.

11 See Table 2-7 for the occupations chosen by men who stress the value of working with people. They largely correspond to the occupations which predominantly appeal to the women.

TABLE 2-9. IMPORTANCE OF VARIOUS OCCUPATIONAL REQUIREMENTS
AMONG WOMEN *
(Cornell Women, 1952: Total = 420)

CONSIDER TO WHAT EXTENT A JOB OR CAREER WOULD HAVE TO SATISFY EACH OF THESE REQUIREMENTS . . .	PERCENTAGE ** RANKING EACH GOAL AS:			
	Highly Important *First*	*Other High*	*Medium*	*Low*
Goal Values				
Provide an opportunity to use my special abilities	29	56	15	1
Permit me to be creative and original	12	45	33	11
People-centered Values				
Permit me to work with people rather than things	24	40	22	15
Permit me to be helpful to others	11	44	36	10
Reward Values				
Stable, secure future	13	31	46	11
Chance to earn a good deal of money	3	20	56	22
Give me social status and prestige	1	16	55	28
Other Values				
Leave me free of supervision	2	31	54	12
Give me a chance to exercise leadership	—	27	54	18
Provide me with adventure	1	17	43	38

* See also page 27, Table 2-3, for similar distribution among all men.
** Percentages are to be added horizontally.

This is a rather apt illustration of how individual motivation is socially shaped. American society, by inculcating the recognized and accepted roles appropriate to the sexes, encourages men and women to *want* different things from their work. Women today may seek equality of opportunity in professional life, but this by no means implies that the needs and goals of their occupational lives correspond—or need necessarily correspond—to those of men.

CAREER GIRLS

But what about the career woman—the girl who rejects the overwhelming emphasis on family relations characteristic of most college women and who expects her work to be a major source of life-satisfaction? We classified our female respondents according to how seriously they said they approached the idea of a career.[12] Several important ways in which the career women differed from the other girls were revealed.

Among college students, no definite set of social characteristics appears to predispose a girl toward a career. Slight differences between career girls and other coeds begin to show up when we compare them in terms of classroom achievement. The distribution of grades is always limited by the normal curve, so that by definition few students receive top marks. Yet 18 per cent of the girls who were rated as seriously career-minded reported cumulative averages above 85—a proportion twice as high as the proportion of high achievers among girls who do not stress a career. It may be that many career girls stress intellectual achievement either because they have special abilities, or because it is

TABLE 2-10. CAREER ORIENTATION AND CUMULATIVE AVERAGE GRADE
AMONG WOMEN
(Cornell Women, 1952)

WHAT IS YOUR CUMU-LATIVE AVERAGE?	INDEX OF CAREER-ORIENTATION *		
	High	*Intermediate*	*Low*
Total =	(108)	(182)	(130)
	(Percentage giving indicated response)		
85 or over	18	8	9
80-84	46	47	44
75-79	28	37	41
up to 74	8	8	6

* The index of career-orientation was constructed as follows:

What three things or activities in your life do you expect to give you the most satisfaction?	1952	1950	Classification
Career selected as first choice	25	56	High
Career selected as second choice:			
Plan to go to graduate school	83	154	High
Do not plan to go to graduate school	96	134	Intermediate
Career selected as third choice	86	105	Intermediate
Career rejected as possible major satisfaction	130	301	Low

12 The construction of this index is explained in a footnote to Table 2-10.

particularly to their taste. In other cases, the causal sequence may be reversed: they may be particularly highly motivated to do well in the classroom in order to be accepted for professional training.

Even though the career girl is likely to be an academically superior student, it would be a mistake to assume that she buries herself in her books, ignores social activities, and disdains everything irrelevant to the advancement of her career. The career girls in our sample reported dating nearly as often as did their opposites: 58 per cent of the former compared with 64 per cent of the latter dated at least once a week—obviously no group of wallflowers.[13] The career women, in addition, engage in just as many extracurricular activities as other women do. In other words, there is every indication that career women are just as likely as any other group of girls to associate with men on the campus.[14]

NON-CONFORMITY AND CAREERS FOR WOMEN

There are certain important respects, however, in which the career women differ sharply from the family-centered women. In a nutshell, the career girls are more likely to present themselves as non-conformists. Not all of them, certainly. Not even the majority. But as a group they include a greater proportion of women who indicate a certain irreverence for rules and conventions.

Take a simple matter like respect for rules and regulations which most colleges set up for their students: limitations, for example, on the number of classes one can skip, special permission for weekends away from the campus, the requirement to return to the dormitory at a given hour, and so on. Many students gripe about such rules but the majority accept them as perhaps an irritating necessity. When we asked the Cornell students, "Do most of the rules and regulations at Cornell seem useless to you?" only a negligible minority checked, "Yes, they do." Since the rules for women are stricter and more pervasive at Cornell than are those for men, they came in for sharper censure. About one quarter of all the students at Cornell (24 per cent) said they considered these

---

[13] This may be characteristic of Cornell girls rather than of coeds in general, since the Cornell women have the advantage of an imbalanced sex ratio.

[14] See Chapter 4 for a full discussion of dating and courtship.

particular rules "useless." Still, that means that the vast majority of the Cornell students are willing to conform in the sense of accepting the need for such rules, with better grace or worse.

Among girls who do not seriously consider a career, however,

TABLE 2-11. CAREER GIRLS ARE MORE LIKELY THAN OTHERS TO
EXPRESS NON-CONFORMING ATTITUDES
(Cornell Women)

	INDEX OF CAREER-ORIENTATION * (Based on 1952 responses)		
	High	*Intermediate*	*Low*
Total =	(108)	(182)	(130)
Do most of the rules and regulations at Cornell seem useless to you?			
Yes, they do	18	18	7
No, they don't	82	82	93
What about those for women only?			
Yes, they seem useless	33	32	18
No, they don't	67	68	82
	(Based on 1950 responses)		
Total =	(210)	(239)	(301)
If you discovered that the man you were engaged to had had previous sex relations, would you break the engagement?			
No, I wouldn't break it	70	62	60
I'm not sure	27	36	35
Yes, I'd break it	4	2	5
Check any of the following circumstances under which you consider pre-marital sex relations justified **			
For women			
Never justified	38	52	50
If they're in love at the time	32	18	15
If it's not purely physical	16	14	8
If he is not promiscuous	17	13	6
For men			
Never justified	29	38	39
If they're in love at the time	33	21	17
If it's not purely physical	21	18	15
If he is not promiscuous	26	21	15

* For construction of this index see footnote to Table 2-10.
** Percentages should not be cumulated owing to multiple responses.

almost all accept the need for such rules. Only 18 per cent say they are "useless." In contrast, among the career girls the proportion of non-conformists, while still a minority, is much higher. It is 33 per cent. Their greater tendency toward non-conformism is noticeable, too, when it comes to more serious matters—their ideas about pre-marital sex relations, for example.

Detailed discussion of the students' attitudes toward pre-marital sex relations appears in Chapter 4. Since we are anticipating matters somewhat by broaching the subject here, we shall content ourselves with a simple example.

We asked the students to express their attitudes toward pre-marital sex relations. The questions and the distribution of responses appear in Table 2-11. Note that whereas half of the least career-oriented women said that pre-marital sex relations for women were never justified, only 38 per cent of the career women expressed this view. Moreover, the career girls were more likely than others to say that they would not feel it necessary to break the engagement upon learning that their fiancé had had pre-marital sex relations.

OCCUPATIONAL VALUES OF CAREER WOMEN

In all these respects—class average, sexual permissiveness, and rejection of rules—the position of the career girls differs sharply from the position of other college women. This is true also of her general approach to her work. For, unlike the girls who do not take the idea of a career so seriously, career women tend to approach their work in virtually the same spirit as the men do. Indeed, they are particularly close to the career-oriented men. Like them, the career women tend to emphasize the goal-values of their work, to stress the appeal of a chance for creativity and the possibility of exploiting one's own capacities at work.

Security, status, and monetary gains are values which an American woman usually derives through her husband, not her job. Hence, few of the girls, career-minded or not, say they find these reward-values particularly compelling in considering vocational activity. Even so, however, the girls who say they consider these reward-values of primary importance turn up even more rarely among the career-minded girls than among coeds who do not emphasize their future occupational activities.

Details can be seen in Table 2-12. There the occupational values considered most important by career-minded women are compared with those of the other coeds. At the same time, the profiles of these women are contrasted with the comparable profiles of men who express different degrees of commitment to their own careers.

In other words, although sex-roles are among the most important determinants of occupational choice and occupational values, their power for women who have adopted a "male" attitude toward their occupations begins to weaken. The career woman is a non-conformist almost by definition, first insofar as she values work over and above the social norm for women; and second, in the sense that she seeks in her work many of the same values that are sought by her male counterparts. The values that appeal to other women are less likely to appeal to her.

But then what about the coed who does not really take very seriously the notion of pursuing her occupation with the same earnestness that seems to characterize the girls we have called here "career women." Why should these girls consider a career at all?

One important reason is to mark time before marriage. A second is insurance against the possibility (considered very remote) of remaining single. Another is insurance against possible adversity that might occur during marriage.

> I want to go into social work even though I know it requires a long training period and if I marry I'll give it up. I'd probably give it up for good, but kid myself that I'd be going back. But then I think: suppose I don't get married? Or suppose something might happen to my husband? Then I'd have a career which is worthwhile and interests me and I'd be able to live a full life anyway.

> It's important to me to have a career, even though I expect to marry and have a family and will only give it up. If you know you can always get a job if you have to—in case of financial reverses, for example, you feel more secure.

But there is still another cluster of more significant reasons be-

TABLE 2-12. IMPORTANCE OF VARIOUS OCCUPATIONAL REQUIREMENTS, ACCORDING TO DEGREE OF EMPHASIS ON ONE'S CAREER (Cornell Women, 1952, Compared with Men at eleven universities)

CONSIDER TO WHAT EXTENT A JOB OR CAREER WOULD HAVE TO SATISFY EACH OF THESE REQUIREMENTS (Ranked first in importance)	MEN — WHAT THREE THINGS OR ACTIVITIES IN YOUR LIFE DO YOU EXPECT TO GIVE YOU THE MOST SATISFACTION (First choice)			WOMEN — INDEX OF CAREER-ORIENTATION *		
	Career (850)	All Other Responses (490)	Family Relations (1635)	High (108)	Intermediate (182)	Low (130)
Total =						
Goal Values	49	36	35	48	40	35
Provide an opportunity to use my special abilities	35	24	27	32	30	24
Permit me to be creative and original	14	12	8	16	10	11
Reward Values	31	30	44	13	18	22
Stable, secure future	20	15	32	11	15	15
Chance to earn a good deal of money	10	12	10	2	2	5
Give me social status and prestige	1	3	2	—	1	2
People-centered Values	8	28	15	36	36	39
Permit me to work with people rather than things	5	10	7	23	25	27
Permit me to be helpful to others	3	18	8	13	11	12
All other values	5	6	5	3	6	4

* For the construction of this index see footnote to Table 2-10.

hind the coed's wish to work even if she does not, strictly speaking, view herself as a career girl. Many of these young women wish to prepare themselves for a career because they feel they need more than family life to give them a feeling of being personally worthwhile.

> I'm studying bacteriology and I enjoy it. If I marry and have a family—and that's what I hope for—of course I won't be able to work full time, maybe not for many years. But I feel definitely that I need a chance to show myself that I can do a real job and can make my own way in the world, to be able to have respect for myself.

> I think one tragedy for many women today is that they feel useless. . . . I think a woman who has a profession, even if she doesn't work at it, even if she is just a housewife, feels more at home in her husband's world . . . She is more of a companion, more understanding . . . more worthwhile.

Though most college women unhesitatingly choose marriage and the family, this wish to find a sense of worth in professional work rather than simply in family life, stays with many. The conflict, therefore, if it exists at all, is likely to occur much later, during the years when the young, college-trained mother is raising her pre-school children. It is at this point that the college women expect to feel stifled. It is in this context that they wonder whether they will long for the day when they can take up or resume some sort of professional life.

> I know I hate housework. It's not that I expect to set the business world on fire when I get a job. I'll probably end up as a glorified secretary. But at least it will be a challenge. Raising kids is a twenty-four hour job that is challenging maybe one hour out of the twenty-four. The rest is drudgery. I've seen it with my friends. They can't wait to get back to part-time work. Anything, anything at all to get out of the house again. And I wonder whether I'll be the same way.

> I love being with children, and I hope to have dozens, and I wouldn't think of leaving them until they're out of grade school. But I guess I'll be just like everybody else—finding myself dreaming of the day when I can go back to work, when I can get really

dressed up every day and become a human being instead of a sort of housework-and-scolding machine.

I've seen so many girls becoming literally *stupid* when they get tied up with babies and husband and housework. Recently I had dinner with a friend who now has two children. All through dinner her only topic of conversation was whether she should get a clothes dryer or a dishwasher. What a topic for dinner conversation! She realized it, too. After dinner when we were doing the dishes she told me she can't wait to go back to work as soon as the children are old enough. She said: "When I had a job I was more interesting to myself," and I can understand her point of view. And she even worries about whether she'll be able to hold a job if she stays away from working until the kids go to school.

But, no matter how many misgivings the girls may have, they still have no doubt that the game is worth the candle.

Yes, I know lots of young marrieds who gripe over their ten o'clock coffee about how utterly *stultifying* it is to be stuck with the house and kids all the time. But not one of them regrets having gone to college. And I feel that way too. I guess I'll end up like everybody else, in the suburbs with a house and kids, but I think I'll make my husband's life pleasanter, understand my children better, and be a more active and more interested citizen and person because of having gone to college.

There is no question that college girls count on building up equity in family life, not in professional work. A dedicated career-girl is a deviant: in a real sense she is unwilling to conform to her sex-role as American society defines it. For professional work among women in this country (and the college-trained women agree) is viewed as an interlude, at best a part-time excursion away from full-time family life—the family life which the coeds yearn for, impatiently look forward to . . . and define as largely monotony, tedium, and routine.

It is this basic contradiction which makes it difficult for college women to come to terms with themselves. They measure family life by standards that leave no doubt about its important—indeed its primary—value to them. At the same time, however, they apply to it other standards which determine value in our culture: self-expression, self-esteem, prestige, status, income, power, recognition and respect from others. In our culture these values are imbedded in the institutional complex of occupation, not of family.

The plan of combining family-raising with professional work, so widespread among college women today, is one technique of escaping from this dilemma. The girls see no way, apparently, of incorporating values institutionally tied to occupational life, into the occupation of wife and mother which they unanimously choose as their life's work.

3

The Fraternity System:
A Style of Life

COLLEGE INVOLVES MUCH MORE than the serious consideration of curriculum and career. It is the bull session, the football weekends, the drinking parties. It is dating, courtship, love, and often marriage. Many students made this abundantly clear to us. Time after time we were told quite literally:

> I have no intention of letting my studies interfere with my college education!

THE FRATERNITIES

The hub of social life and the guiding principle of community organization on many American college campuses is the fraternity system. In many universities the fraternities set the patterns of social life and strongly influence the modes of behavior even of the "independent" students who are not officially members of the system.

An increasing number of schools are attempting to parallel the fraternity system, which rests ultimately on a principle of exclusion, with some other more widely based forms of associational living and eating arrangements. Yet the fraternities remain well entrenched on many campuses. In the universities we studied, membership ranged from a low of 23 per cent of the student body at Wayne State to a high of 85 per cent at Wesleyan University.

Harvard and Yale do not have fraternities in the literal sense; but they have exclusive-membership "eating clubs" which are similar in many respects to the fraternities on other campuses.

There is no doubt that the fraternities perform needed functions in the campus community. They provide housing and shelter for many students; and since certain colleges have inadequate or insufficient housing facilities for their students, the administration may rely on fraternity housing to fill the gap. But, what is perhaps their principal function from the students' viewpoint is that the fraternity often acts as a substitute for the primary group.

THE FRATERNITY AS PRIMARY GROUP

The adolescent who leaves his home community, his family and his friends to go off to a large university, often experiences a major social transition. Even if he does not literally leave his home, he is very likely to be in the process of loosening his ties to his family —leaving it psychologically, so to speak. On campus he rarely has primary ties. The fraternity is one of the major institutionalized devices for reknitting the primary bonds that may have been cut on the way to college.

This theme recurred continually when students told us why they joined "the house."

> The campus is so big, you can get lost in it. But in the house, you feel that they accept you. It's like a family.

> You really get to know people. Not so impersonal—like a family.

> You have a place where you feel at home and people you feel at home with.

> You feel you belong somewhere. You're not so all alone any more.

> . . . a group of people you feel really close to.

> . . . people who really mean something to you.

The very terms, "fraternity brother" or "sorority sister" imply this function of the fraternity as a substitute for the primary group.

"The House" possesses the ideal conditions for the establishment of such primary bonds—small size, physical proximity, frequent interaction, special symbols, rights and duties which focus upon togetherness and exclusiveness—even a common name ("he's a Deke; she's a KA"). For the essence of fraternity life is the pattern of "togetherness"—living together, eating together, studying together, going to movies and parties or games together. As a result, powerful bonds of loyalty to the group and solidarity among its members tend to be established. Fraternity membership gives the individual a sense of belonging.

AN ASIDE ON HOW IT WORKS

Since the next few pages discuss fraternities, we must explain some of their special folkways and, above all, their special vocabulary.

The student body is a floating population which partially renews itself every year. The graduating senior leaves a vacancy in his house which must be filled if the fraternity is to keep going—not only socially and psychologically, but as an economic unit as well. Recruiting new members is therefore very important.

This is done by "rushing." The rushing session is a brief interview during which a committee of fraternity members evaluates freshman newcomers in terms of their suitability as future "brothers." A brief interview—usually about five minutes—serves to size up the freshman. The cues may be: his secondary school training (prep school or public school); his father's social status; where he lives; his high school or prep school record; his interests; the way he dresses and talks and looks; his religious, national, or racial origins. If his father is an alumnus of the fraternity, or if he has been recommended by an *alum,* his chances of being chosen are improved.[1]

This five-minute rush interview will result, if the newcomer "looks OK," in an invitation to cocktails or dinner at the house. The purpose is mutual inspection which may run from one to several visits. If everything goes well—if the brothers think the freshman looks like "good material"—he will receive a "bid," or an invitation to join the house. If he accepts the bid, he becomes a

---

[1] Many fraternities in advance of rushing, compile more or less extensive background data describing potential recruits and provide the rushing committee members with this information before the interview.

pledge—that is, he has pledged himself to join the fraternity, again assuming that certain conditions are met by both sides.

He and the other newcomers who have been invited to join at the same time constitute "the pledge class" for the year. They usually take their meals at the house at a special pledge-table. They are exhorted to spend a certain number of hours a week "getting to know the brothers," are given specific chores and duties to perform about the premises, are expected to learn the school and fraternity songs and rules, are taught to be deferential to the brothers for the duration of the pledge period.

The "pledge-master" keeps a record of their defaults or successes and from time to time conducts a "shaping-up session." During these sessions the brothers make specific criticisms and suggestions designed to bring about a closer fit between the pledge and the ideals of the house. This is how it looks to the pledge:

> He said I'd have to get the lead out and start getting on some committees.
>
> He gave me a rough time. Said I was not getting into the spirit of the thing. Was taking it too lightly.
>
> He said I should spend more time at the house.
>
> He said I was not making enough of an effort to get to know the brothers.
>
> He said I ate like a pig—have to improve my table manners.
>
> He said I was goofing off and gave me some more hours (i.e., chores about the house).
>
> He did not have much to say last week. Just that I ought to get a haircut.

If the pledge gets through this trial period successfully, he is initiated into the fraternity; and—if there is space, and if the campus rules permit—he moves into the house.

Hazing and other dangerous practices associated with the pledge period and final initiation rites used to be much publicized. In recent years, however, these ordeals have been toned down considerably, although even now an occasional story of excessive trials comes to the attention of the campus authorities. The general idea is to solemnize the transition from pledge to brother by making it necessary for the neophyte to undergo some kind of ordeal. These ordeals are more than just tricks or cutting-up; they have been socially shared by all the members, they are exclusive only to members, and they have certain elements of *trauma* or shock which (as most *rites de passage*) serve to commemorate and solemnize the event. For all these reasons, therefore, they tend to increase the sense of identification that the newly initiated members feel with their group and thus to enhance the sense of cohesiveness within that group.

PERSONALITY IN A WORLD OF IMPERSONALITY

The sense of exclusive membership, primary social interaction, the rituals and symbols of togetherness, and the fact that the fraternities fill important housing, psychological, and social needs for the college student contribute to this sense of identification and solidarity with the organization. It will be recalled (see p. 2 and Appendix 1) that one question this study asked was: "This group has its own personality, something over and above the individual members in it. Does this statement express the way you feel about any of the following groups?" The proportions of students on each campus who say they feel this way about their fraternity are listed in Table 3-1. Note that this sense of "the house's" separate identity is characteristic particularly of the students at the heterogeneous state campuses, and at Wesleyan—which is close to 100 per cent fraternity.

The fraternities busy themselves on the campus in many ways—for example, in campus politics. This does not refer, we hasten to explain, to national political groups, such as Young Republicans or Young Democrats. When the students say that they "politic," they are referring to their attempts to influence the distribution of power and acclaim in the various extracurricular aspects of student life.

In the colleges, as in the adult community, there are many specialized groups serving almost every interest and taste. Athletic teams, glee clubs, student government, dramatic clubs, debating societies, newspaper groups, radio groups—the list is almost endless. Participation in groups of this sort forms the essential part of

TABLE 3-1. TENDENCY TO PERSONIFY THE FRATERNITY
(Eleven universities)

This group has its own personality . . . *

	Percentage of Fraternity Members Choosing "Your Fraternity"	Total
North Carolina	71	(198)
Texas	70	(176)
Wesleyan	68	(236)
UCLA	67	(170)
Michigan	66	(209)
Wayne	58	(120)
Dartmouth	56	(187)
Yale **	56	(75)
Cornell (men)	55	(376)
Fisk	52	(61)
Harvard **	33	(107)

* See also page 2, Appendix 1 and Chapter 7 for further discussion of responses to this question.
** Yale and Harvard do not have fraternities in the strict sense of the word, but they do have eating clubs which are similar in function. The question at these universities referred to membership in these eating clubs rather than to fraternity membership.

what are called extracurricular activities. In the afternoons after classes, during the evenings, and on weekends, students drop their classroom assignments and rush off to meetings with others sharing their particular special interests: for these extracurricular activities represent one of the most important sources of satisfaction in college life for the student. These organizations also provide many coveted positions of power and popularity on the campuses. For example, about three out of four students said they participate in one or more extracurricular activities, and well over half reported two or more.

While such participation is by no means monopolized by fraternity members, they are much more likely than independents to engage in them. This is partly because of the explicit and vigorous effort made by the fraternities to secure members who have political power or potential political power, in the campus sense, and to motivate their members to seek and retain such power. These are the kinds of comments the students made:

When we have shape-up sessions they tell you, "You're not going out for enough activities. Better get on it."

That house is crooked. They've monopolized all the cheer leader jobs for the past seven years. Someday the scandal is going to break.

That job (chairman of a certain committee) always goes to an XXX. They try to keep it for their men.

Our house is an athletic house. We have the lettermen and we always try to get the fellows who'll make lettermen. We take as pledge-class those who are interested in sports and who look like good bets. And we put the pressure on. We have to keep up our reputation.

Our house is BMOH (Big Man On the Hill). That is, we try to get the wheels. We pledge the ones who look as if they could make it.

I'll tell you frankly, we're a party house. Just out for a good time. We don't rush men to go out for things. I'd say we're the only house on the hill that doesn't.

It is also, of course, because extracurricular activities attract students who *value* sociability and interaction and who *feel secure* about their social skills—qualities which are also more prevalent, whether by pre-selection or through socialization, among the fraternity members than among the independents. Yet, regardless of how secure they feel about their social skills, fraternity members are consistently more likely than independent students to engage in extracurricular activities.

DATING, DRINKING AND HAVING FUN

Another important function of the fraternities, perhaps the most important one, is to help the dating patterns. Courtship and dating are among the most salient aspects of student life.[2] Dating, the student feels, is not only a means of finding temporary association with the opposite sex, but is also a preparation for marriage. Many students state explicitly that they approach every date as a possible mate. The status system on the campus provides the members of similar status groups with access to suitable dates—suitable in the

---

[2] For a full discussion of courtship and dating, see Chapters 2 and 4.

sense of possible husbands and wives—and the fraternities are an intrinsic part of this status system.[3]

Members of fraternities and sororities are more likely than non-members to have active dating lives; fraternities are influential in determining dating patterns. For example, the fraternity system acts as an important framework for the choice of a dating partner. Fraternities are informally "rated" on the campus; some girls restrict their dates to members of the higher status fraternities. There are girls, for example, who "date a fraternity" at a time—they restrict their dating to various members of a specific fraternity during a semester or a year. Fraternities also hold frequent parties, the locus of much campus dating.

Dating is an important focus of attention especially in a co-educational institution. We asked, "How important a part of your college life do you think dating is?" Less than a third (29 per cent) of the men said very important," 44 per cent called it "moderately important" but only 20 per cent considered dating "not important." [4] Fraternity men are more likely than independents to say they feel that dating is an important part of college life.

Fraternity life gives "the brothers" something of an advantage in dating too. Only six per cent of the fraternity men said they had no dates; 18 per cent of the independent students reported none. Nineteen per cent of the fraternity men had fewer than one date a month; 25 per cent of the independent students reported dating this infrequently. In part this is because of the parties, dances, and organized channels for dating available to the fra-

---

3 Willard Waller, "The Rating and Dating Complex," *American Sociological Review,* 1937 II, pp. 727-734 and in *Readings in Social Psychology,* Theodore H. Newcomb and Eugene L. Hartley (eds.) (New York: Henry Holt & Co., 1947), pp. 388-394.

4 Women are more likely than men to stress dating activities. Only a negligible proportion of the women did not consider dating important. Sorority girls do not differ from unaffiliated women in this respect. This is based on comparison of men's and women's responses at Cornell, the only campus where women were interviewed. Their greatest emphasis on the importance of dating may be specific to the distorted sex ratio at Cornell—five men to every two girls. We are inclined to doubt, however, that the tendency of Cornell women to emphasize the importance of dating more than the men do is unique to this campus. We are more inclined to believe that although the magnitude of the difference in attitude among men and women may be greater at Cornell, it is probable that college women in general tend to attach more importance to dating than do the college men.

ternity man—further evidence of the degree to which the pace of social life is set by the fraternities.

We asked the students what sorts of things they actually did on dates. It turns out that on the whole the dating activities of fraternity men and independent students are quite similar, differing principally in two major respects. First, the reports the fraternity men gave us of their activities fit a more discernible pattern; independent students are less likely to state that any single activity is part of their most frequent dating behavior. Second, fraternity men are more likely than independent students to say they often take their dates places to dance or to drink. These activities are decidedly part of the fraternity dating pattern, although by no means exclusive to it.

TABLE 3-2. WHAT STUDENTS SAY THEY DO MOST FREQUENTLY AND WHAT THEY SAY THEY WOULD PREFER TO DO ON DATES. FRATERNITY MEN COMPARED WITH INDEPENDENT MEN

(Cornell Men, 1950)

	ACTUALLY DO MOST FREQUENTLY ON A DATE		LIKE BEST TO DO ON A DATE	
	Fraternity Members	*Independent Students*	*Fraternity Members*	*Independent Students*
Total * =	(799)	(715)	(799)	(715)
	(Percentage ** giving indicated response)			
Go someplace to dance	57	44	†	†
Go someplace to drink	40	27	14	10
Chance to be alone	35	32	65	66
Go places where you "can be seen"	33	26	10	7
Outdoor activities, picnics, hiking, etc.	25	23	72	76
Relax in someone's house, talk, listen to radio, read	18	19	59	60
Go to concerts, lectures, discussions	8	10	25	31

* Omits 185 fraternity members and 161 independent students who because of marriage or engagement said they did not participate in the dating system.
** Percentages should not be cumulated owing to multiple responses.
† Not asked.

What is perhaps more significant is the discrepancy between what the students say they most frequently do on a date and what they would really like to do—a far cry in many cases from their customary behavior. It would appear that the campus dating patterns over-supply, so to speak, drinking, partying, and going to places where you "can be seen." Many more students say they would prefer forms of dating which are not quite so formalized: outdoor activities, for example, relaxing in a home situation, having a chance to be alone together, even going to lectures and concerts. Notice, that the preferences expressed by the fraternity men vary little in these respects from the preferences of the independent students. Table 3-2 shows the way the preferences and practices stack up.

Since drinking is for many students part of formalized dating behavior, and since it is particularly entrenched in the fraternity dating pattern, it is to be expected that fraternity men report more drinking than independent students. And they do. (See Table 3-3.)

MONEY AND STYLE OF LIFE

It begins to become clear that fraternity membership implies a certain *style of life*: participation in campus activities, dating, drinking—in general, "having a good time."

Some of the activities involved in this style of life cost money, and some of the students simply don't have it. For example, 43 per cent of all students reported that during the academic year they held a job of some sort to help them pay their school expenses. Fifty-three per cent said they depend in whole or in part on their own earnings and savings to get through school. Somewhat more than half the students report that their father's income was less than $7,500 a year (median $5,360). Appendix 9 indicates that there is a marked tendency for the fraternities to recruit and to appeal to students who can better afford not only the fixed charges (fees, pins, lodgings, and so on) but also the style of life. "It's not only the initial cost, it's the upkeep."

This opens up another possible interpretation. Perhaps the so-called fraternity style of life is less a matter of belonging to a fraternity and more just a simple matter of having the economic means to allow one the free time and to meet the costs. But, while there is no doubt that having the economic means *is* an important element in determining this "style of life," it is also true that, social class for social class, the fraternity member is more likely to indulge in extracurricular activities, more likely to date, to drink, and to have a good time, than is his opposite number who remains independent. There is, indeed, a preference for the fraternity style of life, quite apart from the bald fact of having the money to indulge in it.

TABLE 3-3. COMPARISON OF FRATERNITY MEMBERS AND
INDEPENDENT STUDENTS

About how many extracurricular activities are you taking part in this term? (Eleven universities)	*Fraternity Members*	*Independent Students*
Total =	(1,114)	(1,809)
	(Percentage * giving indicated response)	
Two or more	73	42
One	15	20
None	11	36
No answer	2	2

Sociability Index ** (Cornell men, 1952)	(Percentage† reporting two or more extracurricular activities)	
High 3	86 (139)	50 (45)
2	72 (233)	47 (109)
1	68 (240)	50 (153)
Low 0	55 (71)	35 (109)

How important a part of college life do you think dating is? (Cornell men, 1950)	(Percentage giving indicated response)	
Total =	(984)	(876)
Very important	33	24
Moderately important	44	44
Not important	16	25
No answer	7	7

How often on the average did you date while at Cornell this year? (Count only pre-arranged meetings with the opposite sex.)		
Total =	(799)	(715)
Not at all	6	18
Less than once a month	19	25

TABLE 3-3—*Continued*

How often on the average did you date while at Cornell this year? (Count only pre-arranged meetings with the opposite sex.)	Fraternity Members	Independent Students
	(Percentage giving indicated response)	
Once a month	16	10
Twice a month	16	14
Once a week	17	13
Twice a week	9	8
More often than twice a week	5	3
No answer	12	9

(Cornell men, 1952) Total =	(683)	(416)
How often do you drink spirits? (whiskey, rum, etc.)		
Frequently	15	5
Occasionally	54	35
Rarely	23	35
Never	8	25

How often do you drink beer?		
Frequently	33	14
Occasionally	42	42
Rarely	16	23
Never	9	21

(Eleven universities) Total =	(1114)	(1809)
What kind of a time are you having in college?		
Very good	44	23
Fairly good	40	41
OK	14	29
Fairly poor	2	6
Very poor		1

About how much was your father's income last year . . . (Eleven universities)	(Percentage† who participate in two or more extracurricular activities)			
Under $3,000	70	(59)	31	(200)
$3,000-4,999	69	(198)	39	(585)
$5,000-7,499	72	(222)	46	(385)
$7,500-9,999	74	(197)	51	(213)
$10,000-19,999	72	(209)	42	(206)
$20,000 or over	74	(186)	51	(139)

TABLE 3-3—*Continued*

About how much was your father's income last year . . . (Eleven universities)	Fraternity Members		Independent Students	
	(Percentage† who say they are "having a very good time")			
Under $3,000	28	(59)	16	(200)
$3,000-4,999	36	(198)	17	(585)
$5,000-7,499	42	(222)	23	(385)
$7,500-9,999	47	(197)	26	(213)
$10,000-19,999	50	(209)	30	(206)
$20,000 or over	49	(186)	38	(139)
	(Percentage† who say they date twice a month or more)			
(Cornell men, 1950)				
Under $3,000	48	(42)	31	(65)
$3,000-4,999	54	(98)	37	(165)
$5,000-7,499	44	(123)	45	(117)
$7,500-9,999	58	(117)	35	(80)
$10,000-19,999	50	(147)	34	(76)
$20,000 or over	36	(98)	35	(23)
	(Percentage† who say they drink whiskey "frequently" or "occasionally")			
(Cornell men, 1952)				
Under $3,000	57	(35)	27	(56)
$3,000-4,999	56	(99)	32	(113)
$5,000-7,499	64	(121)	46	(92)
$7,500-9,999	69	(124)	46	(70)
$10,000-19,999	73	(158)	50	(48)
$20,000 or over	80	(123)	62	(26)

What is your cumulative average? (Eleven universities) Total =	(Percentage giving indicated response)	
	(1,114)	(1809)
Under 70	3	5
70-74	30	24
75-79	33	26
80-84	21	28
85-89	7	10
90 or above	2	2
No answer	3	6

* The percentages in this table are computed on bases which exclude students who could not be classified on all variables simultaneously examined: that is, students who did not answer the question; students whose responses were not

THE "GENTLEMANLY C"

To some extent, the fraternity style of life de-emphasizes the academic side of college life. Fraternity members are somewhat less likely than independents to obtain high grades probably because the tradition of the "gentlemanly C" still prevails in many of the houses.

> We don't pride ourselves on having "greasy grinds" in our house. There are three things we try to teach our men to handle moderately: liquor, women, and courses. Our motto is no excesses in any of them.

> Lots of pledges come in with the idea that fraternity life means all fun and no studying. We quickly educate them. Not that we want grinds—no—we try to get them to maintain a respectable average. Nothing very glittering, of course, just respectable.

> We try to keep our house's grades up to standard. There's plenty of help for the brothers who fall behind. We have files of old examinations in almost every course that they can use in studying. We even assign certain men to tutor any brothers who need help. They don't have to get super grades. After all, when you get out of college nobody asks what your grades were. Just maintain a decent average.

---

classifiable in terms of the categories presented here; and students to whom the question did not apply. Details appear below.

Cross-section of eleven universities: 52 students could not be classified according to fraternity membership; an additional 43 fraternity members and 81 independent students did not report father's income.

Cornell men, 1952: 52 students could not be classified according to fraternity membership; an additional 23 fraternity members and 11 independent students did not report father's income.

Cornell men, 1950: 148 students could not be classified according to fraternity membership; 185 fraternity members and 161 independent students said they did not participate in the dating system because they were married or engaged; 174 fraternity members and 189 independent students did not report father's income.

** This index is based on answers to the following three questions: Would you say you are the sort of person who finds it easier or harder to make friends than most people? How important is it for you to be well liked by different kinds of people? See page 18 for the distribution of responses to these questions. The third question in the index was, How often do you find yourself taking a position of leadership in a group you are with? Responses to this question distributed as follows: often, 26 per cent; sometimes, 42 per cent; occasionally, 23 per cent; rarely, 8 per cent; never, 1 per cent.

† The figures in parentheses give the bases on which the per cents have been computed.

There is, of course, no convincing evidence that fraternity members are less capable than other students. If they get poorer grades, then, it must be owing to their weaker motivation to get better ones. For, despite a pattern in many American colleges which stresses academic competitiveness and achievement, certain subgroups may establish counter-norms, diverging from the dominant ones. All students follow to some degree the modes of behavior appropriate to their own reference groups. All students must perform adequately in college as a pre-condition for remaining. But the fraternity as a reference group, by and large, emphasizes certain other forms of securing recognition and validating prowess over and above grades. These are the norms which stress *more* those values which have to do with style of life, and *less* those which have to do with academic achievement beyond "a respectable average."

CHEATING ON THE CAMPUSES

Concern about grades is, of course, characteristic of most college students, and the fraternity men are certainly not the only ones who are interested in "keeping up a respectable average." Anxiety about grades is always present, for a few points on an examination may mean the difference between passing or failing a course. Failure, in turn, may have wide-ranging consequences for one's social relations, future prospects, and present self-esteem.

Given the stress on grades in American colleges, one might expect a certain amount of cheating to occur on our campuses. And it does. How much? The answer must be imprecise, but to the point: a good deal.

From the students themselves we get varying estimates of how much cheating goes on. At Cornell we had asked: "In your opinion what proportion of Cornell students cheat fairly regularly?" The distribution of responses shows a wide variation in these estimates: more than half the students put the proportion of cheaters somewhere over 20 per cent of the student body. Of course we do not really know what they may mean by "fairly regularly" but it is certain that many students believe that cheating is a reasonably common practice.

Here is further evidence of the student's perception of the prevalence of cheating on our campuses. Thirty-six per cent of the students at all the universities we polled agreed that "Most college students would cheat on an examination if they were sure of not being caught" while 13 per cent weren't quite sure how to respond. (Fifty-one per cent disagreed with the statement.) We may reasonably assume that if the phrase *"most* college students" had been modified or less sweeping, the number agreeing would have been even higher. Again: two-fifths of all students agreed that the "recent charges of widespread cheating among students" were justified.

But this is what students say about others. More to the point is the question of what they say about themselves. Nearly two-fifths of the students we polled admit having cheated in college. And this estimate is almost certainly understated. We asked: "Have you ever used crib notes or copied in an examination while at college?" Thirty-seven per cent of all the students who answered the question [5] admitted that they had done some cheating some time during the course of their college careers. Fourteen per cent claimed to have cheated once, 21 per cent "somewhat more than that," one per cent "much more than that," and another one per cent did not specify how often.

It is certainly not justified to take these figures at their face value as a numerical estimate of the amount of cheating in our colleges. The two-fifths of the students who admitted cribbing or copying on an examination probably represents the lower limit of the proportion of cheaters. Moreover, many of our respondents are freshmen and sophomores who, if they have not copied as yet, have two or three years before them in which they *might* pick up the practice.

But let us try to understand what the implications of these figures might be. Just what does cheating mean? We find that quite aside from the pressure of grades, and quite aside from the moral overtones, cheating, so to speak, "hooks onto" three important value-clusters.

The first is the formal or informal nature of the social controls. For example, students who attend the larger colleges and universi-

---

[5] Two per cent did not answer it.

ties—campuses where an accompaniment of bigness is, presumably, more impersonal relations between student and administration— are more likely than others to admit having cheated. The only exception to this generalization is Harvard where, in spite of the large student body, only 11 per cent of the students admit having cheated. Either Harvard students are more honorable than others, or the "house system" at Harvard [6] succeeds in establishing highly personal social controls in spite of the large student body.

TABLE 3-4. PERCENTAGE OF STUDENTS WHO ADMIT HAVING CHEATED
(Ten universities) *

	Percentage Who Admit Cheating at Least Once	Total ($N = 100\%$)	Total Male Undergraduate Enrollment in 1952 **
Wayne	49	(519)	8692†
Texas	43	(516)	8513
UCLA	39	(467)	5880
Cornell men	38	(1151)	5546
Michigan	36	(488)	6342
Dartmouth	26	(365)	2588
Yale	24	(297)	4197
North Carolina	23	(414)	3038
Wesleyan	13	(277)	725
Harvard	11	(453)	4400

* Information not available for Fisk.
** Based on President's Report issued by each university.
† Includes 3,614 full-time and 5,078 part-time students.

The second cluster which links up with cheating has to do with a tendency to conform to what is perceived as the current practices of one's peer-group. (This is discussed further in Chapter 8.)

Finally, cheating is linked to a general deprecation of the academic experience as such: a certain disenchantment with, or perhaps a jaded approach to, one's school work. It is the student who is unsuccessful, uninterested, and critical who is most likely to cheat. Conversely, the student who enjoys, appreciates, and feels

---

[6] Harvard and Yale both have the "college system." That is, students live in small, tightly knit, almost independent dwellings where they take many of their classes, as well. Thus each house tends to build up a strong *esprit-de-corps*.

serious about learning is especially likely to deny that he has resorted to cheating.

TABLE 3-5. CHEATING IS MORE PREVALENT AMONG STUDENTS WHO GET LOWER
GRADES AND AMONG STUDENTS WHO DEPRECATE CERTAIN
ACADEMIC ASPECTS OF COLLEGE

	HAVE YOU EVER USED CRIB NOTES OR COPIED ON AN EXAMINATION WHILE IN COLLEGE			
	Yes, More Than Once	*Yes ... Once* *	*No, Never*	*Total*
(Eleven universities)	(Percentage ** giving indicated response)			
What is your cumulative average?				
Under 74	27	16	57	(901)
75-79	26	16	58	(856)
80-84	17	14	68	(738)
85 or over	9	15	76	(317)
Having the opportunity to go to college is very important to me				
Agree	22	16	63	(2838)
Disagree or ?	31	7	62	(113)
(Cornell men, 1952) How do you feel about your major or probable major				
Fairly interested or not interested	36	14	49	(345)
Not sure	30	23	46	(69)
Very interested	24	17	59	(647)
How much of the time spent in class and on required assignments this year was spent in doing things that do not seem important to you?				
A lot	40	16	45	(200)
Some	27	17	55	(562)
A little	22	17	61	(341)
None	22	11	67	(45)
Do you ever feel that what you are doing at Cornell is a waste of time?				
Often	38	16	45	(139)
Sometimes	29	17	54	(484)
Rarely or never	24	17	60	(526)

TABLE 3-5—*Continued*

	HAVE YOU EVER USED CRIB NOTES OR COPIED ON AN EXAMINATION WHILE IN COLLEGE			
	Yes, More Than Once	*Yes ... Once* *	*No, Never*	*Total*
(Cornell men 1952)	(Percentage ** giving indicated response)			
Do you think you cut classes more or less often than most students you know?				
More often	41	15	45	(172)
About the same	28	20	52	(328)
Less often	24	16	60	(648)

* Includes 37 cases in the 11 universities sample or 15 cases in the Cornell men 1952 sample who reported cheating but did not specify frequency.

** All percentages in this table are computed on bases which exclude students who could not be classified on all variables simultaneously examined. Details appear below:

Cross-section of eleven universities: 74 students did not answer the question on cheating; 163 did not provide information as to cumulative average; 24 did not answer the question on importance of opportunity to go to college.

Cornell men, 1952: 3 students did not answer the question on cheating; 90 had not selected a major or probable major. The number of students who did not provide information on the last 3 questions in Table 3-5 was, respectively, 3, 2 and 3.

Note that percentages are to be added horizontally.

Since cheating gears in with a de-emphasis of the intellectual side of college life, and since the fraternities, too, tend to de-emphasize the intellectual side of college, one would expect cheating to be more prevalent among fraternity members than among independents. It is. (See Table 3-6)

What accounts for the relationship between fraternity membership and cheating? Is it due to a pre-selection factor or does it reflect a group norm? If people who are disposed to cheat are, for some reason, especially attracted to fraternity life, we would be dealing with a pre-selection factor. On the other hand, it may be that students entering fraternities at the outset, are no more predisposed to cheat than others, but that once in the fraternity, the general lack of involvement with academic values which is associated both with fraternity norms *and* with cheating would encourage them to engage in the practice. In this case we would be dealing with a group norm. The evidence shows that it is probably the group norm rather than the pre-selection factor which accounts for the higher evidence of cheating among fraternity men.

Freshmen entering college are not usually inducted into the fraternities immediately, but they are "looked over" before being asked to join. It is usually in their sophomore year that they actually take up residence in the fraternity house. If we had found cheating to be more prevalent among affiliated freshmen than among independent freshmen, it would be justified to say that some sort of pre-selection process was at work—that there is something in the nature of the student who admits cheating that attracts him to the fraternity. But we found, on the contrary, that there was virtually no difference at all in the proportion of fraternity and non-fraternity freshmen who declared that they had cheated. The differences appeared only in the sophomore year and were maintained throughout the subsequent years of college life. The fraternity man who admits to cheating in classwork tends to find reinforcement in the fraternity environment for this sort of behavior—evidence, certainly, not necessarily of more widespread dishonesty in fraternities, but rather another indication of their deprecation of academic values.

TABLE 3-6. IN EVERY CLASS AFTER THE FRESHMAN YEAR, FRATERNITY MEMBERS ARE MORE LIKELY THAN INDEPENDENT STUDENTS TO ADMIT HAVING CHEATED

(Eleven universities)

Year in college:	Fraternity Members		Independent Students	
	(Percentage * who admit having cheated more than once)			
First	15	(178)	12	(498)
Second	24	(255)	16	(375)
Third	30	(320)	22	(437)
Fourth	32	(306)	23	(440)
Fifth	42	(49)	31	(48)

* The figures in parentheses are the bases on which each per cent was computed. Excluded from these bases are six fraternity members and eleven independent students who could not be classified as to year in college, as well as 52 students who could not be classified according to fraternity membership.

Because feelings are likely to be rather intense on this subject, it might be wise to make explicit the assumptions which underlie this analysis—indeed, all analyses of this sort. When we talk about "the fraternity man," for example, we are dealing with a group classification. The traits we report refer not to a composite person, but to types of persons to be found with greater or lesser frequency in the total system. The classification itself is principally a tool enabling the analyst for the moment to treat essentially disparate units "as if" the differences among them were irrelevant, "as if" their similarities to other units placed in a contrasting category were likewise irrelevant. This by no means obliterates the very real fact that such differences and similarities continue to exist. At Cornell, for example—the campus we know most intimately—it is certainly the case that members of certain fraternities might have much more in common with independent students than with other fraternity members. And certain students who never joined a fraternity come closer to the stereotype of a fraternity man than most affiliated students ever manage to get, or care to get. In many ways the range of individual differences among fraternity members is as wide as the range of individual differences among independent students.

This does not alter the fact that the fraternity system, *as* a system, performs certain clearcut sociological functions. In spite of admitted deviations and exceptions, the system as a whole fills certain needs; it provides a substitute for the primary group; it reinforces the status structures of the campus and influences the distribution of power. It provides housing and social facilities which are in short supply on many of the campuses.

Nor does it alter the fact that as a social system, fraternities are based upon discernible values of exclusiveness. As a system, they set the pace for a characteristic style of life which emphasizes the importance of dating, drinking and "having a good time," and which relegates the academic side of college to "its proper place" in the scheme of things. In Chapter 5 we shall see that this style of life also accompanies a preference for a conservative economic viewpoint and that the system socializes its membership in this direction.

4

Men and Women

AMONG THE MAJOR TASKS adolescents face are these: to solve the problem of their own identity, to achieve economic self-sufficiency, and to establish relationships with the other sex. Particularly in a co-educational institution, this last task is dealt with in highly patterned ways. The relationships between men and women are guided by a system of behavior, values and standards which, in the course of many student generations, have become institution-alized within the college culture. This is the so called dating system.

DATING AGAIN

There are those who feel that the strong emphasis on dating in college interferes with the academic aims of higher education. This view corresponds to a common campus stereotype which views the "social butterfly" and the "grind" as poles apart. The "grind" is the student who allegedly devotes himself exclusively to his academic pursuits and scorns the social whirlpool into which others are swept. The social butterfly is in the social swing, is seen at dances and parties, and spends so much time on dates that he has little left for classes and assignments. In terms of these stereo-types, we would expect the person who has done well in school to lead a meager social life while the person who constantly dates would just scrape by.

On the whole, however, there seems to be little relationship between academic success and dating patterns. With the possible exception of the small group of brainy women (girls with cumulative averages over 85), the students who have an active dating life do just as well in their classwork as those who go out on few dates. (See Appendix 10 and Chapter 2)

We have already mentioned the discrepancy between what the students say they would like to do on dates and what they say they actually do: that even though most students would prefer doing something outdoors, to meet in an informal setting, to relax, to get to know one another, to enjoy one another's company, yet partying, dancing and drinking are the most frequent dating activities. When we asked the reasons why they preferred such activities, 85 per cent of the students who said they like to engage in outdoor activities explained that "it's informal, relaxing." Seventy-nine per cent of those who especially like to be alone with their dates enjoyed it, they said, because it provides a "chance to get to know your date." In addition to this, nearly half of the students said they found it highly enjoyable to "relax in someone's apartment—talk, listen to records, etc."

The most enjoyable dates, then, are not the big shindigs or the drinking parties; they are the situations in which the students can meet in an informal, natural setting and get to know one another. Dating patterns, as they exist on our campuses, may be too formalized, too stereotyped, too artificial for the students' tastes. Probably, too, many men and women have their signals crossed, each thinking the other wants to drink, or dance, or go to parties whereas each would perhaps prefer less frenetic activity.

For one problem in enjoyable dating, of course, is precisely this necessity to coordinate the interests of both sexes—and these may diverge. Women, it turns out, are twice as likely as men to say they enjoy going to a lecture, concert or discussion, even on a date. Whether this interest is a reflection of the women's wish to prepare themselves for their role as cultural head of the family, or whether the Cornell girls are especially serious-minded, the fact remains that many of the coeds seem to belie the stereotype of flighty, intellectual lightweights.

Men, more than women, say they want a chance to be alone

with their dates, although many women also consider this a post-requisite to an enjoyable evening. But both parties do not necessarily have the same aims in mind. The girls are more likely to say they welcome the opportunity to be alone in order to "talk things over more seriously." The men, on the other hand, are more likely than the coeds are to say they want to be alone in order to get to know the girls better and to have an "opportunity to make love."

This is not to say, of course, that the problems in dating mean that the students do not enjoy it. Most of them do: (82 per cent of the women and 74 per cent of the men who dated at all said "most of the dates I go on are enjoyable"). Nevertheless many of them feel that there is something missing in their dating lives and that they could enjoy them more. Dating has, alas, its frustrations. The artificial atmosphere on the campus, the conventions of dating, and, at Cornell at least, the competitive pressure of an unequal sex ratio, tend to force the students into a dating pattern which they sometimes find repetitive and rigid. The students wish for a dating situation that would allow them to be alone, in a relaxed homelike atmosphere, or outdoors. They wish for a "chance to get to know your date better," they refer to "the strain of entertaining your date," and they appreciate situations which "make conversation easier." The dating pattern instead is oriented to parties on Saturday night, big weekends, drinking and dancing. The existence of this pattern may reflect the institutionalization of campus social life more than it reflects what the students think they want.

THE BACKGROUND FOR LOVE

The students consider dating important because it is fun, and because it may lead to marriage. Virtually every student wants to marry some day. Many feel that the sooner, the better. In fact, twelve per cent of the students we studied reported that they were married before graduation, and another 19 per cent said they were "engaged or otherwise going steady." Marrying or becoming engaged before graduation, incidentally, is more characteristic of the large coeducational universities than of the strictly men's colleges. At Wayne, for example, 42 per cent are already committed; at

Texas, 37 per cent; at Yale and Wesleyan only 22 per cent, and at Harvard 19 per cent. (See Appendix 11 for this distribution at the separate universities.)

The students seek in marriage a stable and dependable source of emotional support; the sense of ego enhancement which comes from being chosen by another; the avoidance of the threat of social isolation; the desire for sexual gratification; the desire for roles symbolic of full-fledged maturity (husband and father or wife and mother); the pride and satisfaction in having children. We have already mentioned that the students expect family life to be their most important source of satisfaction as adults and that among women in particular it is of overwhelming significance. Eighty-four per cent of the Cornell women said this. When we talk with the students about marriage and the family, we are approaching the basic stuff of the social content of college life.

WHEN TO MARRY

To these young persons, romantic love presumably outweighs all other considerations in choosing a mate. The decision to marry, like a bolt from the blue, can come at any time. In principle, it can happen to anyone; it is outside the range of rational or conscious control.

In fact, however, the young person has some strongly preconceived ideas about when and whom to marry. He is actually not "ready" to fall in love at any time whatever. This readiness is paced. It is at its peak during a certain age span which he has defined in advance. He does not look forward to falling in love with "anyone"; he expects to fall in love with someone who has certain objective characteristics which are socially defined as appropriate. The college student looking into his marriage future may not know the answer to the question "who," but he has a pretty good idea of "when" and "what kind of person." The students expect the lightning of romantic love to strike mainly at a predetermined place and time.

When will that be? Almost all of the women would like to marry between the ages of 20 and 25. About a fourth of the girls want to marry between 20-21, two-fifths between 22-23, and another fourth between 24-25. Only 4 per cent of the girls choose an age outside the 20-25 range. That not one of the girls said she "didn't know" when she wanted to marry indicates how clear the norms are on this subject.

The male students prefer to be somewhat older when they marry. Although two-thirds of the women wanted to be married by the time they were 23, this was true of less than one-third of the men. The modal age for the women is 22-23, for the men, 24-25. (See Appendix 12)

But it is one thing to ask about the student's image of the ideal age to marry, and quite another to ask about the age he realistically expects to marry. Most students expect to marry at an age somewhat later than they would consider ideal. This is particularly true of the men: whereas only 18 per cent of them wanted to marry after 25, 30 per cent expected to wait so long. For most college people, however, the gap between their reported desires and expectations in this respect is not very wide.

One might assume that the main reason for postponing marriage would be to prepare for a career. Some students must engage in long and costly training for their professions and may not want to marry until they have a firm foothold in their occupations. But their plans for postgraduate training seem to bear little relationship to the age at which they expect to marry. People who are planning to go to graduate or professional school are not much more inclined to say they expect to defer marriage than those who do not look forward to professional training. (See Appendix 12)

The postwar years have seen a radical change in students' attitudes toward the question of marriage. Gone is the caution of the young man who felt that he had to make a mark in business or the professions before he dared assume the responsibility of taking a wife. Today, more likely, many young men consider a wife an economic asset rather than a liability; if the student marries while preparing for a profession, his wife can work while he completes his studies. This system was, of course, particularly prevalent among veterans going to school on the G. I. Bill after World War II, and may be the heritage of that college generation.

If career does not determine when the student expects to marry, then what does? The answer, it turns out, has little to do with objective or practical considerations; it is based on something totally different, namely, the student's concrete experiences with members of the opposite sex. Simply put, the student who dates a good deal is relatively likely to expect to marry early, whereas the boy or girl who reports few dates is disposed to believe that he will marry late. At the extremes, the differences are unusually large. Twelve times as many girls who dated very frequently expected to be married by the time they were 23 as girls who rarely dated. Even for the men, the corresponding ratio is three to one.

TABLE 4-1. FREQUENT DATERS ARE MORE LIKELY THAN OTHERS TO
EXPECT EARLY MARRIAGE
(Cornell 1950)

"How often on the average did you date while at Cornell this year?"
(Percentage who expect to marry at age 23 or younger) *

	More Often Than Twice a Week	About Twice a Week	About Once a Week	About Twice a Month	About Once a Month	Less often Than Once a Month
Men	34 (62)	31 (139)	19 (253)	15 (253)	11 (213)	11 (541)
Women	63 (63)	53 (129)	39 (143)	22 (67)	9 (43)	5 (77)

* The bases on which each per cent has been computed appear in parentheses. Omits 369 men and 167 women who because of marriage or engagement said they did not participate in the dating system. Also omits 178 men and 61 women who did not answer the question on dating.

There are many reasons why this should be so. For one thing, students who have a great many dates undoubtedly find these associations with members of the opposite sex enjoyable; they become more appreciative of the satisfactions to be derived from marriage and are anxious to enjoy these advantages soon.

The causal sequence may also be reversed; those who are eager to marry early may be more strongly motivated to date. There are some people who claim that, particularly for girls, college life is essentially a period of preparation for marriage and that for many of them college is a marriage market. Thus students who wish to marry early may date frequently for two reasons: they may view frequent dating as socialization for marriage; or they may wish to enlarge the horizons of their possible choice of a prospective mate.

Although there is no way of telling how important it is, there is an additional factor which seems worth mentioning. This is that since the dating behavior is highly patterned some students who date very often become bored with it after a time, and are ready to settle down to a married state. When dating starts to lose its appeal, some students may feel that it is about time for marriage.

> After three years of dating, you begin to long for a chance to settle down to one fellow. The Saturday nights and the weekends all begin to look alike. As for me, I've had it.

> Dating is fun, and don't get me wrong; I have lots of dates and and I enjoy it. But it's artificial after all—you begin to think you'll like just to relax with "Mr. Right."

> I've been out with plenty of women, all kinds, not only the college girls. It's fun and I am not sorry. But I find that now I am engaged, I am relieved to give up the chase, can relax and be myself.

> I always managed to have enough dates even when the competition was keen, but I really think I did it because I had to prove I could, not because I really wanted to. I didn't realize this until after we got engaged, and I so much enjoyed not having to keep up the same pace, the same routine.

The association between frequent dates and the expectation of marrying young may also be tied up with the student's sense of prowess or adequacy. Many adolescents, unsure of their identity, are unsure as well of their attractiveness or desirability to members of the opposite sex. They are also aware that the decision to marry means more than simply choosing someone else: it also requires that one be chosen. From this viewpoint, frequent dating takes on a special meaning for them. It is an affirmation that one is worthy, desirable and attractive in the eyes of the opposite sex. The student who has few dates doubts the likelihood that he (or she) will be readily chosen. The student who has many dates has some assurance that when he or she is ready to marry he will be accepted. And, since early marriage is considered desirable, we can understand the strong correlation between frequent dating and expecting an early marriage.

Whether the student wants his future husband or wife to be older or younger is related to the age at which he expects to marry. In our college sample, we find that the norms are exceedingly strong and consistent on this score. Hardly a girl in the sample said she wanted to marry a man younger than she, and hardly a man said he wanted to marry an older woman. There are more girls who look for an older man than men who seek a younger girl.

TABLE 4-2. MEN PREFER YOUNGER WIVES; WOMEN PREFER OLDER HUSBANDS
(Cornell 1950)

	Men	Women
Total =	(1824)	(729)
	(Percentage * giving indicated response)	
Do you prefer a mate who is:		
Older than you	2	75
Same age as you	30	13
Younger than you	59	2
No answer	10	9

* Omits 184 men and 21 women who were married.

How much older? The girls are willing to tolerate a wider gap than the men are. Most of them are willing to marry men up to 5 or 6 years older than they, and a fifth are quite willing to stretch the difference even more. It seems that for the girls who expect to marry at 23 or younger, the ideal age for a husband is 27; for those who expect to marry at 24 or 25 years of age, it is around 29 or 30.

Men are somewhat less flexible in this regard, tending to prefer wives somewhat closer in age to themselves. For men who expect to marry at age 25 or less, the ideal wife is 21 or 22; for men who plan to marry later, the ideal bride is still no more than 24 years old. Still, all in all, these college students find people within a fairly wide age range acceptable as marriage partners. There is only one rule they almost all refuse to violate—the rule that the wife should not be older than her husband.

Just as college students want the husband to be equal or superior to his wife in age, so they want him to be equal or superior in education. Among our students, we find that no woman wants a husband who is less educated than she is, and only one man in a hundred wants a wife who surpasses him in education. We note here, however, that a third of the college girls hoped to find a man whose education exceeded theirs, but almost none of the men desired women of inferior education.

Among college students the overwhelming general conviction is that the male should be superior to his wife in age and education. And this norm is more prevalent among the women than among the men: 75 per cent of the women want a husband who is older, but only 59 per cent of the men want a wife who is younger. Thirty-one per cent of the women want a more educated husband, but only 4 per cent of the men seek a wife inferior in education. The norms about mate-selection are among the clearest and most entrenched on the college campuses.

LOVE AND MARRIAGE

Students have rather definite ideas regarding the characteristics of the person they would like to fall in love with and marry. Of course, love, they feel, may always prove stronger than any or all of these factors. The point is that the young man or the young woman is likely to be more "ready" to fall in love with a partner who meets the objective requirements: possession of these characteristics may be a necessary condition for marriage, even though it may not be a sufficient condition.

But let us probe more closely into the individual's image of the characteristics of his "ideal" mate, the characteristics which the students say they consider important in choosing a husband or a wife. This is the way we put it to the Cornell students.

> Students' ideas about the qualities they are seeking in an ideal mate vary considerably. Here are some, but not all, of the qualities they said they are seeking, *ideally*. As you read the list of qualities, consider what qualities you, yourself, are seeking in an ideal mate. Indicate your ideas by writing:—
>
> H (High)   next to those traits you consider highly important for your mate to have;

TABLE 4-3. QUALITIES OF AN IDEAL MATE AS SEEN BY COLLEGE MEN AND WOMEN

(Cornell 1950)

Percentage * choosing each trait as:

Consider what qualities you, yourself, are seeking in an ideal mate . . .	Highly Important				Highly Important			
	First	Other High	Medium	Low	First	Other High	Medium	Low
	(Men: Total = 2008)				(Women: Total = 750)			
Possess social know-how	1	39	51	9	1	34	58	6
Sexually stimulating	4	53	41	3	1	47	45	7
Has money at the time of marriage	1	2	23	75	—	8	53	38
Interested in having a family	8	68	21	3	5	76	15	3
Competent in his (her) vocation	1	31	52	16	9	69	22	—
Very much in love with you	36	56	8	—	41	54	4	1
Someone with whom you are very much in love	38	56	8	—	34	50	6	1
No previous sex experience	1	19	46	33	—	14	38	47
Well groomed and neat	3	59	34	4	1	45	49	5

*Percentages must be added horizontally.

M (Medium) next to the qualities you consider moderately important;

L (Low) next to those qualities you consider of little importance or even distasteful.

The list of qualities that followed were:

> Possess social know-how
> Sexually stimulating
> Has money at the time of marriage
> Interested in having a family
> Competent in his (her) vocation or profession
> Very much in love with you
> Someone with whom you are very much in love
> No previous sex experience
> Well groomed and neat

Obviously a large number of relevant qualities (such as intelligence, kindness, generosity) have been omitted, as well as objective social characteristics (such as social status). Many people might wonder, too, at the omission of qualities more spiritual perhaps than "sexually stimulating" for example, or "well groomed and neat." Yet, despite these limitations, there is much that can be learned from the responses the students made.

Beyond all question, romantic love is by far the most important criterion for mate selection. Virtually everyone said they considered loving and being loved as highly important criteria in mate selection. This is one of the greatest points of unanimity in the opinions reported by the college students.

Most students say too, that they desire mates who are interested in having a family. Somewhat less emphasis—although still a good deal—is placed on such qualities as social *savoir faire*, respectable appearance, and physical attractiveness.

The quality in a mate which is stressed least as a criterion for choice—in fact, it seems to be emphatically rejected—is "has money at time of marriage." Only five per cent said they considered this highly important, 32 per cent rated it medium in importance, and 64 per cent deemed it "of little importance or even distasteful." This is particularly interesting as a typically American theme. In novels and short stories, in films, on television and the radio, the American confronts a recurrent conflict theme—whether to marry for love or for money. And, invariably, the approved solution is victorious: money is rejected and love is triumphant. The fact that students so strongly declare that money is an unimportant consideration in choosing a mate is to be attributed to their affirmation of the importance of these themes. In American culture, it is important to allow no functional or secondary considerations to enter into what is one of the most purely primary relationships. Students are nearly unanimous in stating the classic love-money conflict is no problem to resolve (see Table 4-3).

What criteria do men apply to women and women to men? By and large, they appear to seek rather similar traits in one another. (If the list of traits had been more complete, however, a larger number of differences might have appeared.) Women are anxious to have their husbands demonstrate competence in their vocations or professions. Men are more concerned about the physical appearance of their future partner. The really central point of the students' testimony, however, seems to be that unless there is mutual love, no other considerations are legitimate grounds for marriage.

HOW MANY CHILDREN WILL THEY HAVE?

Next to love, the most important requirement that the college student demands of a mate is an interest in having a family (see Table 4-3). Men and women are agreed on this point: three quarters of each group emphasize this. Probably most students do not deliberately seek this quality in their respective husbands and wives—they just take it for granted. But it is these taken-for-granted assumptions that reveal the most important parts of the students' value systems—the beliefs that do not have to be put into words, that are accepted without ever being brought into question.

They want and they expect to establish a family—and a relatively large one. We asked: "How many children do you expect to have by the time you are forty?" (assuming that a family would have attained its maximum size by that time). The answers indicate that, if the students' expectations were ultimately to be fulfilled, families of the college population would more than replace themselves. The modal number of children expected is three. Only six per cent of the students say they expect to have fewer than two children (these are the ones who would fail to replace themselves). The overwhelming majority—82 per cent—say they expect to have from two to four children. It is still possible, of course, that the imperious wail of a child in the night may modify the views of these prospective parents; but as they see things now, this is what they tell us they look forward to.

But, again, men and women do not quite see eye to eye on this subject. The women tend to say they want larger families—some extremely large. Nearly one-fifth of the girls say they want five or more children, whereas only one man in a hundred relished such a prospect. And twice as many girls as men wanted four or more children—evidence once more of the greater tendency among women to emphasize family life (see Appendix 12).

ATTITUDES TOWARD SEX [1]

What about sex? We had decided not to ask direct questions about the students' sex habits, and we can report only their attitudes on the subject. For example, how much stress do college students place on pre-marital chastity?

Few students say they insist strictly on chastity in their potential mates. Some readers may have already been surprised to find that so few students say they consider "no previous sex experience" as an important criterion for choosing a mate. Less than one college man in a hundred—and not one college women—selected this as *the* most important criterion. Fewer than one out of five men, and one out of seven women, said it was important at all.

Other evidence leads to the same conclusion. We have already reported (page 54) the students' ideas regarding pre-marital sex relations for men and for women: only 29 per cent of the students said that they felt pre-marital relations were "never justified" for men, and 38 per cent said they considered them "never justified" for women.

And when it comes down to a more acid test of the importance

---

[1] See also Chapters 2 and 8 which present further analysis of the students' attitudes toward sex.

of pre-marital chastity—whether the individual thinks he might break an engagement if he discovered his partner had had previous sex-relations—we find that only one student in twenty said he felt sure that he would do so. Six per cent of the men and 3 per cent of the women said they would do this (Appendix 12). Many—particularly the men—admitted that such a revelation would raise doubts in their minds, but few asserted unequivocally that they would break the engagement.

On the whole, then, the attitudes toward pre-marital sex relations that the students report show a marked relativism. Apparently, violations of the rule of pre-marital chastity do not elicit the wholesale condemnation which the formal rules of behavior in this country may attribute to them. The idea of a "fallen woman" does not seem to carry much weight with most of these students.

This, of course, does not mean that college students are unconcerned about the pre-marital chastity of their mates: after all, even in terms of the simple testimony which we are reporting here, nearly a fifth said that it was a highly important factor to take into consideration in selecting a spouse; about a third said that pre-marital sex relations could *never* be justified; and nearly two-fifths said they were "not sure" whether they would break their engagement if this rule were violated. For many students, clearly, pre-marital chastity is the desirable situation, even if few declare that it deserves to be considered decisive.

THE DOUBLE STANDARD

This brings us to a related point—the question of the double standard. There are those who believe that this is the basic sexual rule in America—that it is permissible for men to have pre-marital sex relations, but not for women. We find, however, that few college students say that pre-marital chastity is important for women but not for men—a clear repudiation of the legitimacy of the double standard.

Let us look at the evidence. As we saw earlier, students were asked how important "no previous sex experience" was in the choice of an ideal mate. Table 4-3 shows that whereas 14 per cent of the women said that an ideal husband would not have had pre-marital sex relations, 20 per cent of the men said that an ideal wife would have followed this rule—a difference of six per cent. And whereas three per cent of the women claimed they would break their engagement to a man who had violated the rule, six per cent of the men said they would readily take such drastic action. (Appendix 12) Finally, 29 per cent of the students declared that pre-marital sex relations for men were never justified, and 38 per cent that they were never justified for women (see Table 4-4)—a difference of eight per cent. All in all, how many students said they could see no circumstances to justify the behavior of a woman who has pre-marital sex relations, yet could justify a man? The answer is: just 6 per cent.

In other words, when it comes to the public expression of attitudes toward sex, any tendency to apply a double standard is certainly very slight among these college students. Yet it is not entirely dead. After all, 44 per cent of the men said they were "not sure" whether they would break their engagement if they discovered their partners had had sex relations, but only 32 per cent of the women said they felt this way. The violation of the pre-marital chastity rule by one's mate would apparently give more men than women "pause for thought," even though they do not consider the rule inexorable.

One difference, however, does appear clearly in our data. Women's attitudes toward the justifiability of pre-marital sex relations *for both sexes* are stricter than those of men. In other words, our students do not express a double standard so much as they express two different standards. There is not one standard *for* men and another *for* women, but rather one standard *by* men and another *by* women. With regard to pre-marital sex relations, men seem to be more relativistic about the subject for both sexes, women more absolute.

Within college, then, courtship and preparation for marriage constitute an important part of campus life. Shared norms, standards, and ideals regarding the characteristics of the future mate and the nature of the family prevail. Many of these norms are sharp and clear. This is, of course, not unique to the college culture but is characteristic of large sectors of American society. It is

TABLE 4-4. WOMEN ARE MORE LIKELY THAN MEN TO EXPRESS CONSERVATIVE
ATTITUDES TO PRE-MARITAL SEX AND TO SUPPORT THE DOUBLE STANDARD *
(Cornell 1950)

	Men (2008)		Women (750)	
Check any of the following circumstances under which you consider pre-marital sex relations justified . . .	For Men	For Women	For Men	For Women
	(Percentage ** giving indicated response)			
Never justified	27	32	36	48
All right if he's planning to marry her anyway	35	35	25	23
All right if they're in love at the time	31	27	23	21
All right if it's not purely physical	19	15	18	12
All right if they're old enough to know what they're doing	44	35	35	24
All right if he/she is not promiscuous	18	16	20	11
No answer and don't know	4	4	8	7

* See also Table 2-11 for responses by career girls and other women.
** Percentages should not be cumulated owing to multiple responses.

possible that the student population may have and may express more relativistic attitudes toward sex than are characteristic of the middle-class, but the general impression is to the contrary. Student culture—and particularly the women—principally supports, reinforces, and conforms to American middle-class courtship and family values and patterns.

5

Political Apathy, Economic Conservatism

THE INVESTIGATOR ATTEMPTING to describe the political flavor of contemporary American campuses is immediately and forcefully struck by two themes. The first is what seems to be a remarkable absence of any intense or consuming political beliefs, interests or convictions on the part of the college students. The second is extreme political and economic conservatism. Both are in marked contrast to the radicalism usually attributed to American college students in the thirties, and said to be a traditional aspect of student culture in other countries.

POLITICAL APATHY

The American college students we studied simply do not, as a group, get "worked up" about political matters. The tendency seems to be for this lack for feeling about politics to become more characteristic of the college students rather than less characteristic. For example, we had asked: "Do you ever get as worked up about something that happens in political or public affairs as you do about something that happens in your personal life?" On all the campuses we studied, students who responded "yes" to this question were in the minority.[1] At Cornell where we can compare

1 See Appendix 13 for the distribution of responses to this question at the universities polled. As this book goes to press, there seem to be some indications that this trend may be beginning to reverse itself and that perhaps college students' concern about political affairs and public issues may be reviving. For example, the Student Council at Cornell University has recognized as a legitimate campus activity (October

responses the same students made to this question at two points in time, it turned out that a majority of the panel (54 per cent) had acknowledged in the earlier questionnaire such feelings of personal involvement in a political occurrence, but after a lapse of only two years, the comparable proportion had dwindled to 42 per cent: and this in 1952, at the height of the McCarthy era. Moreover two-thirds of those who changed at all in this regard (64 per cent) no longer, they said, ever felt "worked up" about political affairs, while only one-third indicated they had developed such feelings while at college.

It is very tempting to interpret this sort of lack of involvement and apparent disinterest in political matters as indicative principally of apathy, complacency, and unquestioning contentment with the *status quo*. Undoubtedly such an interpretation is justified in many cases. But we have found that what seems to be aloofness to political matters may sometimes be coupled with a certain realistic disenchantment with issues and causes, a sober wariness, perhaps even a certain wistfulness.

> Yes, since you ask me, I do sometimes find myself getting worked up about politics. Yes, I'm interested; and when the time comes I'll do everything that has to be done. But everything in its proper place, is my motto. No sense in getting carried away.

> When I read about peace strikes and picket lines on the campuses in the thirties, it makes me feel a little superior because the "causes" turned out to be phony. Sometimes I feel a little envious, too, because they had so much conviction that there was an easy answer. I guess today we know it's much more complicated. Anyway we play it cool.

POLITICAL CONSERVATISM

The students' political beliefs, moreover, are decidedly conservative. Our analysis of their sober conservatism begins modestly, by

---

1959) a self-styled political party for students. The party calls itself *Action*, and declares that it is against discrimination in off-campus housing and against compulsory ROTC. A similar student political party—Slate—exists at the University of California. An Associated Press dispatch dated October 21, 1959, reported that a freshman student at the University of California engaged in a fifty-one hour hunger strike to call to the attention of the Board of Regents of the state his conscientious objection to compulsory ROTC. These sorts of occurrences have been notable for their absence from campuses during the last decade. Are they now straws in the wind?

examining simply their political party alignment. For although many of the students cannot vote, they customarily express sympathy and support for the political parties and the national and local candidates in an election.

At first glance, it may seem that large proportions of the students reject the traditional political parties. "Do you consider yourself a Republican, a Democrat, or an Independent in most political matters?" we asked. On the campuses we polled, 29 per cent said that they were Republicans and 26 per cent said Democrats. The greatest single proportion of responses—42 per cent—clustered in the category "Independent"; less than one per cent checked "other," and two per cent neglected to answer the question. Even at the conservative Eastern universities (Yale, Dartmouth, Wesleyan and Cornell)—the only campuses where the "Independent ticket" did not run ahead of the major parties—still, around 40 per cent of the students declared that they were "Independent" in most political matters.

TABLE 5-1. POLITICAL PARTY PREFERENCE OF COLLEGE STUDENTS
(Eleven universities)

Do you consider yourself a Republican, a Democrat or an Independent in Most Political Matters?
Percentage* who respond:

	Republican	Democrat	Independent	"Other"	No Answer	Total
All students	29	26	42	1	2	(2975)
Dartmouth	47	9	42	1	1	(365)
Yale	47	14	36	1	1	(297)
Wesleyan	44	16	37	1	2	(277)
Cornell: Men	44	15	37	1	4	(655)
Women	35	15	46	1	3	(245)
Michigan	38	17	44	1	—	(488)
UCLA	29	32	37	1	2	(467)
Harvard	28	22	44	2	4	(453)
Wayne	17	27	53	1	2	(519)
Texas	13	42	44	1	—	(516)
North Carolina	13	41	42	2	2	(414)
Fisk	7	36	53	1	3	(134)

* Percentages are to be added horizontally.

The preponderance of students who call themselves Independent, however, does *not* mean that a substantial proportion of the students have any serious disagreement with either of the two major political parties. Our analysis of the beliefs of those who say they are independent shows that when it comes to choosing up sides on specific issues, they are middle-of-the-roaders. They tend to take a position left of the Republicans but right of the Democrats (see Table 5-6). If the college students call themselves politically independent it is decidedly *not* because they are hungry for some different kind of political fare. A more likely explanation is either that their allegiances are not yet fixed, or that they prefer to avoid a party label, liking to think that they consider each issue and each campaign on its own merits.

THE SEARCH FOR THE REBELS

Even if most students have little interest in opposing the official political and social forms of American society, and even if they stand staunchly behind the existing social order, they could still be politically rebellious without necessarily espousing unorthodox political beliefs. For example, it has often been claimed that the social protest of flaming youth in the twenties, and the political and economic protest of college students in the depression years, really was a displaced rebelliousness; that only ostensibly was it directed against society and really had its roots in opposition to one's own parents as surrogates of that society. It could be that such political opposition to one's parents still exists on the campuses, simply taking the more conservative forms which are modish today for college students. Perhaps without abandoning one of the traditional political parties, the students nevertheless rebel against their parents by espousing—not an unorthodox position, but a political position which is opposed to that of their parents.

Even this rather tortured search for some kind of political rebelliousness, however, proves fruitless. Only one out of twenty-five students with Republican fathers favored the Democrats, and only one out of fourteen students with Democratic fathers favored the Republicans. So strong is this tendency to echo one's father's political preference, that three-quarters of the students who had said their fathers were Independent reported that they, too, were Independent.

TABLE 5-2. POLITICAL AFFILIATION OF SONS FOLLOWS POLITICAL
AFFILIATION OF FATHERS
(Eleven universities)

Do you consider yourself, in most political matters . . .	How does your father usually vote? Percentage* who respond:		
	Republican	*Democrat*	*Independent*
Total =	(1025)	(1077)	(412)
Republican	65	7	12
Democrat	4	52	12
Independent	29	39	75
Other	1	1	—
No Answer	1	1	—

* Omits 461 students who did not give father's usual vote.

The present-day college student, then, is not even in political revolt against his parents. If there is any "rebelliousness" it runs the gamut from A to B, culminating in the adoption of an "Independent" political position. And where this mild rebellion does occur, it is more likely to be in the conservative (Republican) direction.

But what about the small group of students who *did* rebel—students who supported a political party different from that of their parents. Perhaps in this group, at least, we might encounter a hard core of youthful rebels—a group of angry, or at least irritated young men who, in liberating themselves from the political traditions of their parents, have likewise declared their independence from the traditional thinking of their sociological status-groups. But no: analysis of the factors related to "rebellion" against father's vote indicates quite an opposite tendency. It turns out that students who go contrary to the political views of their fathers, are finding a way of adjusting their own political views more nearly to the accepted norms of certain sociological groups to which they feel an allegiance.

Here are a few examples which we have selected to illustrate the process. Take the matter of religious affiliation. We know that Jews and Catholics tend to vote Democratic, while Protestants tend to vote Republican. Thus, among the Republican students who came from Republican homes, only one-fifth were Jews, Catholics, or of mixed religious background. But among students who had turned *away* from their parents' Republicanism to take up the Democratic cause, roughly half were members of these minority religious groups. In the same way, among the Democratic students who came from Democratic homes, about half were Protestants. Yet, those who abandoned their father's Democratic position to support the Republican party were principally Protestants (65 per cent). Have they "rebelled" against their fathers, or have they reverted to the traditional vote of their religious group, which their fathers had abandoned?

Now take the matter of economic group. We know that wealthier voters tend to prefer the Republican party, poorer ones the Democratic party. Among the Republican students who came from Republican homes, 21 per cent reported that their father's annual earnings were over $20,000. But among the students who had "rebelled" against their father's Republicanism by turning to the Democrats, only 6 per cent came from such wealthy homes. Similarly, among Democratic students who came from Democratic homes, 67 per cent reported their parents' annual earnings as less than $7,500. But among those who "rebelled" against a Democratic father by turning to the Republican party, only 56 per cent came from these lower income homes. Have they "rebelled" against their fathers, or have they reverted to the traditional vote of their economic class?

As a final example, we consider the dominant political atmosphere of the college campuses. At six of the campuses we studied, the Republican party was more popular than the Democratic; at five, the reverse situation prevailed. (See Table 5-1). Forty-five per cent of the students who "rebelled" against Republican fathers by turning to the Democratic party were studying at one of the heavily Democratic campuses, while only 27 per cent of those who kept up their father's Republicanism were at one of these campuses.

This tendency to adopt the political views more characteristic of the campus where one is studying exists also on Democratic campuses. Again, are they rebelling against their fathers or adopting a campus norm?

TABLE 5-3. POLITICAL AFFILIATION OF FATHERS AND SONS ACCORDING TO RELIGIOUS AFFILIATION, FAMILY INCOME, AND PREDOMINANT POLITICAL PARTY ON CAMPUS *

(Eleven universities)

	Both Republican	Father Rep. Son Demo.	Both Democrat	Father Demo. Son Rep.
Total ** =	(664)	(45)	(565)	(75)
Religious affiliation	(Percentage in each category)			
Protestant	79	51	51	67
Catholic	7	9	16	17
Jewish	2	33	24	8
Mixed	9	6	4	4
Other	2	—	4	4
No answer	1	—	—	—
Father's annual income				
Under $7,500	40	56	67	56
$7,500-9,999	17	13	13	17
$10,000-19,999	20	20	12	12
$20,000 or more	21	6	5	10
No answer	2	4	3	5
Predominant political party on campus				
Heavily Republican †	72	54	25	36
Heavily Democratic ‡	27	45	75	65

* See Appendix 14 for similar distributions of students who said they or their fathers were Independent voters.

** Omits 496 who could not be classified on both variables.

† This category includes Cornell, Dartmouth, Harvard, Michigan, Wesleyan, Yale where the number of students who said they usually align themselves with the Republicans exceeded the number reporting Democratic sympathies.

‡ This category includes UCLA, North Carolina, Texas, Wayne, and Fisk where the number of students preferring the Democrats exceeded the number preferring the Republican party.

This very crude analysis of something as simple as abandoning one's father's political party, sets the stage for the development of the principal theme of this section. The students are conservative, they are not rebellious, they are as little disposed to political non-conformism as they are to social nonconformism.

ECONOMIC LIBERALISM AND CONSERVATISM

A source of confusion in discussions of "liberalism" or "conservatism" is that at least three different components of these beliefs are often treated together. First, the economic and political elements of liberalism may be considered as if they were identical and interchangeable. While it is true that these two strands are frequently intertwined, they are nevertheless conceptually distinct. It is quite possible to hold beliefs which are politically liberal but economically conservative, even though economic laissez-faire today is a conservative philosophy while political laissez-faire is liberal. Thomas Jefferson's position—that governments have no right to restrict *either* free enterprise, *or* individual liberties—would label him today, for example, an economic conservative but a political liberal. Similarly all other combinations are possible and, in fact, do exist.[3]

At the same time, economic liberalism or conservatism may be obscured by certain strands of humanitarian beliefs which may well cut across both positions. Values of rugged individualism, and of humanitarianism, often contradictory to each other, have existed simultaneously on the American scene since the early days of the republic. Parrington has noted, for example:

> At the beginning of our national existence two rival philosophies contended for supremacy in America: the humanitarian philosophy of the French Enlightenment, based on the conception of human perfectibility and postulating as its objective an equali-

---

[3] The following scheme may clarify the point. It grew out of certain ideas suggested in Harold D. Lasswell, *Power and Personality* (New York, W. W. Norton and Co., 1948).

Political laissez faire: Economic laissez faire

		Pro	Con
	Pro	Jeffersonian Democrat	Twentieth century American liberal
	Con	Reactionary	Corporate state, fascist, communist

tarian democracy in which the political state should function as the servant to the common well-being; and the English philosophy of laissez-faire, based on the assumed universality of the acquisitive instinct and postulating a social order answering the needs of an abstract 'economic man,' in which the state should function in the interest of trade.[4]

Discussions of liberalism and conservatism are often further confused by defining what is basically a set of philosophical assumptions as if they were identical with one's opinion on a current issue. While given attitudes and opinions may well be highly correlated with liberalism or conservatism, they are bound by time and space to particular events and situations, and thus can by no means be considered defining characteristics of a philosophy. For example, at the turn of the century, a favorable attitude toward women voting might have been highly correlated with "liberalism." Today, however, for sociological and historical reasons, it is virtually irrelevant in this country.

We shall try to take up in turn each of these strands of liberalism and conservatism among the college students, focussing in this chapter particularly on their economic beliefs, and reserving for a later chapter discussion of their political beliefs and international attitudes. We shall report here as well some indications of their reactions to economic issues, and the stands they take on certain of these issues which have humanitarian overtones, relating them where possible to these basic economic assumptions.

. . . EITHER A LITTLE LIBERAL OR ELSE A LITTLE CONSERVATIVE

The conflicting themes of humanitarianism and rugged individualism which Parrington referred to are quite discernible in the opinions which the college students expressed. They are wholeheartedly *for* rugged individualism of a free-enterprise economic system; but many of them are nevertheless willing to abandon some aspects of a classic laissez-faire philosophy. For example, the majority (62 per cent) agree that "democracy depends fundamen-

---

4 Vernon L. Parrington, *Main Currents in American Thought* (New York, Harcourt Brace & Co. Inc., 1930), Book III, p. xxiii.

tally on the existence of free business enterprise." Considerably fewer, but still a majority (59 per cent), agree that "the 'welfare state' tends to destroy individual initiative." Yet only a minority (38 per cent) are willing to go so far as to declare that "government planning almost inevitably results in the loss of essential liberties and freedom"; and still fewer accept the unequivocal Jeffersonian pronouncement, "The best government is the one which governs least" (31 per cent agree).

Their attitudes towards specific economic issues indicate, moreover, that many students retreat from a strictly laissez-faire position when the issue is put in terms of preferential economic interests. Take labor unions, for example. About 40 per cent agree that "the laws governing labor unions are not strict enough." Yet, neither is student opinion ready to grant to employers the right to operate as strictly free agents. For example, at Cornell—a campus which, compared with other schools, is somewhat more conservative in its attitudes toward free enterprise, business, and labor —53 per cent of the students rejected the principle that an employer's unrestricted right to hire and fire as he sees fit ought to be viewed "a highly important guarantee" which an ideal democracy owes to its citizens. It would certainly be an oversimplification to say that college students support the rugged individualism of a free enterprise economic system and express attitudes on given economic issues which match this basic philosophical position.

There are, too, certain economic policies with social welfare overtones which many students take for granted as essential for a benevolent democratic government. Take the matter of a minimum wage. Those who remember the discussions of whether such a guarantee by government would be desirable will certainly recall the argument: "If people are certain of a minimum wage they might lose their initiative." This argument has retained its freshness for only about a third of the students. And at Cornell in 1950, only 24 per cent rejected as unimportant or distasteful the idea that an "ideal democracy" ought to guarantee a minimum wage to every citizen. Clearly some of the traditional arguments against a minimum wage have lost their freshness.

Responses at Cornell in 1950:
(Total = 2758)
(Percentage who:)

	Agree	Dis-agree	Un-certain	No Answer
It interferes with a man's right to bargain for the price of his own labor	21	69	9	1
It requires more red tape than it's worth	10	71	19	—

Higher education, on the other hand, is still viewed as a private privilege rather than a public right, according to most of these students. Only about a third (35 per cent) agree that "college education should be free for everyone." Some of the arguments against this sort of benevolent "government paternalism" are:

Responses at eleven universities
(Total = 2975)
(Percentage who:)

	Agree	Dis-agree	Un-certain	No Answer
Educational standards would go down	56	34	9	1
It would lead to higher taxes	50	30	19	1
It would make the lower classes too dissatisfied	15	60	24	1

Responses at Cornell 1950
(Total = 2758)

	Agree	Dis-agree	Un-certain	No Answer
There would not be enough executive jobs to go around	28	48	24	—
You get more out of it if you pay	24	61	14	1
The professions are overcrowded	17	58	25	—
Industry cannot absorb more trained people	11	63	25	1

Even so, however, only 25 per cent of the Cornell students said they felt it would be unimportant or distasteful for an ideal democracy to guarantee "free college education for anyone who wants it and meets the requirements." [5]

---

[5] Many of us in this country and in this generation may have overlooked the "welfare state" aspect of government sponsored free education, simply because it is by now so entrenched in the American way of life. But it is an example par excellence of government guaranteeing as a public right something which was formerly

TABLE 5-4. DISTRIBUTION OF OPINION AT 11 UNIVERSITIES ON ITEMS
RELATED TO ECONOMIC PHILOSOPHY, ECONOMIC ISSUES, AND GOVERN-
MENT RESPONSIBILITY FOR EDUCATION AND WELFARE

(Percentage expressing conservative opinions)

	Cross-Section All Universities (2975)	Cornell Men (655)	Dartmouth (365)	Fisk (134)	Harvard (453)	Michigan (488)	No. Carolina (414)	Texas (516)	UCLA (467)	Wayne (519)	Wesleyan (277)	Yale (297)
Total =												
Economic Philosophy												
Democracy depends fundamentally on the existence of free business enterprise · Agree	62	62	59	53	46	67	72	70	61	62	62	60
The "welfare state" tends to destroy individual initiative · Agree	59	60	63	32	48	69	63	60	55	56	57	64
Government planning almost inevitably results in the loss of individual liberties and freedom · Agree	38	34	30	20	23	32	34	40	30	25	25	38
The best government is the one which governs least · Agree	31	32	26	27	29	30	33	35	29	29	32	32
Economic Issues												
The laws governing labor unions are not strict enough · Agree	40	52	55	22	43	54	51	45	42	40	61	55
Labor unions in this country are doing a fine job · Disagree	48	37	48	19	35	45	49	43	32	33	40	43
If people are certain of a minimum wage they might lose their initiative · Agree	35	32	38	34	23	36	51	45	27	31	34	36
The individual employer should sacrifice this right (to hire and fire without restriction) for the social welfare · Disagree		61										
If there is no ceiling on business profits there is a better chance to develop products at lower costs · Agree		38										

(Asked only at Cornell, 1950: Total 2758)

("   "   "   "   )

Statement	Response			
Free enterprise economic system considered as a deterrent to war, considered* ...	Highly important	41	68	49
A minimum wage as a guarantee expected from an ideal democracy considered ...	Little or no importance	27	44	33
Most business corporations do not give the public a true picture of how much profit they make	Disagree	29	57	46

(Asked only at Cornell, 1950: Total 2758)

Education and Welfare

Statement	Response			
College education should be free to everybody	Disagree	59	62	66
Importance attached to each measure listed, "if a government is to be considered IDEAL."**		54	63	65

Free education for everyone under 16:
- High: 83
- Medium: 15
- Low or undesirable: 2

Free medical care for those who cannot afford it:
- High: 28
- Medium: 47
- Low or undesirable: 25

Free college education for everyone who wants it and meets the requirements:
- High: 25
- Medium: 47
- Low or undesirable: 28

(Asked only at Cornell, 1950: Total 2758)

* See Table 6-18 for text of this question and full distribution of responses.
** See Table 6-1 for text of this question and full distribution of responses.

Finally, how do the students react to the idea of government-guaranteed medical care? This is another aspect of welfare government which only a minority (28 per cent) were ready to accept as a highly important responsibility of a democratic government. Still, it is evident that opinion is not crystallized *against* it; for just 25 per cent said they considered such measures "of little or no importance or even undesirable" in an ideal democracy.

Here is the way the students reacted to certain well-known arguments against government-sponsored medical care:

| | Responses at Cornell in 1950 (Total = 2758) (Percentage who:) | | | |
	Agree	Dis-agree	Un-certain	No Answer
It would lower the quality of medical care	58	23	18	1
It would lead to higher taxes	54	25	21	—
People might learn to rely on the government for everything	53	35	12	—
More red tape than it's worth	46	32	21	1
It would perpetuate the unfit	15	60	25	—

The general impression these distributions of opinion convey seem to be this. When it comes to expressions of economic philosophy, student opinion is on the conservative side, but covers a relatively wide range. When it comes to liberalism or conservatism in economic areas involving education and welfare, student opinion is perhaps middle-of-the-road. But when it comes to current economic issues involving business and labor, about half the students consistently express attitudes and opinions which are linked with a conservative position.

Economic liberalism or conservatism in the three senses men-

considered a private privilege. (See, for example, Shirley Basch, "Pains of a New Idea," *Survey Graphic*, 37, pp. 78-79, February 1948. This article shows the marked parallel between early arguments against public education, and modern arguments against socialized medicine.) At Cornell in 1950 all but 17 per cent of the students felt that this was a highly important guarantee which a democracy ought to grant to its citizens. Only two per cent rejected "free education for everyone under 16" as of little or no importance. (See Table 5-4.)

tioned here varies widely among the different colleges. Fisk students are least likely to express a conservative position, whether it is a question of economic philosophy, economic issues, or education and welfare. But here is an interesting point which underlines the usefulness of distinguishing these components of liberalism-conservatism, rather than treating it as a unitary concept. Distribution of opinion on economic philosophy at Harvard resembles the

TABLE 5-5. PHILOSOPHICALLY CONSERVATIVE STUDENTS ARE MORE LIKELY
THAN OTHERS TO TAKE A CONSERVATIVE STAND ON SPECIFIC
ECONOMIC ISSUES

(Eleven universities)

Position on Philosophy of Government Scale *

	Support laissez faire				Do not support laissez faire
	1	2	3	4	5
Total =	(375)	(568)	(772)	(765)	(495)
The laws governing labor unions are not strict enough	(Percentage giving indicated response)				
Agree	61	46	43	35	19
Disagree	28	34	35	40	58
?	11	20	22	25	22
If people are certain of a minimum wage they might lose their initiative					
Agree	52	49	39	27	15
Disagree	42	46	52	62	72
?	6	6	9	11	12
College education should be free to everyone					
Agree	32	32	31	38	45
Disagree	62	61	57	52	40
?	6	8	12	10	15

* This scale cumulates responses indicating agreement with the following statements:
—Democracy depends fundamentally on the existence of free business enterprise.
—The Welfare State tends to destroy individual initiative.
—Government planning almost inevitably results in the loss of essential liberties and freedom.
—The best government is the one which governs least.

Fisk profile more closely than that of any other campus, even though these Cambridge boys are decidedly more likely than, say, UCLA or Wayne to express conservative stands on current economic issues or even on educational ones.

Finally, it is clear that while philosophically conservative students are very likely to take a conservative stand on particular economic issues as well, the generalizing power of a conservative economic philosophy is substantially less when it comes to an issue with humanitarian and welfare overtones. Students who score high on a scale measuring their acceptance of the principles of economic laissez-faire differ little from those at the opposite end of that scale in the stand they take on issues with education and welfare implications.[6] But on issues involving conflicting economic interests of labor and management, their opinions and attitudes tend to match the philosophical stand they espouse (Table 5-5).

PARTY LINES

It is by now well established that supporters of the Democratic Party tend to be more inclined than Republicans to accept government intervention in economic matters.[7] This is equally true of the college students. About one out of every two students with Republican sympathies declared himself in the conservative laissez-faire camp, compared with roughly one out of four so-called Independents, and one out of five who supported the Democrats.

The same sorts of results appear when we consider the stands students take on economic issues linked to such a philosophy. The ones we are considering here for the purpose of illustration are attitudes toward labor unions, a minimum wage, and free college education. Among the students we studied, the results were highly consistent in showing those with Republican leanings to be more conservative than Democrats, and the "Independents" to be somewhere in between the two major parties.

---

6 See footnote to Table 5-5 for an explanation of how the scale was constructed.
7 See, for example, Bernard Berelson, Paul F. Lazarsfeld and William McPhee, *Voting* (University of Chicago Press, 1954). See also Paul F. Lazarsfeld, Bernard Berelson and Hazel Gaudet, *The People's Choice* (New York: Columbia University Press, 1948).

TABLE 5-6. POLITICAL PARTY AFFILIATION AND PHILOSOPHY OF GOVERNMENT
(Eleven universities)

	Do you consider yourself a Republican, a Democrat or an Independent in most political matters?		
	Republican	*Independent*	*Democrat*
Total * =	(859)	(1265)	(760)
Philosophy of Government	(Percentage giving indicated response)		
Scale **			
support laissez faire	49	28	21
intermediate	26	28	24
do not support laissez faire	25	45	55
Laws governing labor unions are not strict enough			
Agree	55	37	29
Disagree	28	40	50
Uncertain	17	23	21
Labor unions in this country are doing a fine job			
Agree	16	30	44
Disagree	68	45	32
Uncertain	16	25	24
If people are certain of a minimum wage, they might lose their initiative			
Agree	47	33	28
Disagree	43	58	65
Uncertain	10	9	8
College education should be free to everyone			
Agree	21	37	45
Disagree	71	50	44
Uncertain	8	12	10

* Omits 91 students who mentioned other political parties or did not answer.
** For construction of this scale see footnote to Table 5-5.

ECONOMIC STATUS AND POLITICAL PRINCIPLES

And yet, other sociological links to economic philosophy and related attitudes are quite different in the college population compared with the general population. Most community opinion studies have shown that an individual's economic position importantly influences his acceptance or rejection of laissez-faire economic principles, his attitudes toward business and labor, and support for government intervention in social and economic matters. If this were as true of college students as of the general population, one would expect the relatively more conservative students to have said they had come from wealthier homes; relatively fewer conservatives among those who said they had come from low income families. We find, however, that this is not necessarily the case. Conservative beliefs and attitudes were virtually as prevalent among students from each economic group. Students who had said their families were in the top income brackets were not correspondingly more likely to be in favor of a laissez-faire economic philosophy; nor were they necessarily more frequently antagonistic to government provisions for free college education. Some differences do appear between the most extreme groups, but these differences are too weak to warrant the assertion that economic position is significantly related to conservatism in these senses. (See Appendix 15)

It is not until we get down to specific questions about wages, business and labor that we find the expected differences among wealthier and poorer students.

In other words, when it is a question of economic issues which reflect conflicting economic interests, then the student's economic background is directly linked to his attitudes and his opinions. But when it is a matter of his approach to the economic role of government in a philosophical sense, or in terms of a broadly humanitarian aim (such as education) then the power of the students' origins to determine or influence their economic liberalism or conservatism seems to become weaker than we know it to be for the general population.

If the social class origins of college students do not appear to engage quite so directly with their economic philosophy and related attitudes, this may be due in part to the greater homogeneity of our campus populations compared with a full community sample. Certainly the population of college students does not mirror the full range of economic levels in the country at large, since so few American college students come from families on the very lowest socio-economic levels. Moreover, the students are probably

TABLE 5-7. FATHER'S INCOME IS LINKED TO ISSUES REPRESENTING CLEAR-CUT ECONOMIC INTERESTS

(Eleven universities)

	Under $3000	$3000- 4999	$5000- 7499	$7500- 9999	$10000- 19999	$20000- 29999	$30000 or More
Total * =	(267)	(799)	(620)	(418)	(417)	(165)	(162)
If people are certain of a minimum wage, they might lose their initiative		(Percentage giving indicated response)					
Agree	31	33	34	36	36	43	48
Disagree	60	57	57	57	55	50	42
Uncertain	9	10	9	7	9	7	10
Labor unions in this country are doing a fine job							
Agree	40	35	32	27	23	22	16
Disagree	40	40	47	51	57	56	67
Uncertain	20	25	21	22	20	22	17

The header spans *Father's Annual Income*.

* Omits 127 students who did not provide information on father's income.

even more homogeneous in their feelings of class identification. By the time a young man of working class origins has matriculated at a university and has committed himself to four years or more of higher education, he has undoubtedly largely taken on the values and the outlook of the future middle-class professional he aspires to be. Thus his actual economic background (in terms of his parents' dollars-and-cents income) has probably already become a minor ingredient in his economic philosophy and related attitudes. If anything, the attitudes of the class to which he relates himself at least in an anticipatory way will have his allegiance.

In addition, the humanitarian themes of American society are particularly entrenched in the culture of all college students regardless of the social class they may have started in, and even quite apart from their present class loyalties. This is probably particularly true of issues involving education.

Here, then, is a further indication of the way in which the college experience may act as a great leveller. (See also Chapter 1.) It can weaken the link between one's social class origins and one's

sympathies for a philosophy of economic liberalism or conservatism, or one's attitudes toward economic policies of a humanitarian nature.

And yet the generalizing power of class origin by no means
disappears as a result of the college experience. It becomes, so to
speak, specialized. On issues that engage conflicting class interests,
the student who comes initially from a relatively poorer home will
tend to take a stand sympathetic to the economic interests of his
family.

To put it more succinctly: you can infer a college student's economic philosophy if you know only what political party has his
sympathies and what college he is attending, and further information about the economic level of his family will not substantially
improve the prediction. The same clues will lead to a rather accurate inference regarding his stand on an economic issue with
humanitarian overtones. If, however, you wish to infer a college
student's attitude towards a current economic issue which reflects
conflicting class interests, then additional information about his
family's economic level will increase the accuracy of your guess.

CHANGES IN POLITICAL PHILOSOPHY

As students move along in their college careers, they are exposed
to a variety of political and ideological influences. They listen to
political lectures in their classes, discuss politics and political
philosophy, react to the communications of the mass media. Does
the total effect of these influences, combined with the maturation
process make them more liberal or more conservative?

Obviously one cannot answer this question for every place and
every era. The period in which our study was conducted was characterized by a dominant atmosphere of conservatism. We found
that new students entering college at this time appeared to have
been enveloped in this atmosphere, and to have become increas-
ingly conservative as they passed through college. We illustrate this
process by examining how students changed their beliefs regarding
a laissez-faire philosophy of government.

We begin the story by turning to the Cornell panel members,
since there we can examine what happened to the opinions of each

student between the first study and the second. As we compare the responses the students reported when they were underclassmen with the equivalent responses they gave us as upperclassmen, three kinds of patterns emerge which illustrate their tendency to become more, rather than less, conservative. First, as these students passed from class to class, their viewpoint, as a group, seems to have become firmer. The opinions of students who were initially "on the fence" tended to crystallize as recognizably conservative opinions. Second, those who started out with a conservative stand were more likely to have maintained it. And third, those who did change their minds, tended to switch to a more conservative position.

The details are these: as freshmen and sophomores, about a third of the panel (35 per cent) reported opinions that placed them in an intermediate position on the scale we used to measure their philosophy of government.[8] By 1952, however, this proportion had declined to 26 per cent. This is a slight decline, but it indicates nevertheless that at the end of a two-year period, there were fewer "straddlers"—fewer students, that is, with ambiguous views or contradictory opinions about a liberal or conservative philosophy of government. Within the short period of time that had elapsed between these two studies, relatively more students had come to take a definite laissez-faire stand. For, among the panel members who changed their minds during these two years, the majority (55 per cent) switched to a more conservative position, while a minority (45 per cent) switched to a more liberal position.

Moreover, the conservative viewpoint on this subject was more likely to have remained unchanged, perhaps unchallenged. Roughly half of the panel members had not altered their beliefs between the two studies. Of these "stable" students, 44 per cent were initially in favor of an outright laissez-faire philosophy and retained that opinion. In contrast, 34 per cent were staunch about maintaining a contrary opinion.

These small per cent differences indicate only a possible trend, and obviously do not by themselves constitute a compelling argument. It is mainly in tracing the shiftings and balancings of

---

8 See footnote to Table 5-5 where the construction of this scale is explained.

TABLE 5-8. STABILITY AND CHANGE IN POSITION ON PHILOSOPHY OF GOVERNMENT SCALE ACCORDING TO DEGREE OF INVOLVEMENT IN POLITICAL MATTERS

(Cornell panel)

Initial position on philosophy of government scale * as freshmen and sophomores

Later position on philosophy of government scale as juniors and seniors	Supported laissez faire				Did not support laissez faire				Were in intermediate position			
	Degree of involvement in political matters **											
	Always Involved (103)	Became Involved (50)	Became Apathetic (81)	Always Apathetic (98)	Always Involved (87)	Became Involved (34)	Became Apathetic (66)	Always Apathetic (86)	Always Involved (98)	Became Involved (37)	Became Apathetic (63)	Always Apathetic (131)
Maintained same position	61	72	58	65	75	56	58	48	34	24	29	35
Changed position on laissez faire												
Support laissez faire	–	–	–	–	6	15	10	21	39	46	46	42
Intermediate	19	18	31	22	19	30	32	31	–	–	–	–
Did not support laissez faire	19	10	10	13	–	–	–	–	27	30	25	23

* For construction of this scale, see footnote to Table 5-5.
** Do you ever get as worked up about something that happens in politics or public affairs as you do about something that happens in your personal life?

Response at second interview	Response at first interview	
	Yes	No
Yes	always involved	became involved
No	became apathetic	always apathetic

opinions that the case develops convincingly. For it turns out that conservative students, regardless of whether or not they were emotionally involved or concerned in political matters, found it relatively easy to maintain their conservative ideology. In contrast, only the liberal student who was able to feel and to maintain some kind of emotional involvement in these matters, had an equivalent chance of maintaining his liberal outlook. The more apathetic liberal, on the other hand, had a fifty-fifty chance of becoming a conservative by the time he was a senior. It looks as if the initially conservative student may never have felt the need to question his own ideas, while the liberal student must have been sufficiently concerned to be able to defend his.

''INSULATING'' SUBSYSTEMS

One reason for this may be that the involved liberal tends to hold himself aloof from the campus subsystems which possess explicitly conservative norms; for these shifts towards conservatism do not occur to the same degree throughout the diverse social groups that make up the campus social structure.

The fraternities are a case in point. They constitute a social system whose political and social norms are in general clearly conservative. Such norms, it is true, are relatively widespread throughout the Cornell campus and of course are not characteristic solely of the fraternities. But there is an important difference. The fraternities tend explicitly to socialize any members who may deviate from these conservative norms *away* from liberalism and *toward* conservatism. This is not necessarily true of the campus in general.

Here is an illustration. Let us trace what happened to the opinions of students in the panel who had started college with a generally liberal philosophy about what the role of government ought to be. Some of these liberal underclassmen joined fraternities; and if they did, about half (51 per cent) abandoned their liberal viewpoint to adopt a position closer to a strictly laissez-faire philosophy.

A few others had at first remained outside the fraternity system, joining it only as they became upperclassmen. Two-thirds of these late-comers (64 per cent) accompanied their change to fraternity membership with a parallel change to a more sympathetic attitude toward laissez-faire economics; they became more conservative.

In contrast, among the liberal students who remained unaffiliated with the fraternity system, only a small minority (23 per cent) found on the campus any reason to abandon their liberal position; the remainder (77 per cent)—by far the majority—retained their liberal viewpoint about the role of government, in spite of the fact that this was a deviant position to take on the Cornell campus. One would infer that they were able to find spheres of social circulation whose norms were not antagonistic to their liberalism, but, on the contrary, encouraged and reinforced it.

This does not imply that groups outside the fraternity system are uniformly conducive to the maintenance or development of a liberal economic philosophy. Remember, we have traced so far the opinions of only 260 students who started college with a liberal viewpoint (in this case about laissez-faire government) and this group represents only 29 per cent of all the students in the panel. Relatively more started school with conservative views (36 per cent) or with ambiguous or contradictory ideas on the subject (35 per cent). It is in tracing what happened to the opinions of the initially conservative students that it becomes clear that the Cornell campus includes many groups other than the fraternity system and even quite apart from it, which serve to reinforce conservative ideas almost to the same degree. In the fraternities these norms may be more undifferentiated, or perhaps even more explicit or intense. But they are not so widely divergent from those prevailing in other groups and other organizations on the campus.

For example, it is true that students who start out as conservatives in the fraternity system are most likely to maintain their conservatism; some 64 per cent do. But if they are independents, the proportion who continue to support laissez faire as a philosophy of government is but slightly lower (55 per cent). Even if we trace what happens to the intermediate students—those who started college with ambiguous or contradictory views on the subject—the same sorts of trends are apparent: of those who were in a fraternity 45 per cent became more conservative as they passed through college while only 24 per cent became more liberal. Yet among those who were unaffiliated with any fraternity the equivalent proportions are only slightly smaller: 34 per cent became more conservative while 27 per cent developed a more liberal philosophy of government.

TABLE 5-9. PHILOSOPHY OF GOVERNMENT: LIBERAL OR CONSERVATIVE OPINION AS UNDERCLASSMEN COMPARED WITH OPINION AS UPPERCLASSMEN, FRATERNITY MEMBERS COMPARED WITH UNAFFILIATED STUDENTS

(Cornell panel)

Position on Philosophy of Government Scale *	Fraternity Members Throughout	Initially Independent, Joined Fraternity	Unaffiliated Students
Initial opinion as underclassmen			
Did not support laissez faire	(Percentage ** in each group)		
Total =	(127)	(22)	(111)
As upperclassmen:			
Became more conservative	51	64	23
All others	49	36	77
Supported laissez faire Total =	(182)	(37)	(110)
As upperclassmen:			
Remained conservative	64	70	55
All others	36	30	45
Intermediate position Total =	(192)	(23)	(106)
As upperclassmen:			
Became conservative	45	39	34
Became liberal	24	26	27
All others	31	35	39

* See footnote to Table 5-5 for the construction of this scale.
** Excludes 34 panel members who could not be classified according to fraternity membership.

In short, one could conclude that there are at least three types of spheres of circulation on the Cornell campus. There are the fraternities which reinforce conservatism in two ways; they insulate their conservative members against change and socialize their liberal members away from liberalism. There are the spheres of social circulation that attract the liberal students, encouraging their point of view, strongly reinforcing it, and insulating them against the impact of conservative norms apparent elsewhere on the campus. Finally, there is the rest of the Cornell campus, with many organizations and social sub systems, that provide spheres of social circulation whose norms are undoubtedly at least as conservative as fraternity norms. They serve to insulate their participants against liberalizing influences, but they do not necessarily socialize them away from liberalism as explicitly—or perhaps the point is, as effectively—as the fraternity system does.

There is no reason, of course, why the pattern reported here for Cornell should be assumed to have prevailed as well in the other universities which participated in the research. We are aware that other investigators have reported that college students tend to develop political and economic beliefs and attitudes that are compatible with the consensus of their own campus. Theodore Newcomb's now classic study of students at Bennington College,[9] for example, showed that students at this college in the thirties, when the climate of opinion was generally liberal, became socialized toward liberalism. A recent study of students' political beliefs at UCLA reported that liberal political beliefs and attitudes on current political issues associated with liberalism tend to be more prevalent among seniors than among underclassmen, suggesting that the college years might now be reinforcing liberalism on that campus, rather than conservatism.[10]

Yet our analysis shows that at least as far as economic philosophy is concerned, and at least during the conservative period of American history during which our data were gathered, liberal opinions were less prevalent among seniors. At all the universities we studied, even at the such relatively liberal campuses as UCLA, the same trend seemed to occur. Had we been able to observe the development of opinion among all these students as we did at Cornell, we suspect that a similar pattern of socialization toward conservatism, particularly among fraternity men, might have been found at these schools as well.

Table 5-10 shows that the proportion of liberal students (those

---

[9] Theodore M. Newcomb, *Personality and Social Change* (New York: Dryden Press, 1943).

[10] Hanan Selvin and Warren O. Hagstrom, *The Bulwark of Liberty* (Berkeley: University of California, January 1959. Manuscript.)

who reject a laissez-faire philosophy of government) tends to decrease year by year among the fraternity men with the possible
exception of those at Wayne; the equivalent decline among unaffiliated students is not only slighter but the pattern, year by year,
shows much less regularity.

TABLE 5-10. PROPORTION OF STUDENTS WHO REJECT LAISSEZ-FAIRE PHILOSOPHY
OF GOVERNMENT DECREASES FROM FRESHMAN TO SENIOR YEAR. FRATERNITY
MEN COMPARED WITH INDEPENDENT STUDENTS *

	First	Second	Third	Fourth
	(Percentage scoring in two least conservative positions on philosophy of government scale) **			
Wesleyan, Cornell, Dartmouth				
Fraternity members	47 (173)	34 (238)	39 (193)	32 (171)
Independent students	49 (220)	44 (83)	48 (66)	42 (67)
Texas, North Carolina				
Fraternity members	32 (65)	32 (96)	32 (94)	27 (102)
Independent students	42 (120)	27 (103)	39 (166)	40 (130)
UCLA, Michigan				
Fraternity members	44 (58)	43 (66)	43 (116)	32 (123)
Independent students	39 (99)	51 (108)	40 (159)	50 (174)
Wayne				
Fraternity members	— (11)	— (10)	54 (45)	46 (37)
Independent students	43 (91)	52 (91)	45 (98)	54 (83)

*Excluded from this tabulation are Harvard and Yale, which do not have
fraternity systems. Appendix 16 shows the proportion scoring in the two most
liberal positions on the philosophy of government scale at these two universities,
among students in each year in college.
** For construction of this scale, see footnote to Table 5-5. The bases on which
these per cents have been computed appear in parentheses. Excluded from consideration are fifth-year students, special students, foreign students, and other non-
matriculated students.

Our study suggests, therefore, that the overall impact of the
college years, at least during this period of widespread conservatism in the country at large, nurtured a conservative economic
philosophy, and was unsympathetic to a contrary viewpoint. In
special subsystems of campus life, this tendency was strongly reinforced. The fraternities provide one such example, reminding us
of an important sociological truism. In studying the development

of liberalism or conservatism in a special milieu such as the college campus, it is essential to consider as relevant context not only the climate of opinion of that institution as a whole, and not only the climate of opinion in the country at large, but also the explicit norms of particular social subsystems.

6

National and International
Attitudes

IN THE PRESENT PERIOD of American history, the issue of conservatism and liberalism has come to center around the degree of governmental activity and control, particularly as such activity
tends to affect the economic system. Either liberalism or conservatism, in this sense, however, is entirely consistent with a
democratic system of government. For, among other things, democracy involves a certain relation of the individual citizen to his government, including his rights, privileges, immunities, obligations,
and powers. "Styles" of government may change—the government
may be more or less active in economic affairs at various times—
but the hard core of the political system remains. It is these democratic values, as they are differentially interpreted by college
students, that are the central interest of this chapter.

DEMOCRATIC PRIVILEGES

We begin with an analysis of data gathered mainly at Cornell in
1950, for it was in that earlier study that we collected the most detailed information about the students' political beliefs. At that
time, we asked them in this manner to specify the kinds of rights
and privileges they thought an "ideal government" ought to
guarantee to its citizens.

Here is a list of civil, political, and personal privileges which
some students say they would require a government to guarantee

before they could consider that government *ideal*. Read the list of privileges below. Indicate in the first column the relative emphasis which you, personally, think a government should place on each of these privileges. Do this by writing

H (high)   next to those which you consider of the highest importance;

M (medium)   next to those you consider of somewhat lesser importance;

L (low)   next to those you consider of little or no importance, or even undesirable in a government.

Table 6-1 shows the frequency with which each of the rights and privileges was chosen by the students. Note that the first five "privileges" are paraphrases of guarantees appearing in the Bill of Rights. All are rated as highly important by large majorities of the students, yet there is still a range of opinion on some of these rights. Whereas there is virtual unanimity on the importance of freedom of religion and trial by jury, when it comes to public hearings, freedom of expression, and freedom from search and entry, the solid front begins to waver.

Certain other political privileges, economic rights, and welfare guarantees are also declared to be highly important by the students. These are: the right to vote, freedom to choose one's job, universal education, and freedom of movement.

On the democratic significance of some of these rights and privileges there are widespread differences of opinion. Only about half the students consider that the unrestricted right to run for public office should be guaranteed by a democratic government. Furthermore, governmental guarantees that touch upon conflicting economic interests become controversial: hiring and firing, unrestricted right to earn as much money as one can, for example. Access to medical care and higher education are not generally considered criteria by which a government is judged to be democratic, even though many students do not view these measures as irrelevant.[1] Finally, the right of conscientious objectors to be excused

---

[1] See also page 106 for earlier discussion of these matters in connection with the philosophy of economic conservatism.

from military service during wartime is considered important by only a negligible minority of the students. These figures suggest certain general principles that underlie the students' approach to democratic government.

Traditional privileges which are formally incorporated as an intrinsic part of the American creed are most widely accepted as legitimate values. The importance of every one of the Bill of Rights guarantees is attested by these students. A democratic government is judged in terms of them. Conversely, no Bill of Rights guarantee is rejected as a relevant standard for evaluating the democratic character of a government by any significant proportion of the students.

Special privileges and conflicting interests tend to be considered private matters rather than the business of government. For example, the right to earn money, to hire and fire employees, to be paid a minimum wage, referring particularly to the profit of the individual, are considered by only a minority of the students as rights which the government need guarantee.

Finally, *if a widely accepted democratic value can be said to come into conflict in some important way with the survival of the society, its legitimacy tends to be weakened.* For example, we asked these same students which values they would give up in a state of war. "We have been attacked," they were told. "Circle any of the H's you would be willing to give up in such a war-crisis."

Relatively few people checked right to vote, to run for public office, or freedom of religion; presumably they could not see how such a sacrifice would help a war effort. However, about half of those valuing free speech say it should be relinquished in wartime, as well as roughly two-thirds of those highly valuing the right to accept or resign from a job and the right to move and live where one chooses. Over half would yield the right to earn as much as possible. In other words, since economic activity has consequences for production, and since free speech may refer to military secrets or national morale, the basic value of social survival assumes priority.

TABLE 6-1. THE IDEAL DEMOCRATIC GOVERNMENT
(Cornell 1950: Total = 2758)

Privileges to be guaranteed by an ideal government:	Percentage* considering importance of each privilege			*Percentage Who Consider Each Privilege Highly Important yet Would Relinquish it in Wartime*
	High	*Medium*	*Low*	
Bill of Rights Guarantees				
Unrestricted freedom to practice one's own religion, for everybody	92	7	1	2
Unrestricted right to trial by jury	90	8	2	5
Unrestricted right to a public hearing and to summon one's own witnesses	79	19	2	13
Unrestricted right to deny entry and search of one's home without a warrant	74	20	6	31
Freedom to express or communicate any opinion on any subject for everyone	76	21	3	53
Political Participation				
Unrestricted right to vote, for every citizen	80	14	6	3
Unrestricted right to run for public office for every citizen who meets age requirements	49	32	19	13
Economic Rights				
Unrestricted right to accept or resign from any job	77	20	3	67
Unrestricted right of any employer to hire and fire his own employees	46	40	13	55
Unrestricted right to earn as much money as one can	39	40	21	53
Everyone entitled to a minimum wage	27	49	24	16
Education and Welfare				
Free education for everyone under 16	83	15	2	10
Free medical care for those who cannot afford it	28	47	25	7

TABLE 6-1—*Continued*

Privileges to be guaranteed by an ideal government:	Percentage * considering importance of each privilege			*Percentage Who Consider Each Privilege Highly Important yet Would Relinquish it in Wartime*
	High	*Medium*	*Low*	
Education and Welfare				
Free college education for everyone who wants it and who meets the requirements	25	47	28	35
All Other Rights				
Unrestricted right to move and live where one chooses	81	16	3	63
Right of conscientious objectors to be excused from military service in wartime	14	44	42	8

* Percentages "High," "Medium," and "Low" add horizontally to 100%.

ABSTRACT VALUES AND CONCRETE CASES

In general, these results indicate that, by and large, college students affirm their allegiance to the traditional democratic rights and civil liberties of our society. Apparently, they feel it is legitimate to judge a government's level of democracy in terms of the degree to which it guarantees these rights to its citizens. But, when it comes down to concrete cases, just how pervasive are these values?

Take, for example, the most widely accepted democratic value—"unrestricted freedom to practice one's own religion, for everybody." Ninety-two per cent of the students say they consider this to be a highly important characteristic of a democratic government. Only two per cent said they would be willing to give up this right even if the nation were under attack. We have here, ostensibly, overwhelming validation of a democratic value.

Yet, here are some related opinions expressed by the students in the universities studied:

	Responses at eleven universities: Total = 2975 Percentage who:			Cornell 1950 Total = 2758 Percentage who:		
	Agree	Dis-agree	Uncer-tain	Agree	Dis-agree	Un-certain
Religions which preach un-wholesome ideas should be suppressed	23	59	17	19	58	23
Americans must be on guard against the power of the Catholic Church	24	63	13	18	65	16

Even though few students subscribe to the vocabulary of religious suppression, still, when it comes down to the concrete case of "unwholesome ideas," or "the power of the Catholic Church," then something begins to chip away at what looked, at first, like an overwhelmingly unanimous pledge of allegiance to the integrity of individual religious beliefs and institutions.

We do not mean to slur over the very important fact that freedom of religion nevertheless remains a value whose legitimacy is unambiguously attested: just under one-quarter of the students agree with any *one* of these statements whose implications might cast doubt on whether acceptance of the value of religious freedom is as unqualified as it seems to be. And of course the students who turn out to have provisos in mind may still sincerely *believe that they believe* unqualifiedly in freedom of religion. The point is that there is a certain amount of "play," as it were, rather than an exact fit between the general value and the particular case.

This gap between the value in the abstract and the case in particular appears when we examine certain other beliefs as well. For example, 80 per cent of the students said they considered it highly important for an ideal democracy to guarantee "the unrestricted right to vote, for every citizen." An equivalent proportion (76 per cent) reported that they highly valued the guarantee of "freedom to express or communicate any opinion, on any subject, for everyone." Yet here is the way the students reacted to some concrete cases.

Responses at eleven universities:	Percentage who:		
(Total = 2975)	*Agree*	*Disagree*	*Uncertain*
The general public is not really qualified to vote on today's complex issues	47	46	7
People who talk politics without knowing what they are talking about should be kept quiet	30	62	8

Responses at Cornell in 1950			
(Total = 2758)			
People should be kept from spreading dangerous ideas because they might influence others to adopt them	18	62	20
Unrestricted freedom of speech leads to mass hysteria	6	78	15

At Cornell in 1950 we asked: "How far do you think a college professor should be free to express his own ideas and convictions?" The responses (in percentages) were:

A college professor should be free to express his opinion on any subject . . .	
Providing he is not violently opposed to accepted beliefs	10
Providing he does not go out of his own field to express divergent ideas	29
Providing he agrees with accepted beliefs	2
Regardless of whether he agrees or disagrees with accepted beliefs	59

This gap between the abstract value and the concrete case is illustrated even more neatly in Table 6-2a. There is nothing equivocal about the statements, "People who talk politics without knowing what they are talking about should be kept quiet," or "people should be kept from spreading dangerous ideas." They clearly justify limitations on unrestricted freedom of speech. Nor is there anything equivocal in the phrase, "freedom to express or communicate any opinion on any subject, for everyone." The wording is deliberately extreme: ". . . *any* opinion . . . *any* subject . . . for *everyone*." Yet, overwhelmingly, students who agreed that "people who talk politics . . . should be kept quiet," nevertheless stoutly maintained that unrestricted freedom of speech was a value of highest importance to them. And students who agreed

that "religions which preach unwholesome ideas should be suppressed," equally staunchly maintained that they cherished unrestricted religious freedom. This type of relationship turned up
repeatedly in the analysis of the other requirements of an ideal
government which the students say they find "highly important."
But we spare the reader the burden of studying the tables. The

TABLE 6-2a. STUDENTS WHO ARE WILLING TO SUPPRESS "PEOPLE WHO TALK
POLITICS . . ." "PEOPLE WHO SPREAD DANGEROUS IDEAS," OR "RELIGIONS WHICH
PREACH UNWHOLESOME IDEAS," MAINTAIN THAT THEY VALUE FREEDOM OF
SPEECH AND FREEDOM OF RELIGION

(Cornell 1950)

	Freedom to express or communicate any opinion on any subject for everyone Percentages * who say:		
	Highly Important	*Medium, Low or Irrelevant*	*Total*
People who talk politics without knowing what they are talking about should be kept quiet			
Agree	85	15	(562)
Disagree	94	6	(1832)
Uncertain	90	10	(352)
People should be kept from spreading dangerous ideas because they might influence others to adopt them			
Agree	82	8	(497)
Disagree	94	6	(1705)
Uncertain	90	10	(541)

	Unrestricted freedom to practice one's own religion for everyone Percentages * who say:		
	Highly Important	*Medium, Low or Irrelevant*	*Total*
Religions which preach unwholesome ideas should be suppressed			
Agree	88	12	(515)
Disagree	94	6	(1578)
Uncertain	94	6	(644)

* Percentages are to be added horizontally.

evidence shows that the students find it decidedly easier to support the legitimacy of an abstract value than to apply this value consistently to any and every concrete case.

> Sure, I believe in freedom of speech, but somebody ought to shut that guy up. He doesn't know what he's talking about.

> It's all very well to talk about religious freedom—and nobody believes in it more than I do—but there ought to be a law against people who believe some of the crackpot religious ideas you run into.

> Yes, I believe everyone should have the right to vote . . . But people would be happier, and we would probably be better off all around, if uneducated people didn't have so much of a chance to get their way. They are easily taken in by anyone.

MISANTHROPY AND POLITICAL IDEOLOGY [2]

Political ideology is inextricably linked to certain basic assumptions about the nature of human nature. Most of these assumptions are empirically unprovable, resting on a point of view and aimed at bulwarking it.[3] For example, a democratic doctrine *assumes* that most citizens are sufficiently rational so that their efforts to govern themselves will be, in the long run, more in the general social interest than some other alternative. A democratic political system functions best when people *believe* that it is functioning well, when they *believe,* for example, that most of their elected representatives can be trusted on some level to be sufficiently and sincerely concerned with the wills and needs of their constituents. A democratic system must acknowledge the possibility that mankind is not fundamentally vicious, self-seeking, unworthy of trust; for if this were so, how could one be counted on to be concerned for his neighbor's welfare as well as his own?

In a functioning democracy there is ample room for wide variation in the degree of faith in the goodness, worthiness and

---

[2] This section is based on an article, "Misanthropy and Political Ideology," by Morris Rosenberg, *American Sociological Review,* December 1956, pp. 690-695.

[3] See, for example, John Dewey, *Freedom and Culture* (G. P. Putnam's Sons, New York, 1939). Dewey makes the point that the predominant themes of the culture at any given era tend to be placed in evidence as "proving" that the corresponding human traits are inexorable and determining elements, native to human nature. (Chapter 2.)

improvability of human nature. It might range from a dewy-eyed, naive refusal to acknowledge the seamier side of life, at one extreme, to a tongue-in-cheek, cynical willingness to acknowledge a vast amount of human viciousness, at the other. But without some minimal amount of *faith in human nature,* democratic ideology is self-contradicting and highly vulnerable.

The college students report viewpoints covering the full range from the dewy-eyed to the tongue-in-cheek extremes. When it comes to expressing a general faith in the goodness and cooperativeness of mankind, they are close to the positive end of the range. Eighty-one per cent feel that "most people can be trusted"; about two thirds agree that "human nature is fundamentally cooperative" and reject the notion that "a person does not know whom he can count on these days," or that "No one is going to care much what happens to you when you get right down to it."

Many of the students acknowledge, however, that most people are motivated predominantly by their own self-interest rather than by care or concern for others. Seventy-two per cent agree, for example, that "most people are inclined . . . to look out for themselves"; about 60 per cent agree that "if you don't watch yourself, people will take advantage of you."

On the whole, these college students are trusting, even though they temper this trust with a certain, perhaps realistic wariness.

> You can't expect that people are going to hand anything to you on a silver platter. Too many are looking out for number one. But on the whole, I'd say there's more decent people in the world than people who are out to get you.

We used responses to five questions (those marked with asterisks in Appendix 17) in a scale which we called "faith-in-human nature." [4] Notice that each of the questions that make up this scale is phrased in very general terms, quite devoid of any specific political or ideological reference. The references are to "people," to "human nature," to "a person," and so on.

Our analysis shows that a student's position on this scale is highly predictive of important aspects of the way he looks at the public

---

4 See Appendix 17 for a full explanation of how this scale was developed.

and legislature; of his attitudes toward freedom of speech, and his readiness to justify calling the State's repressive functions into action.

THE EFFECTIVENESS OF REPRESENTATIVE GOVERNMENT

Take, for example, the assumption that men are not sufficiently rational to be trusted to participate in the political decisions which affect them. Students were asked to agree or to disagree with the following statement: "The general public is not qualified to vote on today's complex issues." Those who score low on the faith-in-human-nature scale are much more likely to agree with this statement than their counterparts who score high on the scale.

Consider next the responsiveness of public officials to the will of the people. It is mainly the mistrustful students who tend to deny that elected or appointed officials are concerned with the interests of most of the people. They were nearly three times as likely as their more trustful counterparts to agree that "There's little use in writing to public officials because often they aren't really interested in the problems of the average man." Moreover, they are more likely to say they believe that political representatives are usually pawns in the hands of special interests. As Table 6-2 indicates, the lower one scores on the faith-in-human-nature scale, the more likely he is to agree that "Political candidates are usually run by political machines."

Finally, those who agreed with all three of these statements were classified as "dubious" about the effective operation of representative government. Table 6-2b shows 76 per cent of those who scored lowest on the scale of faith-in-human-nature were also in the "dubious" category compared with 32 per cent of the more trustful students. Students who are disenchanted with human nature, it would appear, are also more likely to express disenchantment with the classical liberal description of the processes of a democratic society.

In considering these data, one may get the feeling that all they show is that students with little faith in the nature of man also have little respect for the men who are involved in politics—that the results are simply tautological. This is quite true—in the same sense that any clarifying equation is also a tautology. We should not expect a more cynical person to approve of building a bridge or of shifting the gears of a car any differently from the more trustful person. But we would expect him to be skeptical about any practice which involves the trustworthiness or corruptibility of mankind. And in so far as certain issues in a democratic society seem to engage this basic philosophy about human nature, the more cynical students may be vulnerable as well to the persuasiveness of more cynical opinions on the effectiveness of the democratic process.

FREEDOM OF SPEECH

The democratic concept of freedom of speech implies that exposing most men to different points of view will enable them to arrive at a judgment of their own, not hinder them. The principle underlying the "free market of ideas" is precisely this: that exposure to diverse points of view in this manner presumably provides the soundest basis for arriving at a decision.

We know already that not all students believe this—that, for example, 30 per cent agree that "people who talk politics without knowing what they are talking about should be kept quiet." But the mistrustful students are twice as likely as the more trustful ones to agree that it is reasonable to restrict the free market of ideas, in this sense.

"THERE OUGHT TO BE A LAW"

In time of stress it is not unusual to hear voices urging that the government should "do something about" certain deviant or unpopular groups. The public's reactions to such measures is usually interpreted in terms of liberalism or conservatism, isolationism or internationalism, or other themes associated with the manifest content of the issue. However, what sometimes escapes attention is the fact that readiness to "do something about" restricting a deviant group may also reflect one's attitude to the notion of law, itself. In other words, the question of whether the government

TABLE 6-2b. FAITH-IN-HUMAN-NATURE IS LINKED TO IMAGE OF THE PUBLIC
AND LEGISLATOR AND TO WILLINGNESS TO RESTRICT POLITICAL EXPRESSION
(Eleven universities)

	Scale of Faith-in-Human-Nature *					
	High					Low
	1	2	3	4	5	6
Total =	(303)	(597)	(844)	(613)	(415)	(203)

"The general public is not qualified to vote on today's complex issues." (Percentage in each scale group giving indicated response)

	1	2	3	4	5	6
Agree	35	41	44	49	58	59
Disagree	59	52	48	43	35	32
Undecided	6	7	8	7	7	9

"There's little use writing to public officials because often they aren't really interested in the problem of the average man."

Agree	14	20	25	31	38	41
Disagree	73	67	60	51	44	46
Undecided	13	13	15	18	18	13

"Political candidates are usually run by political machines."

Agree	63	69	74	76	81	85
Disagree	27	23	18	13	9	7
Undecided	10	8	8	10	9	8

Scale of belief in the feasibility of democracy **

Dubious	32	42	49	56	61	76
Sanguine	68	58	51	44	39	24

"People who talk politics without knowing what they are talking about should be kept quiet."

Agree	18	24	30	32	40	38
Disagree	73	68	61	61	53	56
Undecided	9	8	9	7	8	6

* See Appendix 17 for the construction of this scale.
** See page 135 for the items in this scale.

should suppress certain groups is not only a matter of partisan sympathy, not only a matter of tolerance toward the groups under consideration. It also touches upon readiness to employ the restraining power of law as a means of suppression. We would therefore expect the students who mistrust man's ability to control himself, irrespective of their own political views or party allegiances, to be more sympathetic to the idea that "there ought to be a law" restraining some deviant group.

In another context we reported that 40 per cent of all students agree that, "The laws governing labor unions today are not strict enough." Responses to this statement, we said, are linked to a philosophy of economic liberalism or conservatism, and we showed that agreement with this point of view is also linked to sympathy and support for the Republican party. (See pages 112-113)

Table 6-3a which makes it clear that, irrespective of political party affiliation, mistrustful students are more likely than others to declare that "there ought to be a law"—in this particular case, stricter controls against labor unions. Among them, in fact, the party-linked nature of this opinion is substantially weakened.

Note that the opinion that certain religions should be restrained, or that the right to run for public office should be limited only to "desirables" is not associated with political party allegiance. Regardless of their party sympathies, it is the students who mistrust people in general who show greater readiness to advocate restrictions against "religions which preach unwholesome ideas," or the right of certain kinds of people to be considered for public office.

On a variety of issues, then—unlimited freedom of speech, unlimited freedom of religion, unlimited right to run for public office—the student who is cynical about the nature of human nature, seems to find the idea of suppressing deviant people or groups less distasteful than do other students.

There remain, of course, many political matters which are unrelated to the individual's view of humanity. For example, what we have called here faith-in-human-nature has little to do with being a Democrat or a Republican, little to do with being a liberal or a conservative when the issues do not involve advocacy of repressive or restrictive measures. But the type of mistrustfulness we are talking about nurtures a skepticism about the good-will of the public and of public officials, a cynicism about

TABLE 6-3a. FAITH-IN-HUMAN-NATURE IS LINKED TO A WISH FOR STRICTER
CONTROLS: OF LABOR UNIONS, OF RELIGIONS, AND OF THE RIGHT
TO RUN FOR OFFICE

(Eleven universities)

Do you consider yourself a Republican, a Democrat, or an Independent in most political matters?	Scale of Faith-in-Human-Nature *		
	High 1, 2	*Medium* 3, 4	*Low* 5, 6
	Percentage ** who agree that "the laws governing labor unions today are not strict enough."		
Republican	51	54	60
Independent	35	35	42
Democrat	9	31	42
	Percentage ** who agree that "religions which preach unwholesome ideas should be suppressed."		
Republican	18	23	32
Independent	20	21	26
Democrat	20	25	30
	Percentage ** who agree that "it's unwise to give people with dangerous social and economic viewpoints a chance to be elected."		
Republican	38	43	58
Independent	28	40	47
Democrat	36	45	51

* For the construction of this scale see Appendix 17.
** The bases on which the per cents are computed are:

	Scale of Faith-in-Human-Nature		
	High	*Medium*	*Low*
Republican	259	406	194
Independent	392	631	242
Democrat	225	387	148

Omits 91 students who could not be classified.

freedom of speech, and a willingness to see the reasonableness of
suppressing certain political and religious liberties in certain
cases. We shall see in Chapter 8 that it may be part of a total
ideological structure.

It is linked, also, to crucial attitudes about war and peace and
to convictions about how international conflicts and tensions
should be handled—as we shall see in the section which follows.

WAR AND PEACE: A CONTRAPUNTAL MOTIF

American college students today live in the atmosphere of the cold war. It is a part of their very lives. Our pilot research at Cornell was begun in May 1950, just one month before the beginnings of hostilities in Korea. By the time we made our nationwide study in 1952, all but 24 per cent of the men we interviewed fully expected to be called into military service within a very short time. What did they think about war and peace?

While they are decidedly opposed to war, these students are caught in the contradiction between an unequivocal rejection of the morality of waging war, on the one hand, and their acceptance of certain basic assumptions and ideological positions which make war philosophically tenable, on the other.

Consider first the morality of waging war. Here most of the students are on the side of the angels. Three-quarters flatly disagree that "there are lots of good things about war." About three-fifths agree that "War is morally wrong," and reject the statement, "Peace and war are both essential to progress." But when an important assumption implicitly underlying the waging of war is brought into question—the sacrifice of human lives for the sake of a principle—their apparently steadfast front begins to waver. Only a very small minority agree, for example, that "human lives are too important to be sacrificed for the preservation of any form of government."

There can be no doubt either that these young people see no glamor in the military life. Only twelve per cent expressed attitudes toward serving in the Armed Forces that could be called favorable, by any stretch of the imagination.[5] Yet they are philosophically resigned to the legitimacy of requiring each citizen to perform his unquestioned obligation to do his duty. True, they do not relish the prospect; but they take it in their stride as an un-

---

5 Appendix 18 illustrates the use of the intensity component of an attitude measure to establish is zero point justifying division of the population into those with positive and negative attitudes. For an analysis of the students' attitude to military service, see also Edward A. Suchman and others, *Student to Soldier*, Department of Sociology and Anthropology, Cornell University, 1952.

pleasant necessity—perhaps in the same spirit as most adults pay their income taxes.[6]

Yet, granted that war is held to be immoral and militarism and military life distasteful, most of the students nevertheless accept the necessity for war under certain conditions. This means not that they are spirited flag-wavers, but that there is very little evidence of any of the bitter disillusionment with war aims that presumably followed World War I. Few students said, for example, that they felt World War II "was not worth fighting." Although they seemed to be somewhat less positive about the worthwhileness of the Korean conflict, most of them still declared that they accepted the necessity for armed intervention in this case as well.

If one is realistic in the face of the cold war, he must accept the effectiveness of power as a means of preventing hostilities: a substantial minority of the students take this position; and—as a final indication of what may underlie the contrapuntal nature of all these themes—at least an equivalent proportion of these young people felt at the time of our research that we were living in the shadow of war.

The counterpoint that we have noted—the simultaneous rejection and acceptance of the various elements that gear into attitudes toward war—becomes very apparent in the students' ideas on what steps should be taken to prevent war. The two methods most likely to be considered effective are something as forceful as "strong leadership," and something as elusive and intangible as "understanding on the part of every citizen of other peoples . . ." Two almost equally popular measures for preventing war are an idealistic one (world government) and a coercive one (military power). The pragmatic approach, "stop Russia," is paired with the more idealistic "emphasis on spiritual values and inner resources." The "free enterprise economic system" is rated effective by the same proportion who select "long range social planning." Notice,

---

6 This is a rather exact parallel. In both cases special subgroups of the population are called upon to fulfill an obligation the conditions of obedience to which are legally specified and defined. The attitude ultimately engages assumptions about the legitimacy of the authority of law, as well as favorable or unfavorable feelings toward the issue itself.

TABLE 6-3b. STUDENT OPINION ON WAR AND RELATED ISSUES

War as a Moral Issue	Percentage * who:			
	Agree	Dis- agree	Uncer- tain	No Answer
(Eleven universities: Total = 2975)				
There are lots of good things about war	15	74	9	1
War is morally wrong	60	23	18	—
Peace and war are both essential to progress	25	63	11	1
Human lives are too important to be sacrificed for the preservation of any form of government	12	75	12	1
An insult to our national honor should always be punished	13	69	17	1
(Cornell 1950: Total = 2578)				
It's a sign of weakness in a people's character to instigate a war	34	40	26	—
Acceptance of Obligation to Serve in Armed Forces (Eleven universities)				
A soldier should obey all rules and regulations without questioning	40	47	13	—
You owe it to your government to protect it in return for more important privileges	66	20	14	1
Anyone who serves in the armed forces is doing something worthwhile for his country	61	20	18	1
If you refuse to support your government in a war you shouldn't continue to live in a country	32	52	15	1
Too many people use conscientious objection as a loophole to escape serving	33	42	25	1
It's not fair for one man to be excused from military service while others are not	24	65	9	1
Only a moral coward would refuse to protect his government	21	68	10	1
Acceptance of Ideology of War Aims				
We are fighting today for an ideal, the free peoples of the world against dictatorship	61	27	11	1

* Percentages are to be added horizontally.

TABLE 6-3b—*Continued*

(Percentage giving indicated response)

How much do the things that the Korean war is being fought for mean to you, personally?

Tremendously important	20
Quite a bit	41
Don't mean very much	22
They mean nothing to me	5
Undecided	12

Do you ever get the feeling that the war in Korea is not worth fighting?

Never	19
Only once in a great while	18
Sometimes	36
Very often	26
No answer	1

Do you think it would be worth fighting an all-out war to stop Communism, or do you think an all-out war to stop Communism would not be worthwhile?

Very worthwhile	26
Fairly worthwhile	14
Undecided	12
No opinion	4
Hardly worthwhile	18
Not at all worthwhile	24
No answer	2

Effectiveness of Power

Which do you, personally, count on as the more effective deterrent against war: the atom bomb or the U.N.?

The atom bomb	51
The U.N.	45
No answer	4

(Cornell 1950: Total = 2758)

A nation's rights are determined by the nation's power

Agree	29
Disagree	59
Uncertain	12

TABLE 6-3b—*Continued*

(Percentage giving indicated response)

The Shadow of War

(Eleven universities: Total = 2975)

Do you, personally, expect that this country will be in another great war within the next ten years or so, or do you think there is a good chance of avoiding it?

We're in it now	16
Expect war within 10 years	28
Depends	18
Good chance to avoid it	36
No answer	2

The most we can hope to accomplish is the partial elimination of war

Agree	49
Disagree	40
Uncertain	10
No answer	1

In spite of all our efforts for peace, nations just can't live together peacefully so we might as well expect a war every few years

Agree	16
Disagree	73
Uncertain	10
No answer	1

incidentally, how few students take an outright ethnocentric or imperialistic position. Only eleven per cent chose "increased U.S. influence over the affairs of other nations" as a way of preventing war.

What happens to these opinions as the students go through college? The answer for Cornell students (the only campus where we could trace changes of opinion) is this: their faith was noticeably shaken in the effectiveness of virtually all solutions. Only two of the suggested measures were more effective in retaining the faith of their supporters than in corroborating the disenchantment of those who had rejected them. They were: "trained and expert

TABLE 6-4. SUGGESTED MEANS FOR PREVENTING WAR
(Eleven universities: Total = 2975)

Write an H (high) next to each suggestion which you think is highly important for the U.S. to rely on if we are to prevent another war . . .

	Percentage who consider each measure highly important
Leadership	87
Understanding on the part of every citizen, of other peoples . . .	69
Military power	46
World government	41
Stop Russia	38
Emphasis on individual spiritual values . . .	34
Free enterprise economic system	35
Long range social planning	32
Increased U.S. influence over international affairs of other nations	11

leadership" and "understanding on the part of every citizen of other peoples at home and in other countries."

The analysis shows other trends, as well. For example, it shows that the general effect of these college years was less disenchanting for those who believed in forceful solutions than for those who had started college stressing the qualitative approaches to international conflict. It reiterates the ambivalence of student opinion by showing how apparently contradictory themes retained, gained and lost adherents to almost the same degree. And, more important, it shows that among all the measures to prevent war that we are discussing, only two were able to attract the faith of enough students to make up the "deficit" left by the defections of the disenchanted. These two measures were: "Emphasis on spiritual values," and "long-range social planning."

The evidence appears in Table 6-5 which answers essentially two questions. Of the students who did not change their minds, is the proportion who consistently supported a certain measure greater than the equivalent proportion of those who consistently rejected that measure? The second question is: were the students who changed their minds more likely to have been attracted *to* the measure than to have been driven away from it? If the answer to the first question is "yes," it is safe to infer that the intervening years encouraged support for that measure. If the answer to the second question is "yes," then the inference is that the ranks were closed—that any loss of adherents to that measure was now more than made up by a gain of new supporters who had developed faith in its effectiveness. If the comparisons turn out the opposite way, then the inference is that its supporters had become discouraged and were not replaced by new ones.

It turns out that the two measures which were best able to retain the students' faith in them were "trained and expert leadership" and "understanding on the part of every citizen of other peoples at home and in other countries." Yet, even these two measures lost some adherents and this "deficit" was not fully replaced by an equivalent gain of new adherents. Note too that those who had initially counted on "leadership" found it easier to maintain their faith in this selection than those who had counted on "understanding."

On all other measures the theme is disenchantment. Students who were initially unimpressed with the effectiveness of a measure found it easier to maintain their viewpoint than students who were initially impressed with its effectiveness. In this sense, disenchantment was reinforced with regard to military power and world government. Yet, faith in "military power" was more likely to have remained unshaken than was faith in world government. Moreover, the power point of view gained more new recruits than did the world government point of view.

Disappointment with the effectiveness of the next counterposed pair of measures for preserving peace was also registered during this time. They were "spiritual values" and "stop Russia." But fewer students were disillusioned with the first alternative; relatively more were disillusioned with the second. The evidence appears in the first two columns of figures in Table 6-5.

The second pair of columns in Table 6-5 contrasts the proportion of students who increased their faith in each measure with the proportion who lost faith in it. "Emphasis on spiritual values" and "long range social planning" are the only two measures where the first group exceeds the second—the only two measures, in short, where the "deficit" left by the defection of the disenchanted was made up by the advent of the newly enchanted.

TABLE 6-5. CHANGES IN RELIANCE ON CERTAIN MEASURES OF PREVENTING WAR
(Cornell panel)

Write an H (high) next to each suggestion which you think is highly important for the U.S. to reply on if we are to prevent another war	Opinions students reported as underclassmen compared with their opinions as upperclassmen				
	Percentage* who did not change among those who initially said:		Among those who changed, percentage* of responses		
	"High"	All Other Responses	Originally "Low" or "Medium," Changed to "High"	Originally "High," Changed to "Low" or "Medium"	Total
Beliefs which were encouraged					
Trained and expert leadership	91 (846)	32 (80)	43	57	(126)
Understanding on the part of every citizen of other peoples	80 (676)	47 (246)	49	51	(265)
Beliefs which were discouraged					
Military power	64 (428)	74 (483)	45	55	(279)
World government	55 (493)	74 (424)	33	67	(320)
Spiritual values	59 (318)	77 (586)	51	49	(257)
Stop Russia	58 (399)	66 (506)	44	56	(288)
Free enterprise economic system	55 (370)	73 (535)	46	54	(299)
Long range social planning	55 (291)	75 (623)	54	46	(279)
Increased U.S. influence	19 (116)	95 (884)	27	73	(128)

* The bases on which the per cents are computed appear in parentheses.

Of course, there is no way to disentangle what may have been the contributions of the college environment and what may have been the contribution which world events during this period made to either enchantment or disenchantment with each measure we are discussing. Moreover we know the Cornell campus to be a relatively conservative one, so it is questionable to what extent these generalizations might apply to other student populations. But the findings are clearcut: between 1950 and 1952 the only two war-prevention measures in which these college students were able to maintain their faith were "leadership" and "understanding." Adherents to all the other ways of preventing war which we have been discussing up to now tended to fall away; and but few of the students initially unimpressed by the effectiveness of any other war-prevention measures were able to find reason to take a less jaundiced view of them.

POWER, COOPERATION, AND HUMAN NATURE[7]

College students' attitudes toward peace and war are clearly ambivalent. They declare that they oppose war and have little taste for military service, although, if conditions require it, they declare they are ready to do their duty. Their ideas about how to maintain peace range from the coercive to the spiritual. In short, student opinions and attitudes toward issues of war and peace seem to range as widely and to be as much in conflict as are the opinions of the general population. They seem to be as contented or as resigned as are adults to going along with existing approaches to international conflicts.

These approaches can be conceived of in terms of basically two positions. The first relies mainly on power and force as a solution to international differences; the second relies mainly on mutual cooperation. Each derives from certain principles which are, philosophically speaking, at opposite poles.

In the first case the principles are these: it is the essential nature of men and thus of nations, to pursue their own self-interests. When conflicting self-interests clash, it is the nature of men, and thus of nations, to wield their power. The conflict can be held in check only if one of the antagonistic persons or nations can be forced to capitulate to the greater strength of the other.

This line of reasoning takes for granted that certain constants

---

[7] This section is based on an article by Morris Rosenberg, "Misanthropy and Attitudes Toward International Affairs," *Conflict Resolution*, Vol. 1, No. 4, December 1957, pp. 340-345.

characterize communities of nations as well as communities of people. All are assumed to be competitively engaged in an inexorable struggle for existence in which the strong will survive and the weak will be "selected out." Since this is a natural state of things, any nation is justified in exercising force by virtue of the very fact that it is strong enough to do so: for it must avoid being itself "selected out." In the last analysis, every nation—like every man—is "looking out for number one."

The summary is deliberately schematic to make apparent the parallel with an oversimplified version of the notion of the survival of the fittest. Strength alone ensures survival; survival is synonymous with fitness; thus strength is synonymous with fitness. If "fit" is then given its connotation of "deserving," it follows that the strong *deserve* to survive, the weak to perish.

The second view rejects the assumption that conflicting self-interests are necessarily equivalent to a competitive struggle for survival in the evolutionary sense. It takes for granted certain other constants, and stresses them over and beyond admitted conflicts and antagonisms. For example: all people, and thus all nations, wish essentially to dispense with force and to live in peace. All men, and thus all nations, are by nature potentially capable of accomplishing this. There is in the nature of men, and thus of nations, a powerful potential to cooperate for the common welfare, an equivalent potential for rational, just and equitable resolutions of conflicting interests. Tawney put it this way: ". . . no change of system or machinery can avert those causes of social malaise which consist in the egotism, greed, or quarrelsomeness of human nature. What it can do is to create an environment in which those are not the qualities which are encouraged." [8] In the long run, solutions which build on these potentials and encourage them will be the more effective ones.

It is interesting that the first set of arguments considers the effectiveness of power to be apparent, and justifies mainly the morality of wielding it The second set of arguments considers the morality of cooperation to be apparent, and justifies mainly its

---

[8] R. H. Tawney, *The Acquisitive Society* (New York: Harcourt Brace and Co., 1920), pp. 180-181.

effectiveness. But both sets of arguments have in common the beliefs about the nature of human nature that we have referred to earlier and measured in the college population by means of the scale of faith-in-human-nature.

These philosophical links between reliance on power or reliance on cooperation in international affairs and the corresponding beliefs about human nature, are clearly discernible when the testimony of the college students is analyzed. Equating power with rights, for example, is more characteristic of students who declare their mistrust of man's essential nature. Or take the matter of international co-operation. For most students this principle is symbolized by the idea of the United Nations, whether or not they believe it is actually accomplishing it. In contrast, "the bomb" is today the symbol of supreme force and violence. The mistrustful students are more likely to count on the bomb as a deterrent to war; the more trusting students on the United Nations.

We have pointed out the contrapuntal themes in students' ideas of what are effective measures for peace: strong leadership but also understanding; world government but also military power; stop Russia but also spiritual values, inner resources and long-range planning. The counterpoint is less evident when the opinions of the cynics are examined separately from those of the more trustful students. For in the former group it is principally those measures that state or imply the wielding of power that are considered "highly effective"; only rarely will these students grant that less forceful measures for maintaining peace might work. At the opposite extreme, the most trustful students stress principally the qualitative measures for peace, and only rarely do they declare that steps which require the wielding of power and force are likely to be effective.

Finally, the mistrustful students are more likely than others to declare that war is inevitable. Few students of any type agree that "in spite of all our efforts for peace, nations just can't live together peacefully so we might as well expect war every few years." But those who believe this are more likely than others to be on the low end of the faith-in-human-nature scale. And when it comes to a statement like; "The most we can hope to accomplish is the partial

TABLE 6-6. STUDENTS WHO SCORE LOW ON THE FAITH-IN-HUMAN-NATURE SCALE
ARE MORE LIKELY THAN OTHERS TO COUNT ON POWER TO PRESERVE
PEACE AND TO BELIEVE IN THE INEVITABILITY OF WAR

	Scale of Faith-in-Human-Nature *					
	High					*Low*
	1	2	3	4	5	6
Total =	(303)	(597)	(844)	(613)	(415)	(203)

Eleven universities

Which do you personally count on as the more effective deterrent against war?   (Percentage in each scale group giving indicated response)

	1	2	3	4	5	6
The atom bomb	43	48	51	57	60	60
The United Nations	56	52	48	43	40	40

In spite of all our efforts for peace, nations just can't live together peacefully so we might as well expect a war every few years

	1	2	3	4	5	6
Agree	7	11	14	18	24	28
Disagree	86	82	75	71	62	60
Uncertain	6	8	11	10	14	12

The most we can hope to accomplish is the partial elimination of war

	1	2	3	4	5	6
Agree	36	40	48	54	60	61
Disagree	56	49	40	35	30	26
Uncertain	7	10	11	10	9	13

. . . Write an H (high) next to each suggestion which you think is highly important for the U.S. to rely on if we are to prevent another war **

	1	2	3	4	5	6
Understanding on the part of every citizen of other peoples at home and abroad	76	72	71	70	64	58
World government	48	42	43	40	36	36
Military power	37	46	45	49	49	53
Stop Russia	26	38	37	40	44	48
Increased U.S. influence	5	8	9	13	13	19

Cornell 1950 †   Total = (431) (752) (689) (413) (303) (170)

A nation's rights are determined by that nation's power

	1	2	3	4	5	6
Agree	18	28	37	36	40	44
Disagree	68	58	55	56	50	47
Uncertain	14	14	8	8	9	9

* For construction of this scale, see Appendix 17.
** Per cents should not be cumulated owing to multiple responses.
† Since this item was asked only in the 1950 study, we have used the scale of faith-in-human-nature which was developed in that study. This differs somewhat from the 1952 scale (Appendix 17).

elimination of war," the majority of the cynics are agreed that this is the case. Only a minority of the trustful students take this position.

There is a great temptation to moralize here about the implications these findings may have if the generalizations true of college student opinions and attitudes were to hold true, as well, for international policy-makers. Without succumbing to it, however, this point does deserve to be made: to the extent that there is any margin at all for policy-makers to influence the behavior of their nations in the international scene, it is not at all unlikely that their own very fundamental attitudes and beliefs about the nature of man will affect the way they exercise that influence. Nor is it far-fetched to conjecture that realization of cooperative measures for maintaining peace will be paced to the rate at which the social and psychological milieux within which all peoples live and develop are such that they justify every man's belief in every man's essential worthiness.

7

Secular Religion

IN CONSIDERING the religious beliefs and values of students, we
found ourselves, when we began the study, confronted with certain clearly apparent social facts in the college community. The
college students with whom we talked, whom we interviewed, observed, and made friends with, readily told us about sets of values,
beliefs, precepts and practices which they considered religious.

They told us that they believe in God. Some of them described
Him as a Divine, Omniscient, Omnipresent, and vigilant kind of
Being; others visualized Him as a more mystical Power; but in
either case, they said they believed.

They told us that they go to religious services, many of them
with a high degree of regularity. Some said that they derived from
their church attendance, or simply from being part of an identifiable religious group, certain strong feelings of identification and
belongingness.

They said that they were aware of a need for some kind of religious faith or personal philosophy. They told us that they talk
about it, grope for it, and some of them eagerly seize upon this or
that organizational means of finding it.

We were struck, too, by the observation that even in this allegedly secular society of ours, certain students nevertheless declared (some solemnly, some quite casually) that their religious
beliefs and activities constituted for them a sort of focal point
around which their major life-goals and life-satisfactions, they
thought, would ultimately revolve.

We viewed these statements and self-descriptions as social facts which it was our job to fit into a conceptual scheme that could be called "religiousness."

MEASURING RELIGIOUSNESS

The students told us that they *believe in God*. In American society a central core of our religious system—indeed of our whole social system—is human recognition of a superhuman controlling power, especially of a personal God entitled to obedience. Hence we considered this belief as one essential defining characteristic of "religiousness." [1]

The questionnaire, therefore, asked, "Which of the following statements most closely describes your ideas about the Deity?" [2] Here are the alternatives which were offered, and the proportions selecting each one.

Responses at eleven universities (Total = 2975)

	Percentage
I believe in a Divine God, Creator of the Universe, Who knows my innermost thoughts and feelings, and to Whom one day I shall be accountable.	48
I believe in a power greater than myself, which some people call God and some people call Nature.	27
I believe in the worth of humanity but not in God or a Supreme Being.	5
I believe in natural law, and that the so-called universal mysteries are ultimately knowable according to scientific method.	7
I am not quite sure what I believe.	12
I am an atheist.	1
All other responses	3

---

[1] De Tocqueville was struck by the fact that the religious basis of our judicial system was not simply a philosophical matter, but could be seen in operation. He quotes a newspaper article which appeared in the *Spectator* of August 23, 1831. "The Court of Common Pleas of Chester County (New York) a few days since, rejected a witness who declared his disbelief in the existence of God. The presiding judge remarked that . . . this belief constituted the sanction of all testimony in a court of justice; and that he knew of no case in a Christian country where a witness had been permitted to testify without such belief." [*Democracy in America* (New York: Knopf 1955), p. 317.]

[2] This question is patterned after a similar question reported in Daniel Katz and Floyd Allport, *Students' Attitudes* (Syracuse, New York, The Craftsman Press, Inc., 1931), p. 259. See also Murray Ross, *The Religious Beliefs of Youth* (New York: Associated Press, 1950), for distribution of responses to a similar question.

The students said that *they get a sense of belongingness from religion.*

A second defining characteristic of religiousness, we felt, must have to do with this awareness of community stemming from religion and things religious. Emile Durkheim made this point very clearly when he referred to the "moral community" of religion, bound together by members' feeling that "we" who share common symbols and beliefs about the unknown, and who participate in common rituals, become a distinguishable and identifiable collective.[3] We have mentioned this feeling of collective identity in discussing the feelings the students reported about their colleges and fraternities. The question we had asked which touched upon these feelings was:

> "This group has its own personality, something over and above the individual members in it." Does the statement above express the way you feel about any of the following groups?

The checklist which followed included as one alternative the response, "Your church or your religion," a category which was checked by 38 per cent of all students.

The relative frequency with which this response was chosen compared with the other possible responses (see Appendix 20) indicates something about what we have implied in the title of this chapter is the secular nature of the students' religious beliefs ("religion" is third in order of choice).[4] Yet at the same time it indicates that these college youth tend to personify, in this semi-mystical way, their religious community (in Durkheim's sense) rather more than their national or ethnic community. More students feel that their church or religion "has its own personality"; relatively fewer say this about their national group.

---

3 Emile Durkheim, *The Elementary Forms of Religious Life* [Glencoe, Illinois, The Free Press (translated from the French by Joseph Ward Swain)] Chap. 1.

4 See, for example, Will Herberg, *Protestant, Catholic, Jew* (New York: Doubleday and Company, 1955). Herberg speaks of the new religious revival but sees its origins as secular. His discussion centers on second-generation Americans. Our analysis suggests that the phenomenon of secular religion may be much more widespread.

Some students told us that *they counted on religion to give them an important sense of satisfaction in their lives.*

Perhaps the most acute aspect of the "religiousness" expressed by the students was this feeling of commitment, the expectation that religious beliefs and religious activities would play an important role in one's total life picture. We have already discussed the family-centeredness and the career-centeredness that the college students revealed when we asked them: "What three things or activities in your life do you expect to give you the most satisfaction?" (See Table 2-2) The comparatively few students (17 per cent) who selected "religious beliefs or activities" *at all,* could be viewed, we felt, as having given expression to this sort of over-all feeling of commitment to religious feelings and beliefs. This does not mean, necessarily, that the majority of students expect to derive no satisfaction from religion or their religious activities.[5] But it does mean that, just as there is a certain absence of identification with religion, there is an even more marked absence of intense commitment to it. The students' beliefs are "secular" in the sense that religious activities cannot compete with the family-centeredness, the work-centeredness, and even the leisure-centeredness of their society.

Implicitly underlying the concept of religiousness was, it seemed to us, an unstated assumption. We said that when we talked to the students about religion we found that many of them began the discussion by declaring that *they felt strongly a need for some kind of a religious faith or philosophy* to give meaning to their lives and to bridge the gap between the manifest occurrences of daily life and the ultimate meaning of these occurrences. Each of

---

[5] A study of the general population, conducted by *The Catholic Digest,* reports that 75 per cent of the sample declared religion to be "very important" to them. ("How Important Is Religion to Americans?" *The Catholic Digest,* 8, February, 1953) A study conducted by W. Seward Salisbury, of the State University of New York, polled 1,675 undergraduate students sampled from the student bodies of ten teachers' colleges. Eighty-five per cent of these students said "that they felt religion to be an important ingredient for an adequate and satisfying life." The same study, incidentally, found that in response to the identical question used in the present research ("What three things or activities in your life do you expect to give you the most satisfaction?") "Religious beliefs or activities" was selected by an equivalent proportion—16 per cent—of the students polled. ("Religion and Secularization," *Social Forces,* 36, 3, March 1958, 197-205.)

the other elements of "religiousness" defined thus far rested, it
seemed, on that feeling of need. When we asked "Do you, personally, feel you need to believe in some sort of religious faith or
philosophy?", the vast majority (80 per cent) said "yes." Only 13
per cent unequivocally responded "no," while the remaining
seven per cent checked "don't know."

Four facets of the idea of "religiousness" had been specified
which, we felt, satisfied the requirements of a conceptual scheme,
on the one hand, and, on the other, were close to the kind of information we had been getting spontaneously from the students in
personal interviews with them before fixing our questionnaire.
There still remained, however, the more formal aspect of attendance at religious ceremonies and services as a possible fifth facet
of "religiousness."

We were somewhat dubious about including this as a defining
characteristic of "religiousness": from one point of view there was
reason for viewing active participation in the symbolic rites and rituals connected with religion and religious beliefs [6] as an indicator
of religiousness in our society. From another point of view, however, it could be argued that *belief,* in our society, although undoubtedly highly correlated with practice, is really quite different
from it conceptually, and should thus be treated separately. The
matter was decided ultimately in a strictly empirical manner; but
meanwhile we had tentatively included as a fifth possible facet to
be measured in "religiousness" professed attendance at services.[7]

---

[6] In *Structure and Function in Primitive Society* (Glencoe, Ill.: Free Press, 1952),
A. R. Radcliffe-Brown states, for example: ". . . any religion . . . normally involves
certain ideas or beliefs on the one hand and, on the other, certain observances . . .
In European countries and more particularly since the Reformation, religion has
come to be considered mainly a matter of beliefs . . . My suggestion is that in attempting to understand religion, it is on the rites rather than on the beliefs that we
should concentrate attention." (pp. 154-155)

[7] In response to the question, "How often do you attend religious services?", the
students' answers distributed as follows:

(Responses at eleven universities: Total = 2975)

Once a week or more	27
About twice a month	14
About once a month	12
Mainly on important holidays	21
Never or almost never	25

TABLE 7-1. RELIGIOUS BELIEFS OF COLLEGE STUDENTS

	Fisk	Texas	No. Ca.	Wayne	Michigan	Wesleyan	Cornell Men	Cornell Women	UCLA	Yale	Harvard	Dartmouth
Total =	(134)	(516)	(414)	(519)	(488)	(277)	(655)	(245)	(467)	(297)	(453)	(365)
Religion is expected to be "a major source of satisfaction in life."	36	29	27	20	17	16	13	24	13	12	11	10
(Percentage giving indicated response)												
Attend religious services "once a week or more"	49	29	34	27	28	29	29	32	27	24	22	20
Church or religion has "its own personality"	25	43	46	36	41	46	34	46	30	39	35	40
"I believe in a Divine God"	60	62	68	43	45	43	42	38	32	36	30	35
Need for a religious faith	89	88	90	78	79	83	75	83	73	81	70	77

THE RELIGIOUSNESS SCALE

Thus, in terms of the initial problem we had set for ourselves, we had specified five possible facets ranging from what we had felt to be the most elementary minimum condition for "religiousness" (an expressed need for religious faith) to what we felt was a refined measure of "feeling committed to religion." The facets which were tested are repeated below.

	Percentage of Students Giving "Religious" Responses Total = 2975
Need for religious faith	80
"I believe in a Divine God . . ."	48
Church or religion "has its own personality . . ."	38
Attend religious services once a week or more	27
Religion is expected to be a major source of satisfaction in life	17

The pattern of responses to four of these five questions fitted the criteria for a scale. In other words, all these responses referred to the same trait, specified in our conceptual analysis as "religiousness." The item which fell outside the pattern—as indeed we had to some extent anticipated—was the item on church attendance.

Table 7-1 shows the proportion of students at the universities studied who gave the "religious" response to each of these questions. In the sense defined here,[8] the most "religious campuses" are the Southern ones (Fisk, Texas, North Carolina); the least religious campuses are the Eastern universities (Cornell, Yale, Harvard, Dartmouth). UCLA students incidentally, responded very much like the students at these four Eastern colleges. Notice, too, that although at Fisk the "religious" responses tend to be most prevalent, there is an important exception. These Negro students are least likely to say that their religious group provides them with any sense of identification or belongingness—an intimation of the

---

[8] It should be obvious that this scale makes no attempt to define exhaustively the concept of religiousness. Certainly many dimensions of the concept are not included in this scale. The idea of a moral God as a pre-eminently righteous Being is touched upon only by implication. Feelings such as those of awe, reverence and respect are omitted. The idea of man's responsibility to Divine principles is not included—to mention only some examples.

theme of alienation and anomie which is taken up later (pages 169-172).

In principle, the kinds of beliefs which are included in this scale would seem to be free of reference to any set of ideas which are necessarily associated philosophically or doctrinally with one of the three major religious faiths rather than another. Belief in an Absolute Deity, commitment to religious beliefs or activities as a way of life, need for religious belief, personification of one's church or religious group—any and all of these might be considered compatible with the teachings of Protestant, Catholic, or Jewish faith.[9] Yet characteristic differences between Protestant, Catholic and Jewish students appear when their religious belief is measured by the criteria incorporated in this particular scale.[10] The Catholic students are most likely to have a high score; Jewish students are least likely, and Protestants are somewhere in between these two religious groups.

TABLE 7-2. RELIGIOUSNESS SCALE: STUDENTS FROM CATHOLIC, PROTESTANT
AND JEWISH HOMES

	What is your family's religious background?		
	Catholic	Protestant	Jewish
Total * =	(368)	(1793)	(429)
Religiousness scale **	(Percentages in each scale position)		
High: 4	18	10	2
3	34	21	12
2	25	33	30
1	16	22	33
0	7	13	22

* Omits 385 students with mixed religious backgrounds or those who did not provide information.
** The construction of this scale is explained pp. 154-159.

---

[9] The only exception might conceivably be the biasing effect of the word, "church," in the alternative "your church or religious group" to be selected as one of the personified collectivities. (See page 155.) This might have put off some of the Jewish students, even though the alternative "your religious group" was suitable for them.

[10] See, for example, Murray Ross, *The Religious Beliefs of Youth, op. cit., passim.* Daniel Katz and Floyd Allport, *Students Attitudes, op. cit., passim.* The fact that the present scale of religiousness distinguishes the three groups in a manner which corroborates the findings of these and many other investigators validates, in effect, our interpretation of the meaning of the scale.

We shall have occasion, from time to time, to point out other characteristic ways in which these three groups differ from each other. We shall return also to a detailed analysis of the correlates of "religiousness," as measured by this scale. But first we would like to examine some of the requirements which students said they considered essential in a religious or ethical belief system.

RELATIVISTIC RELIGIOUS BELIEFS

We have referred to the generally secular tone of the campuses, pointing out that even if religious belief is widespread, religious commitment is rare. This secular tone is apparent in another sense, as well. When we analyzed the specific content of the beliefs the students reported, we found that the predominant point of view seemed to be relativistic rather than absolute. About 80 per cent said they felt a need for religion; but 46 per cent meant "some sincere working philosophy or code of ethics, not necessarily a religious belief." [11] And in spite of the widespread assertion of

---

11 This proportion, incidentally, is slightly higher than the equivalent proportion at Syracuse where only 36 per cent selected the same response in a study published in 1931. (Katz and Allport, *op. cit.*, p. 288.) The question asked in both cases was: "Which *one* of the following statements most nearly expresses your opinion of what you, personally, need to lead a good life": The percentage responses of both samples were:

	Cornell, 1950	Syracuse, 1931
Total =	(2758)	(1300)
Some sincere working philosophy or code of ethics, not necessarily a religious belief.	46	36
Some religious belief, but it may be purely personal. Church attendance contributes nothing.	7	6
Some individual religious belief. Church attendance helps but is of minor importance.	9	16
An individual religious belief. Regular attendance at church helps but is not absolutely necessary.	21	27
An individual religious belief is not sufficient. You must also be a member and a regular attendant of church.	11	7
I do not wish to check this item.	7	7

The distribution of responses made by both populations are rather similar, even though some differences are statistically significant. However, the methodological differences between the Syracuse study and ours is compounded by the time difference and accompanying changes in measures of meaning, frame of reference, etc. (the Syracuse data were gathered in 1926). Thus the apparent comparability of the two frequency distributions is questionable enough so that we avoid the temptation to interpret the differences as changes.

belief in God, only 47 per cent of the students said they felt that acceptance of the Deity is a highly important component of a religious or ethical system (see Table 7-3).

There is very little evidence that students feel that religious belief must demand absolute conviction or adherence to a fixed set of unchanging or Divine principles or rules. The majority emphasize in an "ideal" belief system chiefly the kinds of elements which might be said to serve the individual's own personal needs. In brief, we found that the elements which students chose as essential to an ideal belief system, are of three main types. They are listed below in descending order of the proportions of students choosing each as "highly important."

Goals which serve highly individual and personal ends.

Goals which imply societal functions.

Goals which emphasize the absolute, and ritualistic or formal practices.

This classification orders a variety of responses which the students made when we asked them: ". . . consider what characteristics you, yourself, feel are essential before you could consider a religious or ethical system ideal." Again they were instructed to rate each characteristic "H" if they considered it highly important; "M" if they considered it of medium importance, and "L" if they considered it only slightly important, irrelevant, or even undesirable.

The data have been arranged in Table 7-3 which shows how the students' religious beliefs cluster around these three "poles." The consensus on the campuses we studied is that the absolute, traditional or ritualistic content of a religious system, more than any other type of content, is "only slightly important, irrelevant, or even undesirable." The range goes roughly from one fourth of the students who minimize the importance of some concept of God as a cornerstone of religious beliefs to 43 per cent of the students who minimize the importance of any concept of salvation [12]

---

[12] (Cornell 1952: Total = 1571)

The following items have been combined in the "Scale of absolute religious belief."

(Percentage)

—Rational premises and propositions considered of low or medium
importance but not highly important   62

or of formal ritual, clergy, and church. Similarly, very few students feel that these elements of religious belief need to be considered "highly important."

These beliefs refer to a single universe of content, measured by a scale of "Absolute Religious Belief." [12] The main difference between this scale and the Religiousness Scale is that the former touches upon certain doctrinal components, while the latter is relatively free of doctrinal references.

Students are most likely to declare that a religious or ethical system ought to do something for the individual—provide him with intellectual clarity, for example, or with a focus for his own personal adjustment and development.[13] This is the kind of belief system about which there is most widespread agreement both positively (well over half of the students hold such beliefs) and negatively (almost nobody considers these instrumental characteristics to be of little or no importance).

Somewhere in the middle range fall the kinds of religious values that we have classified as emphasizing the societal function of "an

	(Percentage)
—Prayer and worship considered of high or medium importance but not of low importance	60
—Based on God as a Supreme Being considered of high importance, not medium or low	47
—Provides salvation or redemption of the soul considered of high importance, not medium or low	26
—Church, clergy, ordained personnel considered of high importance, not medium or low	18

Position on this scale is so highly related to position on the Religiousness scale discussed earlier (pp. 154-159) that we shall have occasion in Chapter 8 to use the two measures almost interchangeably in tracing the correlates of religious belief. Appendix Table 20 shows this relationship.

Note that the items in this scale follow almost literally the definition of religion presented in 1915 by Emile Durkheim. His definition of religion included:

1. Acceptance of the idea that these aspects of religion are beyond reason and thus in the realm of the sacred.
2. Acceptance of the existence of an institution with specialized personnel dedicated to the practice of the sacred.
3. Acceptance of the importance of rites and rituals.
4. Acceptance of the existence of a Divinity.

(See Emile Durkheim, *op. cit.*, Chap. 1)

13 One must be cautious here not to confuse consequence with motive. We do not mean to imply that the search for such instrumental values necessarily *motivates* the student's religious belief. It might well be, for example, that many of the students are thinking in terms of the gratifications they find in their belief systems.

ideal religion." Compared with the more absolute beliefs, there is greater acceptance of religion as "an anchor for family life and children," as a source of social philosophy, as a producer of "strong community feeling," or "welfare services and material aid." Between about a third to a half of the sample agree on these religious values.

There seems to be a significant *lack* of agreement. The students are most in accord in declaring that a belief in God is of first importance in a religious or ethical system—but only 25 per cent say they feel this way. Fifteen per cent emphasize as most important "a focus for personal adjustment and development"; 13 per cent check "intellectual clarity about the fundamental problems of living." From there on, the figures dwindle to a point where they are relatively meaningless. And yet student opinion was much more likely to converge on the characteristics that they felt were most important to seek in an "ideal mate," or the guarantees which they would expect from an "ideal democracy." They were more likely, too, to find areas of agreement about the most important aims of college education or even about the characteristics of an "ideal job" (see Tables 4-3, 6-1, 1-1 and 2-3). It appears that the norms for religious belief among these college students may be much less fixed and much less patterned than they are in these other institutional areas.

DIFFERENCES AMONG RELIGIOUS GROUPS

One reason, of course, for this apparent lack of fixed norms of belief on the campus as a whole is that students who say they belong to one of the three major religious faiths express substantially differing points of view. Table 7-4 lists each religious value again, in descending order of the frequency with which the population of Catholic, Protestant, and Jewish men and women consider it to be highly important. The profiles provide an unsophisticated but informative sketch of the major doctrinal differences in the approach to religion characteristic of adherents to the three faiths.

The Catholics are most agreed on the necessity for a religious or ethical belief system to be based on absolute and traditional values.

TABLE 7-3. CHARACTERISTICS OF AN IDEAL RELIGIOUS OR ETHICAL SYSTEM
(Cornell 1952: Total = 1571)

Consider what characteristics you, yourself, feel are essential before you would consider a religious or ethical system ideal.	Percentage* selecting each characteristic as				
	Highly Important		*Me-dium*	*Low or Irrele-vant*	*No Answer*
	First	*Other High*			
Personal					
A focus for personal adjustment and development	15	45	29	7	4
Intellectual clarity about the fundamental problems of living	13	43	32	8	4
Societal					
A strong community feeling of closeness with your fellow men	8	43	36	10	4
An anchor for family life, children	8	43	34	11	5
Welfare services and material aid for people who need it	2	31	49	13	4
Absolute, Ritualistic					
Based on God as the Supreme Being	25	22	23	26	5
Prayer and worship	3	28	29	35	4
Provides salvation or redemption of the soul	2	24	26	43	6
Rational premises and propositions subject to logical laws **	7	25	39	23	6
A church, clergy, ordained personnel	—	18	33	43	5

* Note that per cents are to be added horizontally.
** Those who consider this requirement of a religious system as of little or no importance are considered to have given the "absolute" responses. As stated, the phrase "rational premises . . . subject to logical laws" is interpreted to be the opposite of *faith*. Many theologians argue, for example, that to attempt to apply finite human proofs to Divine Manifestations is specious. See *The Theology of Paul Tillich*, Charles W. Kegley and Robert W. Bretall, (eds.) (New York: The Macmillan Co., 1952), esp. pp. 339 ff.

"God," "salvation," and "prayer" appear at the top of the list for Catholics; "rational premises" (the opposite of faith) appears at the bottom—i.e., is rarely considered important by students who come from Catholic homes.

The Jewish students approach religion, apparently, in virtually the opposite way. These young people are most likely to agree that absolute or ritualistic values are *not* important in a religious or ethical belief system. They tend to stress the individual and societal values that a belief system can bulwark. They seem to stress ethical and social content rather than absolute or Divine sanction.

The Protestants appear to be somewhere in between. Many of them resemble the Jewish students in their tendency to approach religion as an individual matter, to say they consider certain absolute religious values ("Salvation" and "Church") of less importance. Yet many others resemble the Catholics in agreeing that belief in God is an essential core of any such system, in marked contrast to the Jewish population.

There is another important way in which the three faith groups differ from each other. In almost every case, consensus among Catholic students is more marked than among Protestants; more marked, in turn, among Protestants than among Jews.[14] To put it another way, the pattern of choices among Catholic students is the most undifferentiated one; the pattern of choices among Jewish students is the most differentiated.

The table reveals two other interesting findings. It is not only when each religious group is compared that this sort of wide variation in the degree of consensus can be noted. When the choices made by the men are compared with those made by the women, differences of the same order of magnitude appear. The religious norms are more clear-cut for Catholic women than for Catholic men; for Protestant women than for Protestant men; and for Jewish men the religious norms are least clear-cut of all.

The second interesting point is this: religion is more likely to be valued by the women as a possible anchor for family life and as a source of personal adjustment. This is so regardless of the particular religious background the girls say they come from. Here again we find a reflection of their greater interest, greater concern, and greater stake in these matters—a pattern which has consistently

---

14 That is, the most marked consensus among Catholic men is that a belief in God is essential to a religious or ethical belief system; 75 per cent feel this way. Among Protestants, not only is this requirement fifth in rank order, and not only is it chosen by only 47 per cent of the Protestant men, but in addition, greatest consensus in this group, that "personal adjustment" is an important requirement, represents the opinion of only 58 per cent of the total.

TABLE 7-4. How Men and Women in the Three Major Religions
See the Requirements of an Ideal Religious or Ethical System
(Cornell 1952)

Catholic		Protestant		Jew	
Men (Percentage* choosing each characteristic as "highly important")					
Total = (120)		(655)		(243)	
God	75	Personal		Intellectual	
Salvation	72	adjustment	58	clarity	62
Prayer	55	Family	53	Personal	
Family	55	Intellectual		adjustment	56
Church	49	clarity	52	Community	
Personal		Community		feeling	46
adjustment	41	feeling	52	Rational premises	44
Community		God	47	Welfare services	36
feeling	40	Prayer	31	Family	33
Intellectual		Rational premises	31	God	24
clarity	40	Welfare services	30	Prayer	11
Welfare services	31	Salvation	25	Church	5
Rational premises	26	Church	16	Salvation	3
Women					
Total = (32)		(231)		(104)	
God	88	Personal		Intellectual	
Family	68	adjustment	78	clarity	70
Salvation	67	Family	68	Personal	
Prayer	56	Intellectual		adjustment	67
Church	53	clarity	62	Community	
Intellectual		God	56	feeling	59
clarity	53	Community		Family	50
Community		feeling	54	Welfare services	42
feeling	50	Prayer	43	Rational premises	35
Personal		Welfare		God	22
adjustment	47	services	39	Prayer	11
Welfare services	28	Salvation	28	Church	10
Rational premises	28	Rational premises	23	Salvation	4
		Church	10		

* Omits 133 men and 53 women who said their religious background was mixed or who did not provide the information. Percentages should not be cumulated owing to multiple responses.

turned up, in whatever institutional context we have studied. Perhaps it reflects, as well, their greater anxiety about family matters and the psychological problems of family life.

In spite of these sex differences, however, (and with the exceptions noted above) the requirements of a religious or ethical belief system turn out to be arranged in virtually the same sort of hierarchy among the men as well as among the women of each religious grouping. Thus, even though the views of Catholic men, Protestant men, and Jewish men tend to be more widely differentiated than the views of the women in each of these faiths, both sexes agree on the *relative* emphasis each element deserves. And, the most impressive point seems to be this: with the exception of the Catholic students, the kinds of beliefs which most of these young people accept as legitimate religious values seem to center around the personal and individual approach to religion. "Personal adjustment," an "anchor for family life," "intellectual clarity"—these are the kinds of criteria which most of the students agree are important. These are also the kinds of approaches which can be expected to appeal to everyone, which everyone can share—perhaps a least common denominator of religious belief and religious feeling; secular values rather than sacred ones.

8

Religious Beliefs and the
Social Fabric

THE STUDENTS, THEN, are believers; and even though the three major denominations differ substantially from each other, the tone of the campuses as a whole is secular. For only rarely are students committed to religion; and they are characteristically more likely to agree on relativistic and individualistic religious beliefs, rather than on absolute and sacred ones.

RELIGION AND ANOMIE

Ever since Durkheim made the term popular, the word *anomie* has been used to describe the condition which exists in a social group whose members feel cast loose from their moorings, purposeless, normless, lonely, and alienated. His analysis indicated that an important social function of religious belief was to provide stable norms which combat any tendencies towards *anomie* in the group.

We ought to be able to check Durkheim's hypothesis with our own college students. If his analysis comes anywhere close to the mark today, at least two types of college students should prove to be more sensitive to the sorts of feelings of personal alienation that are the manifestation in the individual of the social *anomie* he was discussing. To the extent that *anomie* is at all present on the campuses, it ought to show up most clearly among students who belong to marginal groups of this society and among students who are not religious believers.

The questionnaire provided several opportunities to make these checks. Students had been asked whether they agreed or disagreed with a series of statements which touch upon alienation. "Even when I'm with people, I feel lonely most of the time," is one of these statements. It refers precisely to this feeling of being cast adrift. "Since life is so short, we might as well eat, drink, and be merry, and not worry too much about what happens to the world." Here is another statement which touches upon the theme of purposelessness, normlessness, and lack of meaning in society. Leo Srole has pointed out that the feeling that "there is little use in writing to public officials because often they aren't really interested in the problems of the average man" is, in a certain sense, a symptom of alienation insofar as it indicates a feeling of impotence *vis-a-vis* the power figures in American society, and of abandonment by them.[1]

The college population of young students whom we have studied is certainly noteworthy for its freedom from *anomie*. This is certainly not surprising given their youth, their homogeneity, and the especially strong and cohesive milieu of the college campus. Variation among the different universities in this regard is negligible, with one important and predictable exception. Given the Negro's marginal position in what is our essentially white society, the students at Fisk ought to indicate a greater tendency towards *anomie*. We have already seen some suggestions that they do: on page 159, for example, we reported that these Negro students have a weaker sense of identification with their religious group. Here, now, is further evidence to this effect. When it comes to *anomie* expressed as feelings of impotence towards power figures in American society, the students at Fisk are more likely than students at the other campuses we have studied to testify to such feelings. Equally interesting, however, is the fact that Fisk does not differ from other campuses when the measures of *anomie* refer to their interpersonal

---

[1] Leo Srole, "Social Integration and Certain Corollaries: An Exploratory Study" *American Sociological Review, 21,* 6 (December 1956) pp. 709-716.

relations and their relations with private rather than public groups.

When we traced further the anticipated association between religious belief and *anomie* among the students, we again found evidence that tends to support Durkheim's thesis. The minority of students who say they feel powerless to move "public officials" is proportionately greater among the "unbelievers," while believers are much less likely to say they feel this way. In checking this association further, however, we came across what we feel is an interesting amplification of this thesis.

In the Cornell sample, we were able to investigate the link between religiousness and reported feelings of alienation among both sexes, not only among men. Moreover, the more detailed questionnaire used at Cornell provided additional indicators of alienation. (See Table 8-1) We noted in this analysis that in some cases the original correlation between religious belief and these indicators held more strongly for women than for men, or even in some cases virtually disappeared when the men were examined separately. When we analyzed the kinds of items where the relationship did weaken or disappear among the men, we came upon an important insight. There are certain values in American society that seem to be typically male, that are so sex-linked, as it were, that men tend to share them almost in the same way that they share other aspects of the role of American male. And these role-reinforced values of the group seem to be able to combat alienation, perhaps as strongly as religious belief.

For example, American college men of all types tend to declare that they have a good chance "to amount to something." To a certain degree this is simply a part of being a young, American male on a college campus. Even those who may otherwise feel alienated and rootless nevertheless have, in present-day American society, the assurance that their chances of "amounting to something" are pretty strong. Among the college women, however, this assurance is *not* imbedded in the sex role. For the women, therefore, such statements can be said to touch "more purely" upon feelings of being personally worth while.

For these reasons, the correlation between religious belief **and** a feeling that "these days I often find myself giving up hope of amounting to something" is striking among the women, who are testifying to their feelings about their own worth. It virtually disappears among the men who testify not only in terms of their feelings but also in terms of what they think an American college man can expect in the normal course of events.

In the same way, the culture of college youth in this country seems to dictate that indifference to whether "other people care for you" is built into the male role.[2] This is much more strictly a feminine value. Thus, the statement "No one is going to care much what happens to you, when you get right down to it," is purely an indication of despair for the women, less purely so for the men. In both cases, religiousness combats this despair among the women.

This finding, which is borne out in other cases as well, leads to the hypothesis that the norms imbedded in basic social roles (such as the sex role) can also perform socially integrating functions and reduce *anomie* in the same way that religiousness can.[3] In the present case, for example, these norms seem to combat among the men the alienating effect of non-belief which is clearly registered among the women.

RELIGIOUS FAITH AS A GUIDE TO CONDUCT

One way in which a religious belief system serves as a cohesive force in the social fabric is by setting absolute rules to guide moral conduct. By referring to these rules the believer can route himself unreflectively through the maze of possible alternatives, arriving unerringly at what is right and avoiding what is wrong. A more relativistic belief system, on the other hand, provides no such clear-cut guideposts. It may allow for numerous shadings of right

---

[2] This does not mean to imply that men actually *do* have less concern than women whether others care for them. It means only that greater proportions of the men can be expected to testify publicly that they are indifferent on this score.

[3] The finding alerts us to a methodological problem as well. It provides further evidence of the caution with which a single measurement in a heterogeneous population may be interpreted: namely, that identical items may not be equally sensitive measures of the same concepts for different subgroups of that population.

TABLE 8-1. SELECTED RESPONSES OF STUDENTS SCORING IN DIFFERENT
POSITIONS ON RELIGIOUSNESS SCALE

		\multicolumn{5}{c}{Religiousness Scale *}				
		High				Low
		4	3	2	1	0
(Eleven universities):	Total =	(297)	(639)	(935)	(679)	(425)
		\multicolumn{5}{c}{(Percentage giving indicated response)}				
"There is little use in writing to public officials . . ."						
Agree or ?		38	36	43	45	50
Disagree		62	64	57	55	50
(Cornell 1952):						
Men	Total =	(82)	(193)	(309)	(337)	(230)
"I often find myself giving up hope of amounting to anything."						
Agree or are undecided		5	8	8	9	7
"No one is going to care much what happens to you . . ."						
Agree or are undecided		30	34	41	40	48
Women	Total =	(51)	(73)	(118)	(130)	(48)
"I often find myself giving up hope of amounting to anything."						
Agree or are undecided		8	10	5	20	23
"No one is going to care much what happens to you . . ."						
Agree or are undecided		20	30	24	38	42
(Eleven universities)	Total =	(297)	(639)	(935)	(679)	(425)
"Do you feel that you *now* have an adequate faith or philosophy as a guide to your conduct?"						
Yes		76	71	54	52	59
Don't know		8	11	19	18	21
No		16	18	26	30	20
(Cornell 1952)						
Men	Total =	(82)	(193)	(309)	(337)	(230)
How often do you drink spirits (whisky, gin, rum, etc.)						
Never		40	21	13	10	7
How often do you drink beer?						
Never		30	17	10	13	12

TABLE 8-1—*Continued*

(Cornell 1952)	*Religiousness Scale* *				
	High				*Low*
Men	4	3	2	1	0
	(Percentage giving indicated response)				
Do you think you cut classes more or less often than most students you know?					
"Less often"	65	65	61	50	50
If I found the person I was engaged to had had sex relations, I would break the engagement.					
Agree or are uncertain	46	39	33	23	26
Women Total =	(51)	(73)	(118)	(130)	(48)
How often do you drink spirits (whisky, gin, rum, etc.)					
Never	29	18	10	10	—
How often do you drink beer?					
Never	43	29	24	30	26
Do you think you cut classes more or less often than most students you know?					
"Less often"	67	71	57	51	47
If I found the person I was engaged to had had sex relations, I would break the engagement.					
Agree or are uncertain	41	27	21	18	8

* For the construction of this scale, see pages 154-159.

and wrong, may require one to decide anew, for each new set of circumstances, what would be the moral choice.

It is of interest that analysis of the students' own testimony suggests this function of religious belief. When we asked the students: "Do you feel you *now* have an adequate faith or personal philosophy as a guide to your conduct?" 60 per cent said "yes." It turns out that students rated as religious are significantly more likely than others to declare that their belief provides them with an adequate guide to conduct. (The figures are presented in Table 8-1.)

Two further points about this relation deserve to be noted. The students who score in the lower positions of the religiousness scale are consistently more likely than others—not to *deny* that their present faith is adequate, but to indicate uncertainty about it. There must then be many students who reject religious belief, yet whose ideas on the subject are probably vague and unstructured. They are probably *non*-believers rather than *un*believers.

The second point lends support to this interpretation. The relation between position on the religiousness scale and the admission that one's present beliefs are inadequate as a guide to conduct is not linear, but may tend to be U-shaped. That is, it may be that the students whose attitudes are polarized—whether toward religiousness or away from it—are more likely to declare that their ethical guides to conduct are adequate; while those with less structured attitudes are not so likely to feel this way. (Notice that 59 per cent of those who score lowest on the religiousness scale feel they have an adequate guide to conduct, while only 52 per cent of those who score in the next lowest position feel this way. If the measure of religiousness we were using had been more finely calibrated at the "unreligious" end, this figure of 52 per cent might have continued to diminish.)

These findings suggest the hypothesis that it may be not only the *religious content* of belief which provides these students with such security, but also the *structured nature of belief*—religious or otherwise—which does so.

Given the religious student's apparently greater certainty that his guides to conduct are generally adequate, we begin to wonder how the believer faces certain common problems of campus conduct—drinking, sex relations, cutting classes, cheating on exams, and the like. Is his feeling that he has an "adequate" guide to conduct reflected in his testimony regarding his customary behavior and attitudes on these counts?

The answer would seem to be "yes." Believers are more likely than others to say they "never drink" either beer or whisky; more likely to say they cut classes "less often" than other students. They are more likely to say they adhere to an absolute standard of sexual morality. It is the nonbelievers who are more likely to admit to impropriety in each of these practices or attitudes.

We are dealing, it should be remembered, with what may seem to some to be rather less than soul-shaking moral problems; and even these are touched upon only briefly and cursorily in the present questionnaire. Yet the findings corroborate an important generalization about the relation between religious beliefs and public morality: religion lends Divine sanction to social mores. That is, for behavior which is socially dictated, built into the mores of particular cultural subgroups on the campus as proper, religious belief may convert the "propriety" into "morality."

But the generalization that religious belief is consistently linked to the "proper" or "moral" or "ethical" choice cannot strongly be upheld. For when it comes to the matter of cheating on examinations, no relation between confessed cheating and *either* religious belief *or* the conviction that one's guides to conduct are adequate can be discerned (Appendix 22). One might be tempted to speculate that these students see no moral question to be involved in cheating, viewing it rather as a legitimate kind of chicanery.

This sort of conclusion would be unjustified, however. A modest survey, conducted at Cornell in 1953, checked on the matter. The findings indicate that the students unequivocally admit the moral issue involved in cheating.[4] Almost all the students polled (85 per cent) agreed that "It is morally wrong to cheat." Apparently, however, they are caught in a cross-pressure: for, while they consider cheating to be immoral, there is widespread conviction among these students that the practice is fairly prevalent. They are struck, moreover, by the implication of unfair advantage a cheater has over a noncheater. For example, an equal proportion of the same students also agree with the statement, "If everyone else cheats, why shouldn't I?"

Now, the religious students seem to be caught in two opposing currents here. On the one hand, they are more likely than others to see the moral implications of cheating. On the other hand, they are also more likely than others to feel that the currency of the practice among their peers in some way justifies cheating. "If everyone does it, why shouldn't I?", they reason. Apparently they

---

[4] The survey was conducted under the auspices of the Cornell Student Council by Miss Alice Green. The survey questioned 393 entering freshmen.

tend more than non-believers to feel they have a right to conform to what is expressed as a norm. (The figures for the freshmen are given below.)

TABLE 8-2. RELIGIOUS STUDENTS ARE MORE LIKELY TO SEE MORAL IMPLICATIONS IN CHEATING; MORE LIKELY TO FEEL A NORM JUSTIFIES CHEATING

(393 entering Cornell freshmen)

	Religious (135)	Mixed (211)	Non-Religious (56)
Percentage * in each scale position who agree that:			
"It's morally wrong to cheat"	92	81	79
"If everyone else cheats, why shouldn't I?"	87	80	75

* In this study, students were considered "religious" if they indicated an unqualified belief in a Divine God and also reported regular church attendance; students who testified to neither were considered "unreligious." All others were considered "mixed." (Alice Green, *Report on Religion*, 1953, manuscript on file at Cornell University Department of Sociology and Anthropology.)

ELEMENTS OF CONFORMITY IN RELIGIOUS BELIEF

There is further evidence that religious belief is not necessarily linked consistently to the ethical choice. Decisions about drinking, cheating, and sex relations are, after all, by no means to be understood solely as conscious ethical or moral choices. They can be, at the same time, social practices characteristic of the role behavior of different subgroups of the campus world: "propriety" rather than "morality." The preceding analysis, for example, has shown not only that the "proper" choice is more prevalent among students characterized as religious; at the same time the evidence has indicated that conservative attitudes toward these practices are more prevalent among women than among men—in other words, that they are strongly dictated by social rules of behavior appropriate to one's sex. In an earlier chapter (Chapter 3) we showed how drinking patterns also differ among campus subgroups defined by fraternity affiliation; how women's attitudes to premarital sex relations were more absolute than those of the men (Chapter 4) while those of career-girls were less absolute than those of other women

(Chapter 2). Appendix 23 shows, further, that students from homes that are poorer, economically speaking, are more likely than others to score high on the religiousness scale and also to report less frequent drinking and more conservative attitudes toward premarital sex relations (see Appendix 23).

Thus, sociological role factors are at least as closely linked to the "moral" choice as is religious belief. It is partly for this reason that any interpretation that views the association between religiousness and propriety as evidence of the impact of religious belief on moral decisions must be made very cautiously.

Indeed, the relations previously reported suggest another theme that seems common to them all. Religious believers seem to feel more integrated in society; non-believers seem more alienated from it. Religious believers tend to testify to the kinds of behavior and belief that conform to the standards of propriety of American culture; non-believers are less likely to do so. Religious believers are more likely to respond to the pressure of a social norm, even on an issue that they regard as a moral question (such as cheating on examinations). Perhaps these are all aspects of conformity to the dominant values of the social groups to which these students belong. And, when we look at the evidence from this point of view, there seems, indeed, to be justification for such a contention.

We begin our analysis this way: Let us look at these young people in terms of the degree to which their questionnaire responses indicate their willingness to conform to the social roles that are most salient to them.

What are these social roles? College youth are sons and daughters with respect to their parents; they are students with respect to the academic side of the university; and they are participants in the distinctive social milieu of the American college campus.

Take the first major role—sons and daughters of their parents. A minimal indication of conformity or non-conformity to this role is the degree to which they feel that, up to now, they have fulfilled their parents' expectations for them. We had asked, "So far, how well would you say you have lived up to what your parents have expected of you?" The responses of students on the campuses we studied indicate that the vast majority do not hesitate to say that

TABLE 8-3. RELIGIOUS STUDENTS ARE MORE LIKELY THAN OTHERS TO
EXPRESS CONFORMITY TO THE PREVAILING VALUES OF THEIR
MAJOR SOCIAL ROLES

(Cornell 1952)

Indices of Conformity to Three Major Social Roles	Scale of Absolute Religious Belief *				
	High				*Low*
As son or daughter:	4	3	2	1	0
"How well have you lived up to your parents' expectations?"	(Percentage in each scale position giving indicated response)				
Women					
"Very well"	51	49	48	45	33
"Fairly well"	42	39	46	41	50
Men					
"Very well"	47	47	40	36	45
"Fairly well"	45	45	51	52	41
As college students:					
"Most of what I am learning in college is very worthwhile."					
Women	76	73	79	68	60
Men	80	75	70	66	64
"America has the best system of college education in the world."					
Women	27	24	20	20	5
Men	39	37	29	25	25
"Do you ever feel that what you are doing at Cornell is a waste of time."					
Women who say often	11	12	12	18	30
Men who say often	6	12	11	16	13
As an affable social being:					
"It is harder for me than for 'most people' to make friends."					
Women	5	13	9	14	18
Men	7	8	11	17	14

* For construction of this scale, see p. 162, footnote 12. The items in the measure were available only for the Cornell sample. The bases on which per cents have been computed are:

Women	55	103	103	99	60
Men	132	300	200	275	244

their behavior has conformed reasonably well to what their parents have expected. (Forty-two per cent checked "very well," 48 per cent checked "fairly well," and only 10 per cent checked "not so well.") The point is, however, that the students rated as most religious are consistently more likely than others to testify to conformity in this sense. The relationship is particularly marked among the women.

Take the second major role—as students in the academic setting of the university or college. On the whole, these students, we have said, have an extremely optimistic and positive opinion about the value of their college education; the expression of cynical or disenchanted attitudes, then, is *deviant* (see Chapter 1). In every case it is clear that the students who were rated in the lower positions by any of our measures of religiousness are more likely to check these *deviant* responses; students who were rated high on these measures are more likely to check the optimistic, culturally-approved and culturally-approving responses.

Finally, there is the role of a social being in the particular milieu of the campus. On these American campuses we have shown the cultural norm calls for an outgoing, friendly, easygoing approach to interpersonal relations—what has been called "other-directedness" (see Chapter 1). Our analysis now indicates that it is the religiously oriented students who are more likely than others to stress the importance of generalized affability in social relations.

RELIGIOUSNESS AND TOLERANCE

The link between religious belief and propriety, then, owes at least part of its existence to certain elements of conformity to role behavior which also link up with religiousness. We also find further evidence that religious belief is not consistently linked with "the moral choice."

One good example lies in the area of intergroup relations. For, if one of the tenets of Judeo-Christian belief is the principle of equality of all people before God—a principle perhaps better known as brotherly love—then such adherence to the ideals of essential equality should apply, in principle, to all races, creeds and colors. Yet our data show that students who were rated as "believers" are, if anything, *more* likely, not less likely, to testify to feelings of racial and religious intolerance.

We had asked the students to indicate agreement or disagreement with certain statements taken from the vocabulary of prejudice. The consensus of the campuses is decidedly toward expressions of tolerance.[5] Only seven per cent of the students on the eleven campuses polled agreed that "although some Jews are honest, in general Jews are dishonest in their business dealings." Only 17 per cent agree that "generally speaking, Negroes are lazy and ignorant." On the other hand, as many as 23 per cent agree that "some religious groups are inferior," or that "religions which preach unwholesome ideas should be suppressed."

Now, among students from Protestant, Catholic and Jewish homes, it turns out that the believers are more likely than nonbelievers to agree with these statements. The figures reported in Table 8-4 show relatively small differences, but they tell a consistent story.

It is worth calling the reader's attention, incidentally, to the fact that when it comes to the well-known vocabulary of prejudice associated explicitly or implicitly with recognizable minority groups (Negroes and Jews), Jewish students are least likely to express intolerance. When it is a matter, however, of agreeing with a statement that amounts, conceptually speaking, to a declaration of intolerance but which is, perhaps, not recognizable as referring to a specific minority group, ("unwholesome ideas" in a religious sect, for example) there is no discernible difference between the

---

5 Other studies indicate that the college-educated, particularly those now attending college, are less likely than the general population to subscribe to the vocabulary of prejudice. A *Fortune Survey (Fortune,* December 1948) reports that two-thirds of the college students in their nationwide sample agree that steps should be taken "right away" to "see to it that Negroes have the same chance to get good jobs as white people . . ." This is in contrast to 47 per cent of the total sample. The Cornell Studies in Intergroup Relations report a similar tendency for the college-educated to express tolerance toward minority racial and religious groups. Samuel A. Stouffer's *Communism, Conformity and Civil Liberties* (Garden City, N. Y.: Doubleday & Co., 1955) rates two-thirds of a nationwide sample of college graduates as "more tolerant" of civil rights for minority groups, in contrast to 42 per cent among high school graduates and 16 per cent among those who have never gone beyond grade school (page 90).

TABLE 8-4. RELIGIOUS BELIEVERS ARE MORE LIKELY THAN OTHERS TO
AGREE WITH THE VOCABULARY OF PREJUDICE
(Eleven universities)

	Respondents' Religious Background		
	Protestant	Catholic	Jewish
	(Percentage giving indicated response)		
Negroes are lazy and ignorant			
Religious *	22	15	6
Mixed	22	20	5
Non-religious	16	7	3
Some religious groups are inferior			
Religious	27	39	6
Mixed	26	26	7
Non-religious	22	23	5
Religions which preach unwholesome ideas should be suppressed			
Religious	24	28	29
Mixed	24	26	19
Non-religious	19	22	14

* This is a score which refines the religiousness scale by including frequency of church attendance in the original measure. Students who score high on the religiousness scale (positions 3 and 4) and who also attend services at least twice a month, are considered religious. Students who score low on the religious scale (positions 1 and 0) and who attend services never or mainly on important holidays are considered non-religious. All other students are considered mixed.

The totals on which the above percentages are based are given below.

	Protestant	Catholic	Jewish
Religious	405	182	17
Mixed	963	126	190
Non-religious	425	60	222
Totals	1793	368	429

Omitted are 385 students who could not be classified on all three variables.

readiness with which the several religious groups testify to such intolerance.

These findings are all the more significant since the religious students are under both an ideological and a sociological pressure toward tolerance rather than intolerance. On the one hand, they are presumably under a moral pressure to view all men as brothers; on the other hand, they tend more than others to conform to the prevailing norms of the campus—and campus opinion is decidedly toward the expression of racial and religious tolerance. In view of both these kinds of pressures, it is indeed of interest that religious students react in the *opposite* direction from these pressures. What are the opposing factors which pull them toward intolerance?

THE INTOLERANCE OF DEVIATION

One of the basic opposing factors seems to be that the students rated as religious believers tend to be reluctant to countenance any kind of deviation or nonconformity. We have already seen that they are more likely than others to indicate attitudes and opinions that conform to the demands of their social roles. We have seen that they are likewise readier to express intolerance of minority racial and religious groups. If we view these factors now, not in terms of their manifest content, but as perhaps indicative of a more generalized readiness to disapprove of *any* suggestion of deviation or nonconformity—in *others* as well as in themselves—we may be better able to begin to understand these opposing factors.

A case in point is their attitude toward conscientious objectors. Regardless of whether one approves or disapproves of a philosophy which leads a person to refuse to take up arms in defense of his

TABLE 8-5. LINK BETWEEN RELIGIOUSNESS AND ATTITUDE TOWARD
CONSCIENTIOUS OBJECTORS
(Eleven universities)

Position on Religiousness Scale	*Percentage Most Tolerant of CO's* *	*Total*
High 4	15	297
3	16	639
2	17	935
1	24	679
Low 0	27	425

* The distribution of responses to the questions which make up this scale have been presented in Chapter 6 page 142. They are:
You owe it to your government to protect it in return for more important privileges.
If you refuse to support your government in a war you shouldn't continue to live in a country.
Too many people use conscientious objection as a loophole to escape serving.
It's not fair for one man to be excused from military service while others are not.
Only a moral coward would refuse to protect his government.

country, democracy in principle respects the individual's right to live by his personal philosophy, however deviant, as long as it is not subversive or illegal. Students who are rated as "most religious," however, are less likely than their opposite numbers to express such tolerance of conscientious objectors.

TABLE 8-6. CONSTRAINTS AND RESTRICTIONS

	Scale of absolute religious belief *				
	High				*Low*
	4	3	2	1	0
A college professor should be free to express his opinion on any subject . . .	(Percentage** agreeing with each statement)				
(Cornell 1952) Total =	(187)	(403)	(303)	(374)	(304)
Regardless of whether he agrees or disagrees with accepted opinion	38	50	55	68	71
Providing he is not opposed to accepted beliefs	18	13	11	8	3
Providing he does not go out of his field . . .	40	34	31	23	21
Providing he agrees with accepted beliefs . . .	3	2	1	1	1
Other responses	1	1	2	1	4
Protestants Total =	(92)	(268)	(184)	(210)	(131)
"Only trained and competent people should be permitted to run for public office."	80	72	74	69	67
"It's unwise to give people with dangerous social and economic viewpoints a chance to be elected."	59	34	33	32	34
"Only people whose loyalty has been proved should be allowed to run for public office."	67	54	49	46	45
Catholics Total =	(54)	(46)	(26)	(13)	(13)
"Only trained and competent people should be permitted to run for public office."	68	74	78	—	—
"It's unwise to give people with dangerous social and economic viewpoints a chance to be elected."	62	43	41	—	—
"Only people whose loyalty has been proved should be allowed to run for public office."	63	74	59	—	—

TABLE 8-6—*Continued*

A college professor should be free to express his opinions on any subject . . .	Scale of absolute religious belief *				
	High				*Low*
	4	3	2	1	0
	(Percentage ** agreeing with each statement)				
Jews Total =	(9)	(39)	(65)	(118)	(116)
"Only trained and competent people should be permitted to run for public office."	—	80	74	62	60
"It's unwise to give people with dangerous social and economic viewpoints a chance to be elected."	—	35	29	24	17
"Only people whose loyalty has been proved should be allowed to run for public office."	—	47	49	30	22

* For construction of this scale see footnote 12, p. 162.
** Omits 187 students with mixed religious backgrounds or who gave no answer.

Or, take the matter of academic freedom. We had asked the students to indicate the conditions under which they thought a college professor should be free to express his own opinion. The majority of the students (59 per cent) declare their approval of unlimited academic freedom for college professors. But among those classified as most religious, only 38 per cent would grant to this hypothetical professor freedom from the constraint of expressing only "acceptable" ideas. Among students at the opposite end of the scale, however, 71 per cent would do so.

RELIGIOUSNESS AND CONSTRAINTS

It seems, too, as if the religiously oriented students may not only be less tolerant of nonconformity in others: apparently they are also more confident about expressing opinions on what is "right" and what is "wrong" for other people. We find that they are more willing than others, for example, to approve of measures which would restrain someone from doing something. They tend to agree that "there ought to be a law . . ." even when the topic in question may, on the face of it, be rather ambiguous. About two-thirds of the students classified as religious are willing to agree that "only people whose loyalty to the government has been proved should be permitted to run for public office"; but only about a third of those rated as least religious agree with such an unqualified statement.

The same sort of link can be discerned between position on this scale and readiness to agree that "only trained and competent people should be permitted to run for public office," or "it's unwise to give people with dangerous social and economic viewpoints a chance to be elected." (The preceding table shows these correlations separately for students of the three major religious faiths.)

Let us speculate a little further about what might be the significance of these links between a high score on the measure of religiousness and agreement with the kinds of statements we have been discussing. The particular phrases to which the students were asked to react have certain implications or overtones. We have already seen that some of these opinions which seem to be more characteristic of religiously oriented students are particularly compatible with a pessimistic view of the essential nature of mankind (Chapter 5). From another point of view, agreement with these statements could reflect a certain tendency to structure an otherwise ambiguously defined field: after all, none of the terms in these statements is specified. What kinds of beliefs are "accepted?" What would "training" or "competence" consist in, and how would it be recognized? What kinds of social and economic viewpoints would be considered "dangerous"? What might be adequate "proof" of loyalty, and, for that matter, loyalty to what and to whom?

Thus these two strands of thought—pessimism about human nature, on the one hand and a tendency, or a wish, or a need to impose structure on the other—could be engaged in the observed readiness for high scorers on the measure of religiousness to express a certain sympathy for opinions which justify imposition of restraints or controls on others.

RELIGIOUSNESS, FAITH IN HUMAN NATURE,
AND RESTRAINTS

In tracing these relations we begin with this question: Do religious believers accept assumptions about the nature of man which are characteristically different from those accepted by the non-believers? There is a certain rationale for expecting such a relationship, either in a positive or negative direction. Assumptions about man's nature are implicit in the creeds of the Christian belief system. The conception of original sin, for example, implies that man is basically evil, but through service to God and dedication to religious belief and works he can redeem himself. There is also the alternative conception: that it is exposure to the imperfections of man-made institutions which perverts humanity, whose basic nature is intrinsically good and improvable; that religious belief and works help man find again this essentially good, God-given nature.

When we examine the correlation between our measure of religious belief and the measure of faith-in-human-nature, we find a positive association. That is, those who score high on the scale of religiousness are most likely to express their faith in the cooperative and trustworthy aspects of human nature. It is among those characterized as religious skeptics that the less trusting view is more prevalent.

The correlation is mild, but apparent, among students who say they come from Protestant or Catholic family backgrounds. Among those from Jewish homes no such relationship can be discerned.[6]

---

6 Although the doctrine of original sin is official creed in the Catholic church, and not a part of the creed of most Protestant denominations, the correlations between the scale of faith-in-human-nature and the scale of religiousness are of virtually equal strength among Catholic and among Protestant students. It is possible that American Catholics have accepted the more optimistic philosophy about human nature which prevails in the country as a whole. It is equally interesting that among Jewish students—even though they are, for the most part, less religiously oriented than Catholics and Protestants—no correlation between religiousness and faith-in-human-nature can be discerned. The religious basis of Judaism does not explicitly state a position regarding the essentially sinful or essentially Divine nature of man, and one wonders whether this fine philosophical point would be registered among the Jewish students.

Now we can turn to the question posed earlier, re-examining the affinity first observed between religious belief and a willingness to impose restraints, religious skepticism and a distaste for restraints. We can see to what extent these links continue to appear among those who testify to an optimistic view of human nature compared with those who declare that they have a more pessimistic view.

Here the findings are provocative. With impressive regularity the figures show that the higher a group's score on the scale of religiousness, the more prevalent in that group is expressed approval of the idea of constraining, say, "people with dangerous social and economic ideas," or those of unproved "loyalty." With equivalent regularity, the figures show that this association of ideas is clearly more characteristic of students who take a pessimistic view of the nature of man, less characteristic of those who accept more optimistic assumptions; so much so, in fact, that at the point of calibration on the faith-in-human-nature scale which sorts out the most optimistic students, the correlation begins to waver. Here—in this group of students who have in common their consistent assertions that people can be assumed to be essentially cooperative, trustworthy and mutually responsible—one can no longer declare with any confidence that the religiously oriented are more likely than their opposites to express a sympathy for measures which would restrain "undesirables" from doing something.

What might be the meaning of these findings? Why should students rated as most religious show such a marked affinity for measures which impose restrictions *unless* they are optimistic about the nature of mankind? Why should students rated as least religious tend to declare their distaste for such measures *even if* they are relatively pessimistic about the nature of mankind?

Perhaps we must begin to search for answers to these questions by distinguishing between types of religious believers. After all, there are many diverse elements in religious belief systems. Students classified as "believers" by means of a simple measure such as the scale that we are using, could still differ vastly in terms of which elements in religion are salient to them.

Suppose we try to reconstruct first the characteristics of the "religious pessimist," in terms of what we already know about him. He has a high score on the scale of religiousness, a low score on the scale of faith-in-human-nature, and we are speculating about why he should be so predisposed to express his sympathy for measures which imply constraints or controls.

In a sense, all religious belief systems remind mankind of the yawning gap between what one should be and what he actually is; all religious belief systems are the source of controls, restraints and proscriptions which aim to narrow this gap. The believer who assumes that mankind, by nature, cannot be trusted to hold his baser instincts in check might very well select as most salient in his own belief system those aspects of religion which provide such controls, restraints and proscriptions. For, as he sees it, this is what humanity most needs and, for that matter, *deserves*. He would tend to organize his belief system, then, around religion's role in keeping mankind in line, so to speak. This emphasis could, in turn, reinforce in him or even give rise to a more generalized sympathy for all restraints—even those that involve strictly secular issues and have little to do with religious belief.

This sketch can provide a clue to guide our speculations about the second question: Why should a distaste for restraints be more characteristic of unbelievers, even if they share this pessimistic view of the nature of mankind? Perhaps those very elements of religious belief which are most appealing to the "religious pessimist," as we have sketched him, are precisely the elements which impel many of the unbelievers to reject religion. For example, we can conceive of the type of person who has a very broad and generalized distaste for controls and restrictions. Such a person, then, may reject religion principally for those elements in it that he feels impose limitations, restraints and proscriptions—just as he tends to reject in secular life measures that smack of limitations or restraints even on the deviant, the "unproved," the "unacceptable," the "undesirable."

Finally, there is the "religious optimist." With the "pessimistic" believer he shares faith in God; with the "optimistic" unbeliever he shares faith in man. Yet, when it comes to measures which imply constraints or controls which would prevent someone from doing something, he resembles *more* the students who share his apparently secular philosophy, and diverges sharply from students who share his religious philosophy.

This is the main point, perhaps, of our analysis. In order to account for the statistical correlations which so consistently turn up even with the rough and crude measures we have used of beliefs as complex as "religiousness," "faith in human nature," and "willingness to constrain," we have had to resort to explanations which show the impact of secular values, characteristics and beliefs rather than religious ones.[7] It would be very difficult, indeed, to make a satisfactory case for the contention that there is something in the manifest content of religious belief, identification, and commitment which would lead believers more than skeptics to wish to control conscientious objectors, restrain professors with "unacceptable ideas" from expressing an opinion, or to keep "undesirable" types of people from seeking election. The religious believers who feel this way probably do so not because they are religious, but because their assumptions about the nature of man are compatible with the idea of controlling others—particularly deviants. Their religious belief, apparently, does not challenge this, but on the contrary seems, if anything, to reinforce it. The believers who express a distaste for controls probably do so not because they are religious, but because their assumptions about the nature of man are incompatible with the idea of controlling others. Their religious beliefs, apparently, are simply not engaged in these matters. It is this non-engagement which can be considered the principal index of secularization on the campuses and, for that matter, in American life.

RELIGIOUSNESS, CONSTRAINT, AND INTOLERANCE OF AMBIGUITY

We pointed out earlier that the kinds of attitudes and opinions we are discussing here may also imply a tendency to introduce

---

7 This analysis leads to conclusions very similar to those reported by R. Nevitt Sanford, "Ethnocentrism in Relation to Some Religious Attitudes and Practices," in *The Authoritarian Personality* by T. W. Adorno, Else-Frenkel-Brunswick, Daniel J. Levinson and R. Nevitt Sanford (New York: Harper Bros., 1950), pp. 208-221.

structure in what would seem, on the face of it, to be matters that are rather ambiguously defined. Is this trait indeed related to readiness to agree to measures that would have the effect of restraining someone from doing something, for vaguely defined reasons? Do students rated as "religious" exhibit this trait more than others? Analysis of the testimony gathered in this research indicates that the answer to both questions is likely to be "yes."

We had asked these students, "How important is it for you to have your plans for the future known in advance?" The terms of this question are deliberately vague: What plans? Known in how much detail? How far in the future? How far in advance? None of the antecedents was specified. Those who nevertheless say it is "very important" that their future plans be known are, in effect, imposing a structure of their own upon the question. At the same time the response they have selected declares that they attach importance to defining what is essentially undefined: future events.

This tendency is considerably more apparent among students who score high on the scale of religiousness. Among Protestants in this category only 14 per cent said it was relatively unimportant that they know their plans in advance; among skeptical Protestants, 35 per cent gave this response. The corresponding proportions among Catholics are 17 per cent compared with 27 per cent; among Jews, 14 per cent compared with 40 per cent.[8] In other words, in all three religious groups there seems to be an association between religious belief and a need "to know in advance," between religious skepticism and the absence of such a need.

The more interesting point, however, is this: the affinity originally observed between religious belief and sympathy for the idea of imposing restraints or controls can be discerned principally among those who express this "need to know." In contrast, among students who say such a need is relatively unimportant in their scheme of things, the association is so irregular that it can be said

---

8 This same relationship is corroborated in a different sample—the Cornell freshmen polled in 1953. (See page 176.) These students were asked, "How definite are your plans for the future?" Among the religious freshmen, 77 per cent said these plans were "very definite" or "moderately definite." In contrast, among the unreligious students, only 40 per cent checked these responses. (Alice Green, *op. cit.*)

virtually to disappear. In this group, who have in common what may be interpreted as a tolerance for ambiguity, believers and unbelievers alike tend to reject the idea of restraining "people with dangerous social and economic ideas," or people of unproved "loyalty."

TABLE 8-7. ASSOCIATION BETWEEN RELIGIOUSNESS AND RESTRAINING TENDENCIES ACCORDING TO FAITH-IN-HUMAN NATURE AND ACCORDING TO IMPORTANCE OF KNOWING FUTURE PLANS
(Eleven universities)

SCALE OF FAITH-IN-HUMAN-NATURE **		RELIGIOUSNESS SCALE *				
		High				*Low*
		4	3	2	1	0
Protestant:		(Percentage† ratings on scale)				
	Total =	(186)	(383)	(603)	(391)	(230)
Low		14	19	18	19	26
Intermediate		54	47	51	48	50
High		32	34	32	33	24
Catholic:						
	Total =	(68)	(124)	(92)	(57)	(27)
Low		16	19	32	25	30
Intermediate		52	48	40	42	44
High		32	33	28	33	26
Jewish:						
	Total =	(10)⌣(53)		(128)	(143)	(95)
Low		23		16	30	24
Intermediate		51		55	45	51
High		26		29	25	24

Percentage‡ who agree: "It's unwise to give people with dangerous social and economic ideas a chance to be elected"

All religious groups:				
5,6 (Low)	63	62	53	39
4	61	58	52	32
3	44	41	42	33
2,1 (High)	37	38	39	23

Percentage‡ who agree: "Only people whose loyalty has been proved should be permitted to run for public office"

5,6 (Low)	61	62	60	44
4	65	64	55	41
3	55	58	51	38
2, 1 (High)	52	56	46	38

TABLE 8-7—Continued

HOW IMPORTANT IS IT FOR YOU TO KNOW YOUR PLANS FOR THE FUTURE IN ADVANCE ††	RELIGIOUSNESS SCALE *				
	High 4	3	2	1	*Low* 0
Protestant:	(Percentage giving indicated response)				
Total =	(186)	(383)	(603)	(391)	(230)
Very important	37	36	34	24	23
Fairly important	49	46	45	47	41
Not very; not at all	14	18	20	28	35
Catholic:					
Total =	(68)	(124)	(92)	(57)	(27)
Very important	43	44	34	35	31
Fairly important	40	40	45	39	42
Not very; not at all	17	16	22	26	27
Jewish:					
Total =	(10) ⁓ (53)		(128)	(143)	(95)
Very important	38		41	34	25
Fairly important	48		45	48	35
Not very; not at all	14		14	18	40
All religious groups:	Percentage†† who agree: "It's unwise to give people with dangerous social and economic ideas a chance to be elected."				
Very important	51	55	51	44	37
Fairly important	51	46	43	29	28
Not very; not at all	34	38	39	29	27
	Percentage†† who agree: "Only people whose loyalty has been proved should be permitted to run for office."				
Very important	64	64	56	52	42
Fairly important	60	58	52	38	34
Not very; not at all	40	54	43	45	32

* For the development of the Religiousness Scale, see pp. 154-159.
** For the development of the Scale of Faith-in-Human-Nature, see Appendix 18.
† Excluded from this table are 385 students with mixed religious backgrounds, or who did not provide information concerning their religious backgrounds.
‡ The bases on which the per cents have been computed are:

5,6 (Low)	46	127	181	264
4	60	130	192	231
3	93	173	279	299
2,1 (High)	98	209	283	310

†† footnote cont. p. 194

It is worth remarking, incidentally, that here is further evidence of how little religious belief seems to be engaged in other aspects of the students' belief systems. In this group it is the shared psychological trait of tolerance for ambiguity which contributes to their expressed distaste for restraints. There is no evidence that the factor that differentiates them—their religious belief or skepticism —is in any way involved in these opinions.

Once again the findings are tantalizing. Why should religious believers be particularly sympathetic to the idea of controlling other people *only if* they have, at the same time, a generally low tolerance for ambiguity? To infer an explanation we must again speculate about different types of believers.

Many people feel ill at ease, even incapable, of facing anything which they feel to be undefined, unstructured, vague, uncertain. If such a person is a religious believer (and he is likely to be), perhaps he selects as salient for his own system of belief chiefly those aspects of religion that explain for him the vast, otherwise unknowable unknown. An important function of his religious belief, in this case, would be the psychological service it performs by introducing certainty into the many aspects of living and dying which, without revelation and faith, are necessarily uncertain. This sort of person would see religion principally as a roadmap without which he would find it unbearable to face the vast stretches of uncharted terrain in human existence. His religious belief system would serve and reinforce, then, his more generalized need for certainty, a need likewise expressed in his secular opinions—for example, in his apparently seeing nothing ambiguous about measures which would restrain vaguely defined "undesirables" for vaguely defined heresies.

In contrast, one could postulate quite a different type of religious believer; one who can accept ambiguity and make his peace with it; who would willingly spend his life seeking, rather

†† The bases on which per cents have been computed are:

Very important	118	237	323	190	104
Fairly important	131	291	421	318	176
Not very; not at all	47	110	189	168	144

Omits 8 cases who could not be classified in terms of importance of plans in advance.

than insist upon finding; who would turn to religion not to demand of it "What is the answer?" but with the more humble query, "What is the question?"

This type is rarely encountered on the campuses we studied. We venture to say that it is equally rare in American society.

9

Some General Observations

WE HAVE OFTEN REFERRED in this book to "the college campuses."
At this point it is time to remind ourselves of the disclaimer appearing in the introduction: the campuses we studied are not
representative of American colleges and universities.[1] Interpreted,
however, in the light of sociological principles of how societies
function, develop and change, the findings of this research, nevertheless illuminate trends that are dominant in American society as
a whole.

AMERICAN EDUCATION REFLECTS AMERICAN SOCIETY AND MODIFIES IT

What occurs on the campuses cannot be understood solely as individual responses to pressures that are individually felt and acted
upon. The campus culture is to be viewed as one element of an
important institution in our society: education.

Education is also a dominant theme of our culture. That is, the
value placed upon education and the consequences we anticipate
will derive from it, permeate all other institutions of society.[2] We

---

[1] In 1955 there were no less than 760 four-year degree-awarding institutions in
the United States, claiming to provide a liberal arts education. This includes liberal
arts colleges, universities and teachers colleges. It includes "trolley car" colleges,
sectarian and church-affiliated colleges, women's colleges, as well as institutions
which more closely resemble the ones we studied. (Natalie Rogoff, *Board Member
Colleges: A Comparative Analysis.* Mimeographed. New York, Bureau of Applied
Social Research, 1957.)

[2] We are referring here to the sociological meaning of institution: an orderly
system of behavior, relatively enduring through time, specialized to the satisfaction
of certain explicit social needs. Highly patterned rules and norms of behavior are

196

Americans are for education just as we are against sin: education is expected to have positive consequences in all spheres of social life, just as sin is expected to have corrupting ones (granted a certain ambivalence in both cases).

Clustering around education as a cultural institution are characteristic assumptions, standards, values, and norms which validate a traditional aim of our universities: to provide students with a liberal education. That is, colleges and universities traditionally aim to turn out a graduate who can think broadly, effectively, and imaginatively; who can make relevant judgments and communicate his thoughts to others; who can interpret with detachment the idea behind "the fact" yet feel committed to intellectual endeavor and convinced that there can be no legitimate justification for calling a halt to the advancement of knowledge and the search for understanding. In spite of real and very apparent countertrends, these are some of the important aims and assumptions that lie at the heart of the conception of higher education.

AMERICAN EDUCATION IS MODIFIED BY AMERICAN SOCIETY

At the same time, campus culture and the traditional values of higher education must be analyzed within the context of all other social institutions. These institutions in turn possess their own dominant norms and values. Particularly those generated by our economic institutions appear as themes permeating all aspects of our culture. Productivity and practicality, for example, have come to be incorporated as values appropriate to all other institutions, including the educational. When our religious or our educational institutions attempt to "rationalize their productive processes," they are acting in the service of these values.

It is this idea which is implicit in the meaning of terms such as "mass culture," "mass entertainment," "mass participation," "mass media." And now "mass education." Used as a modifier,

---

associated with the satisfaction of these needs and are transmitted through education to all members of the society. The justification for the behavior, rules and norms dictated by the social institutions are ultimately enforceable by the moral sanctions of the society. This technical meaning of the term is in contrast to its common meaning—a group or association which serves the public.

"mass" refers not only to the numbers of people involved, but also to at least two further considerations: the process has been rationalized (as in mass production); and the cultural product is impersonally directed toward an anonymous consumer without regard to his inner experience in using or applying it.

These norms and values exist side by side with the academic ones on our campuses as in our society. To say, as this study finds, that the students we studied come to acknowledge the legitimacy of academic norms and values and to adopt them, does not deny the existence of such conflicting norms and values. Nor does it deny that counter-norms and values are likewise transmitted to many students.

Many perceptive critics focus their attention on these counter-norms and values, declaring that they have succeeded in drastically distorting the central idea of what a university is and should be. They point to the current emphasis on technique and on size, on status and social relations.[3]

But the findings of the present research call attention to what is almost a sociological truism and yet is often overlooked: that if young people are exposed for four years to institutional norms and values in the very milieux in which they are explicit and authoritative, they will become socialized to the predominant values of that milieu and will come to acknowledge their legitimacy. The present study shows that this occurs with regard to academic educational values.

This very finding, however, suggests certain corollary questions which are left to future research. To what extent does this process occur only in some institutions of higher education and not in others? What are the characteristics of those colleges and uni-

---

[3] See, for example, Jacques Barzun, *The Teacher in America*, Boston, 1945, and more recently, *The House of Intellect* (New York: Harper and Bros., 1959). See also Theodore Caplow and Reece J. McGee, *The Academic Market Place* (New York: Basic Books, 1958). See Philip E. Jacobs, *Changing Values in College* (New York: Harper and Bros., 1957) and also Alan Barton's excellent critique of this book, *Studying the Effects of College Education* (The Edward W. Hazen Foundation, New Haven 11, Connecticut, 1959). See also Richad Hofstadter and C. DeWitt Hardy, *The Development and Scope of Higher Education in the United States* (New York: Columbia University Press, 1952). Paul F. Lazarsfeld and Wagner Thielens, *The Academic Mind* (Glencoe, Ill.: Free Press, 1959).

versities which successfully transmit the liberal values of education? How do these institutions differ from others which may
undermine the authority of these educational values? What specific elements in the complex structure which is the university are
effective in transmitting these values? In inhibiting them? What
kinds of students are open to such influences? What kinds of students resist them? What happens after they leave college: do they
maintain the same educational values and with what degree of
intensity? For how long? Do their educational values differ in any
important ways from those of people who have not been exposed
to college education?

These are only a few of the questions which our study suggests.
At the same time, its findings call attention to a point which deserves to be reiterated. Among the students we studied, and in the
colleges and universities we covered, the academic ideals and
values of liberal education are very much in evidence. No matter
what else is also conveyed to the students, these academic educational values are vigorous, have authority and continuity.

UNFORESEEN SOCIAL CONSEQUENCES AND CONSERVATISM

The present generation of college students, this study finds, is politically disinterested, apathetic, and conservative. Social movements
and social philosophies do not arouse their interest or command
their commitment. Certainly one cannot claim that this is because
there are no current issues that deserve serious attention and concern. Vast areas of the world are ill fed, ill clothed, ill housed, and
face a future without hope. In our own country there is no longer
mass unemployment; but there are the looming problems of auto-
mation, threats to civil liberties, social injustices; and there is
racial segregation. There is the fundamental conflict between
totalitarian and democratic ideologies and values; and, most important of all, there is the ever present threat of war and destruc-
tion on an unimaginable scale. Nor can it be claimed that the
students are unaware of these issues. They are part of the atmosphere the students breathe.

But this generation of college students sees no easy or immediate solution to these problems. In the postwar world in which they have developed, at least one thing has become clear. The economic and political situations throughout the world and the alignments of power have become so intricate, so delicately interdependent and precariously balanced, that policies and programs cannot claim exhaustive command over their own social effects. There are sure to be totally unforeseeable consequences, perhaps even the contrary of what was intended. This has happened in one country after another, with one promise after another, and with one ideology after another.

It is partly because of these developments that liberal programs today are on the defensive. They have not yet recovered from the blow of realizing that many of the programs they urged and fought for in the twenties and thirties have been accompanied by social effects which today they find themselves forced to deplore.

A widespread reaction in liberal ranks is to assign responsibility to the personal corruptness of the executors of these programs, without acknowledging the need to re-examine and revise basic assumptions. This results in sharp and cogent criticisms of the *status quo*—but not in equally sharp and cogent alternatives. Another widespread reaction is to assume complete bankruptcy of everything about their own social philosophy; to abandon *all* their earlier assumptions; to justify total abdication from liberalism.

It is this atmosphere in which the students have developed and are maturing. If, then, they are conservative and apathetic, they are so, in part, by default. There are no clearly defined programs around which to rally, no clearly defined answers to the problems their generation confronts. In social psychological terms we would say that they react to baffling complexity by withdrawing. In the slogan of their own campus culture, they "play it cool."

The generalization, however, that the college students we studied are, by and large, withdrawn from political and economic issues and uninvolved in them, conceals certain complexities which are often overlooked. For example, the present study finds that their economic and political beliefs are quite differentiated. They avoid identifying themselves with a political party label of any kind, preferring to think of themselves as independent voters. Many who agree with the most extreme clichés of laissez-faire economic philosophy, nevertheless accept important inroads on a strictly conservative position. Support for humanitarian and welfare measures cuts across liberal as well as conservative campuses and subgroups and across the lines of social class. The prevailing climate of opinion throughout the campuses we studied favors tolerance of racial and religious minority groups and accepts in principle the basic assumptions of democratic government. Outside the social subsystems on the campus which explicitly reinforce conservative norms and values, the students register liberalizing social influences.

Again one wonders whether these findings may be characteristic only of the campuses and the students we studied, or whether, on the contrary, they would prove to be widespread among other types of colleges and universities. Does the climate of opinion on the college campuses differ noticeably from that among a comparable group of non-college youth? How do the political and economic beliefs of these American students differ from those of students from other countries? To what extent are the opinions, philosophies and attitudes reported in this study held with any intensity of conviction? To what extent are they formal echoings of the democratic credo?

How many of these students have found it necessary, during college, to hold their beliefs up to the light of critical appraisal? Are they aware of the implications their beliefs may have for their future behavior as responsible citizens? Many of the findings of other research studies, which contrast the behavior and beliefs of the college educated with those of less well educated adults, can be re-examined to cast light on these questions. But in the long run we must count on long term future research on these subjects to provide the answers to these important questions, amplifying and extending the findings reported here.

THE PHILOSOPHICAL CLIMATE

We have noted in this volume that religious belief on the campuses is widespread. At the same time, we have characterized the philosophical climate of the campuses as essentially non-religious. First, the religious values the students prefer seem to be broadly dispersed, highly personal, relative and vague. Second, the analysis has shown that these beliefs and values seem to be only weakly engaged in the opinions, attitudes and behavior they report in other spheres of life.

At the same time, we have reported certain indications that the young people on these campuses are dissatisfied with this sort of philosophical climate. Almost all the students feel, they say, a need for religious or philosophical guides to provide orientation and meaning to their lives. It is as if they were aware that empiricism, rationalism and relativism do not provide this sense of meaning; that it must be sought in a belief system that specifies irreducible standards of value, not relative ones. One senses a certain nostalgia for such absolute guides and for the guarantees of certainty that only faith can provide.

It is perhaps this nostalgia which makes much of what passes for religious belief today compatible with—perhaps the cornerstone of—secular beliefs which also guarantee certainty. The reasoning is by analogy; they both provide the same thing, therefore they are alike—a correspondence which has been noted by many other investigators.

The present analysis, however, goes somewhat further. It suggests that such a correspondence may exist for certain types of religious believers, and not for others. It points to the importance of differentiating among ostensibly similar "believers" in terms of the psychological function which their belief is called upon to perform: to reduce ambiguity, for example; or to provide a source of controls for essentially unruly mankind.

Again we are forced to raise more questions than we can answer: for it becomes relevant to ask whether the college experience has any impact not only on the content of religious beliefs, but—perhaps more important—whether it is relevant in any way to the psychological function which religious beliefs may be called upon to serve. This may, in fact, be an important respect in which campuses differ from each other. Certainly one would expect the small, denominational colleges to vary markedly from the large state universities and the more cosmopolitan Eastern campuses in this regard. It may, as well, be an important characteristic differentiating the college educated from those who are less educated.

Man today has conquered the atom and invaded space. Yet the basic problem of the human condition remains unchanged: how to live with uncertainty and make one's peace with it; how to invest the days of one's life with meaning. Perhaps these questions encompass the basic criteria for measuring the success of education.

APPENDIX 1. DISTRIBUTION OF OPINION SHOWING STUDENTS' EVALUATION OF COLLEGE EDUCATION

	Har-vard	Yale	Dart-mouth	Wes-leyan	Cornell Men	Cornell Women	No. Car.	Texas	UCLA	Mich.	Wayne	Fisk
Total =	(453)	(297)	(365)	(277)	(655)	(245)	(414)	(516)	(467)	(488)	(519)	(134)
	(Percentage giving indicated response)											
1. GENERAL EVALUATION												
Having the opportunity to go to college is very important to me.												
Agree	95	98	96	98	93	94	95	99	96	97	94	97
On the whole, the colleges are doing a good job.												
Agree	76	78	84	83	77	71	79	80	80	84	85	76
Most of what I am learning in college is very worthwhile.												
Agree	75	76	66	78	77	67	71	74	70	75	77	80
Proportion who consider charges that "colleges don't keep up with the times . . ."**												
Justified	9	10	9	10	11	11	15	22	14	14	14	28
Not justified	91	90	91	90	89	89	85	78	86	86	86	72
I think that college does not really equip you for life outside the campus.												
Agree	16	15	11	12	18	23	16	28	27	21	20	20
Disagree	66	73	72	74	67	60	68	59	57	63	63	63
Uncertain	17	11	16	13	14	15	13	13	16	16	16	15
No answer	1	*	1	1	2	2	3	*	*	*	1	2
America has the best system of college education in the world.												
Agree	32	38	38	32	33	19	48	39	37	38	30	22
Disagree	21	24	21	20	24	36	18	25	22	20	27	31
Uncertain	46	37	39	48	42	43	32	36	40	41	43	46
No answer	1	*	1	*	1	2	3	*	1	*	*	1

* Less than one per cent.
** The question was: "Recently colleges and universities have been under fire. Some of the charges and complaints which have been made against them are listed below . . . Place a checkmark next to any of these charges which you think are justified."

	Har-vard (453)	Yale (297)	Dart-mouth (365)	Wes-leyan (277)	Cornell Men (655)	Cornell Women (245)	No. Car. (414)	Texas (516)	UCLA (467)	Mich. (488)	Wayne (519)	Fisk (134)
Do you ever feel that what you are doing at Cornell is a waste of time? (Asked only at Cornell 1952)												
Yes, often					13	18						
Sometimes, not often					41	49						
Rarely or never					46	32						
How much of the time you spent in class and on required assignments this year was used in doing things that do not seem important to you? (Asked only at Cornell 1952)												
A lot of it					17	20						
Some of it					49	51						
Only a little					29	27						
None of it					4	3						
2. UNIVERSITY'S ROLE IN EDUCATING FOR VALUES												
I am disillusioned about college life.												
Agree	6	7	9	8	11	14	9	9	10	10	8	9
Disagree	87	89	82	85	81	78	79	85	82	84	85	75
Uncertain	6	5	8	6	8	6	9	5	7	6	7	12
No answer	1	*	1	*	1	2	3	*	1	*	1	4
College education does more to break down values than to build up ideals.												
Agree	20	15	17	12	12	20	15	15	15	15	14	13
Disagree	59	70	61	75	67	61	64	63	65	67	67	60
Uncertain	20	15	20	13	19	16	19	21	19	18	19	26
No answer	1	*	2	*	2	3	3	1	1	*	1	1
Too many college teachers lack respect for religious values.												
Agree	18	15	17	12	14	16	29	25	13	17	15	29
Disagree	67	67	63	70	59	63	50	52	64	58	60	43
Uncertain	15	18	18	18	26	19	19	23	22	25	24	26
No answer	*	*	1	*	1	2	3	*	1	*	1	2

	Harvard (453)	Yale (297)	Dartmouth (365)	Wesleyan (277)	Cornell Men (655)	Cornell Women (245)	No. Car. (414)	Texas (516)	UCLA (467)	Mich. (488)	Wayne (519)	Fisk (134)
I don't have as much respect for college education as I did before I came here.												
Agree	13	15	19	13	26	25	30	30	23	25	22	21
Disagree	79	81	75	82	68	66	64	65	68	71	74	69
Uncertain	7	4	5	5	5	7	3	5	8	4	4	7
No answer	1	*	1	*	1	2	3	*	1	*	1	2
American colleges today should place more emphasis on teaching American ideals and values.												
Agree	17	28	26	26	42	47	43	41	33	33	35	28
Disagree	64	52	47	51	35	30	33	38	46	45	43	36
Uncertain	18	19	25	22	22	20	22	21	21	22	22	34
No answer	1	1	2	1	1	3	2	*	*	*	1	2
3. IDENTIFICATION WITH COLLEGE OR UNIVERSITY												
This group has its own personality, something over and above the individual members in it. Does this statement express the way you feel about any of the following groups? Check as many as apply....												
"Your college"	63	58	77	63	44	54	57	42	40	52	45	38
Rank order among all choices	1	1	1	1	2	1	1	3	2	1	1	1
4A. OPINIONS REGARDING OFFICIAL POLICIES: IN EDUCATIONAL ADMINISTRATION †												
Proportions who consider the following charges justified: †												
"Production line teaching methods ..."	45	52	41	43	64	70	50	58	63	55	37	43
"People in the educational profession are underpaid ..."	77	86	78	80	73	81	72	78	68	73	67	72
"Overemphasis on athletics .."	76	73	60	76	48	42	53	58	45	52	51	49

† The percentages should not be cumulated owing to multiple responses.

	Harvard (453)	Yale (297)	Dartmouth (365)	Wesleyan (277)	Cornell Men (655)	Cornell Women (245)	No. Car. (414)	Texas (516)	UCLA (467)	Mich. (488)	Wayne (519)	Fisk (134)
How many of your instructors do you think take a personal interest in their students? (asked only Cornell)												
All of them					2	3						
Most of them					24	17						
About half of them					24	24						
Few of them					45	53						
None of them					4	2						
4B. OPINIONS REGARDING OFFICIAL POLICIES: RELATED TO THE LIBERAL OR CONSERVATIVE ATMOSPHERE OF THE UNIVERSITY												
"Racial and religious discrimination in admissions policies . . ."	31	32	38	33	44	63	44	43	25	32	25	62
"Suppression of academic freedom . . ."	37	26	32	40	26	36	28	32	31	32	26	40
I think college teachers are afraid to say what they really believe these days.												
Agree	19	15	21	14	23	20	27	35	33	23	33	46
Disagree	67	74	64	78	61	58	62	52	55	65	53	41
Uncertain	12	10	14	8	14	20	9	12	13	12	14	13
No answer	1	*	2	*	1	2	3	1	*	*	1	*

APPENDIX 2. EDUCATIONAL GOALS STRESSED BY CROSS-SECTION OF MALE STUDENTS AT EACH CAMPUS POLLED

(Eleven universities)

CONSIDER WHAT EDUCATIONAL GOALS YOU THINK THE IDEAL COLLEGE OR UNIVERSITY OUGHT TO EMPHASIZE Total =	Wes-leyan (277)	Yale (297)	Har-vard (453)	Dart-mouth (365)	Cornell Men (655)	No. Car. (414)	UCLA (467)	Michi-gan (488)	Texas (516)	Wayne (519)	Fisk (134)
					(Percentage ranking each goal as highly important)						
Provide a basic general education and appreciation of ideas	90	88	85	84	73	74	70	69	65	64	59
Provide vocational training, develop skills and techniques directly applicable to your career	36	31	30	32	62	65	68	66	67	74	80
Develop your ability to get along with different kinds of people	76	69	59	75	74	77	64	72	75	70	66
Develop your knowledge and interest in community and world problems	58	57	55	67	48	49	49	47	45	47	57
Help develop your moral capacities, ethical standards and values	60	51	48	45	44	53	41	42	45	44	52
Prepare you for a happy marriage and family life	18	19	11	18	20	27	24	19	24	24	28

APPENDIX 3. STRICTLY EDUCATIONAL GOALS GAIN IN POPULARITY
AMONG UPPERCLASSMEN

(Eleven universities)

STUDENTS' RANKING OF EDUCATIONAL GOALS		YEAR IN COLLEGE			
	Total =	First (684)	Second (644)	Third (770)	Fourth (761)
		(Percentage* ranking each goal as indicated)			
Provide a basic general education					
First importance		25	28	34	42
Other high importance		39	43	40	37
Medium importance		31	26	22	19
Low importance		5	3	4	2
Provide vocational training					
First importance		36	35	34	27
Other high importance		29	27	24	25
Medium importance		29	29	32	36
Low importance		6	9	10	12
Develop your ability to get along with different kinds of people					
First importance		19	17	14	13
Other high importance		56	53	55	56
Medium importance		23	28	28	26
Low importance		3	2	3	5
Knowledge and interest in community and world problems					
First importance		3	3	3	4
Other high importance		43	46	47	52
Medium importance		47	45	45	40
Low importance		6	6	5	4
Help develop your moral capacities					
First importance		10	9	8	9
Other high importance		34	36	38	39
Medium importance		41	38	40	41
Low importance		15	17	14	12
Happy marriage and family life					
First importance		1	1	2	1
Medium importance		21	20	21	20
Other high importance		43	42	42	42
Low importance		35	37	35	37

* Omits 116 students who were in their last year of 5 year programs, special students, non-matriculated students, or those who did not answer the question.

WHAT THREE THINGS OR ACTIVITIES IN YOUR LIFE DO YOU EXPECT TO GIVE YOU THE MOST SATISFACTION?

APPENDIX 4. IMPORTANCE OF CAREER COMPARED WITH OTHER BASIC LIFE SATISFACTIONS *

(Percentage of students ranking each activity as first in importance)

	UCLA	Wayne	Fisk	Harvard	Wesleyan	Cornell Men	Michigan	Yale	Dartmouth	No. Car.	Texas
Total =	(467)	(519)	(134)	(453)	(277)	(655)	(488)	(297)	(365)	(414)	(516)
Your career or occupation	35	33	33	31	31	30	28	27	25	24	24
Family relations	48	49	43	51	56	58	60	54	61	62	55
Leisure time recreational activities	6	4	4	7	1	4	3	5	2	2	4
Religious beliefs and activities	5	4	10	3	3	3	3	3	2	5	8
Participation as a citizen in the affairs of your community	—	2	2	—	1	1	—	1	1	1	—
Participation in activities directed toward national or international betterment	2	1	1	3	2	1	2	3	1	1	1
No answer	6	6	7	4	6	4	4	6	8	6	8

* See Table 2-2 for comparison with nationwide cross-section.

APPENDIX 5. OVERLAPPING VALUES AND PSYCHOLOGICAL DISTANCE
(Total = 4585)

	Creative	*Abilities*	*Helpful*	*People*	*Status*	*Money*	*Security*
Creative and original	—	.470	.140	−.078	.007	−.177	−.386
Abilities and aptitudes	.470	—	.105	−.126	−.107	−.141	−.199
Helpful to others	.140	.105	—	.580	.002	−.336	.073
Work with people	−.078	−.126	.580	—	.245	−.126	.123
Status, prestige	.007	−.107	.002	.245	—	·594	·331
Good deal of money	−.177	−.141	−.336	−.126	·594	—	·342
Secure future	−.386	−.199	.073	.123	·331	·342	—

The measure of the adequacy of the matrix in the table is the degree to which the figures in any line or column grow progressively less positive (or more negative) as they proceed away from the diagonal dashes. Theoretically, "the values on the base line (the diagonal adjacent to the dashes) would be high, and these values would progressively decrease, proceeding toward the point of the pyramid (extreme upper right- and lower left-hand corner)," [Babette Kass, "Overlapping Magazine Reading," in *Communication Research 1948-1949* (P. F. Lazarsfeld and F. Stanton (eds.), New York, Harper and Bros., 1949), p. 140] at which point the most negative relationship would appear.

An examination of this matrix shows that it approximates this model, although it is by no means perfect. If we assume that a failure to decrease positively, or increase negatively, as one moves away from the diagonal dashes, represents an error, then we find that there are seven errors out of a possible forty-two, an error of 17 per cent.

Kass (*ibid.*, pp. 140) has noted that the pattern can be highlighted "by taking the averages of the diagonals parallel to the dashes. Were the correlation perfect, the diagonal immediately adjacent to the dashes would yield the highest average, the next diagonal the next highest, and so on to the most distant diagonal whose average would be the lowest." Going from the outermost to the innermost diagonals, we obtain the following averages:

Diagonal farthest from dashes −.386
−.188
−.020
−.099
−.040
Diagonal adjacent to dashes −.389

As one proceeds away from the diagonal adjacent to the dashes, the degree of positive relation decreases (or negative relation increases) with the exception of the third diagonal (average −.009). The reason for this unexpectedly high average is that it includes the very strong negative relation existing between a desire to be "helpful to others" and to "earn a good deal of money" (Q = −.336). From M. Rosenberg *et al.*, *op. cit.*, p. 14.

APPENDIX 6. IMPORTANCE OF VARIOUS OCCUPATIONAL REQUIREMENTS

(Eleven universities)

CONSIDER TO WHAT EXTENT A JOB OR CAREER WOULD HAVE TO SATISFY EACH OF THESE REQUIREMENTS....	Cornell (Men)	Dart-mouth	Fisk	Har-vard	Michi-gan	No. Car.	Texas	UCLA	Wayne	Wes-leyan	Yale
Total =	(655)	(365)	(134)	(453)	(488)	(414)	(516)	(467)	(519)	(277)	(297)
	(Percentage ranking each occupational requirement as highly important)										
Self expression values											
Permit me to be creative and original	49	39	51	56	47	36	39	52	51	50	53
Provide me with an opportunity to use my special abilities or aptitudes	77	74	76	82	81	65	74	80	83	77	78
People-Centered values											
... opportunity to work with people rather than things	35	55	54	40	39	49	55	40	45	57	47
... opportunity to be helpful to others	35	38	72	36	42	49	38	38	45	54	43
Reward values											
... look forward to a stable, secure future	56	64	77	46	62	75	64	62	60	56	51
Give me social status and prestige	25	33	18	25	21	30	33	23	28	20	23
... a chance to earn a good deal of money	35	41	37	33	36	44	41	39	37	36	39
Other											
... relatively free of supervision	39	42	38	42	34	38	42	40	34	35	38
... chance to exercise leadership	32	35	23	27	29	29	35	34	34	28	33
... provide me with adventure	16	16	16	18	13	17	16	18	12	13	18

APPENDIX 7. OCCUPATIONS RANKED ACCORDING TO INDEX OF INCONSTANCY
(Cornell panel)

Expected Occupation	Index of Inconstancy *
Advertising, public relations	2.43
Business	1.51
Journalism	1.31
Personnel	1.30
Natural science	1.16
Farming	1.00
Teaching	.96
Law	.83
Medicine	.81
Architecture	.77
Food, restaurant, hotel administration	.70
Engineering	.51

* This index has been computed by dividing the number of students entering or leaving a field, by the number originally choosing it. An index of 1.00 means that the number of constant students was exactly equivalent to the number of "shoppers." An index of more than one means that the number of "shoppers" exceeded the number of constant students. An index of less than one means that the number of constant students was greater than the number of "shoppers." Based on M. Rosenberg *et al.,* *op. cit.,* p. 64.

APPENDIX 8. OCCUPATIONS CHOSEN BY WOMEN AND BY MEN

WHAT BUSINESS OR PROFESSION WOULD YOU MOST LIKE TO GO INTO?	*Men at Eleven Universities*	*Women at Cornell (1952)*
Total =	(2975)	(420)
Engineering	14	*
Medicine	14	4
Business unspecified	12	4
Law	7	1
Teaching	9	21
Natural sciences	7	7
Art	4	8
Sales, Promotion	3	4
Government	3	6
Personnel	3	4
Architecture	2	2
Advertising	2	2
Farming	2	1
Real estate, Finance	2	*
Social work	1	5
Journalism, Drama	1	2
Food, Hotel	1	8
Social sciences	1	2
Other	1	1
Secretarial work	*	1
Don't know	12	14
Housewife	—	3

* Less than one per cent.

APPENDIX 9. FRATERNITY MEMBERSHIP IS LINKED TO ECONOMIC STATUS
(Eleven universities)

	Fraternity Members	Independent Students	Total
About how much was your father's income last year . . .	(Percentage * giving indicated response)		
Under $3,000	24	76	(267)
$3,000-4,999	25	75	(799)
$5,000-7,499	39	61	(620)
$7,500-9,999	49	51	(418)
$10,000-19,999	53	47	(417)
$20,000-29,999	63	37	(165)
Over $30,000	57	43	(162)
Do you depend more upon your own earnings or your own savings to put yourself through school, or more upon the support of your parents?			
Own earnings or savings	27	73	(974)
Equally on both	39	61	(605)
Support of parents	50	50	(1362)
In which of these four groups do you consider your family to be?			
Upper class	60	40	(384)
Middle class	41	59	(1895)
Working or lower class	24	76	(661)

* The percentages in this table are computed on bases which exclude students who could not be classified on all variables simultaneously examined: that is, students who did not answer the question; students whose responses were not classifiable in terms of the categories presented here; and students to whom the question did not apply. Details appear below.

   127 students did not provide information on father's income;

   34 students did not provide information on main source of support;

   35 students did not provide information on social class identification;

   52 students could not be classified according to fraternity membership.

Note that per cents should be added horizontally.

APPENDIX 10. NO RELATIONSHIP BETWEEN ACADEMIC ACHIEVEMENT AND
DATING, EXCEPT FOR WOMEN WITH HIGHEST AVERAGE

(Cornell 1950)

How often on the average did you date at Cornell this year?

What is your cumulative average?	Not at All	Less Than Once a Month	Once a Month	Twice a Month	Once a Week	Twice a Week	More Often
Men	(Percentage * giving indicated response)						
Total =	(192)	(349)	(213)	(253)	(253)	(139)	(62)
Under 75	22	23	25	26	24	25	26
75-79	33	35	35	34	34	41	34
80-84	29	27	24	26	31	23	31
85 or over	16	14	16	14	11	11	9
Women							
Total =	(32)	(45)	(43)	(67)	(143)	(129)	(63)
Under 75	20	11	15	9	15	16	18
75-79	32	46	39	40	45	41	39
80-84	16	30	37	42	31	33	33
85 or over	32	14	10	9	9	11	10

* Omits 369 men and 167 women who because of marriage or engagement said they did not participate in the dating system. Also omits 178 men and 61 women who did not answer the question. Percentaged on bases which exclude 62 men and 21 women who did not report their cumulative averages.

APPENDIX 11. MARITAL STATUS OF STUDENTS

(Eleven universities)

Percentage * at each university who are:

	Married	Engaged, Pinned, or Otherwise Going Steady	Single and Un- attached	Total
Wayne	24	18	57	(519)
Texas	19	18	64	(516)
UCLA	13	16	71	(467)
Michigan	12	23	65	(488)
North Carolina	10	25	65	(414)
Fisk	6	29	65	(134)
Cornell: Men	5	18	77	(655)
Women	1	36	63	(245)
Dartmouth	2	20	78	(365)
Wesleyan	2	20	78	(277)
Yale	2	20	78	(297)
Harvard	2	17	81	(453)

* Percentages are to be added horizontally.

APPENDIX 12. SOME OPINIONS ABOUT MARRIAGE, FAMILY SIZE, AND SEX
RELATIONS. MEN AND WOMEN COMPARED

(Cornell 1950)

Desired and Expected Age of Marriage *

		Men		Women	
		Desired	*Expected*	*Desired*	*Expected*
	Total =	(1824)	(2008)	(729)	(750)
Age		(Percentage ** giving indicated response)			
19 or under		2	1	1	1
20-21		10	6	25	14
22-23		19	18	42	31
24-25		41	36	23	28
26-27		11	15	1	8
28-29		4	9	2	4
Over 30		3	6	—	3
Don't know		—	2	—	4
No answer		9	7	5	7

"Are you planning or considering going to
graduate or professional school?"

		Yes	*No*	*Yes*	*No*
	Total =	(868)	(1048)	(339)	(400)
. . . How old do you think you will be when you do get married?					
21 years or younger		7	7	14	18
22-23		20	21	32	37
24-25		38	41	35	28
26-27		17	16	11	8
28 or older		18	15	8	9

"Do you prefer a mate who . . ."	*Men*	*Women*
Total =	(1824)	(729)
Is more educated than you	1	31
Has about the same amount of education	86	64
Is less educated than you	4	—
No answer	9	6

* The questions were: "If it were up to you, at what age would you like to get married?" "Looking at things realistically, how old do you think you will be when you *do* get married?"

** The percentages in this table are computed on bases which exclude students who could not be classified on all variables simultaneously examined. Details appear below:

184 men and 21 women were already married and did not answer the question on desired age of marriage.

92 men and 11 women did not state their plans for graduate school.

164 men and 82 women did not state age at which they expected to marry.

APPENDIX 12—*Continued*

How many children do you expect to have by the time you are 40?	*Men* (Percentage **	*Women* giving indicated response)
Total =	(2008)	(750)
None	2	1
One	5	—
Two	25	13
Three	38	27
Four	23	31
Five or more	1	18
Don't know	2	1
No answer	3	8

If you discovered that the man (woman) you were engaged to had had previous sex relations, would you break the engagement? †

Total =	(2008)	(750)
Yes, I'd break it	6	3
I'm not sure	44	32
No, I wouldn't break it	48	62
No answer	2	2

† See also Table 2-11 for these opinions among career-women compared with others.

APPENDIX 13. PROPORTION OF POSITIVE RESPONSES AT EACH
UNIVERSITY TO:

Do you ever get as worked up about something that happens in politics or public affairs as you do about something that happens in your personal life?

(Eleven universities)

	Percentage who say "yes"	*Total*
Wayne	46	(519)
Yale	44	(297)
Wesleyan	44	(277)
Cornell Men: 1952	42	(655)
Harvard	41	(453)
Dartmouth	39	(365)
Texas	39	(516)
UCLA	38	(467)
Michigan	38	(488)
Fisk	37	(134)
North Carolina	34	(414)

APPENDIX 14. FATHERS WHO ARE USUALLY "INDEPENDENT" VOTERS AND SONS WHO ARE USUALLY "INDEPENDENT" OF POLITICAL PARTY ALIGNMENT, ACCORDING TO RELIGIOUS AFFILIATION, FAMILY INCOME, AND PREDOMINANT POLITICAL PARTY ON CAMPUS

(Eleven universities)

	Both Independent	Father Independent Son Rep.	Father Independent Son Demo.	Father Rep. Son Indep.	Father Demo. Son Indep.
Total =	(308)	(51)	(50)	(302)	(419)
	(Percentage * in each religious, economic and political group)				
Religious affiliation					
Protestant	54	63	36	73	51
Catholic	11	6	12	9	15
Jewish	22	4	28	6	23
Mixed	7	25	12	8	5
Other	5	2	12	4	5
No answer	1	—	—	1	—
Father's annual income					
Under $7,500	56	53	56	48	72
$7,500-9,999	17	16	16	18	9
$10,000-19,999	15	10	18	15	10
$20,000 or more	10	20	8	15	5
No answer	3	2	2	5	3
Predominant political party on campus					
Heavily Republican **	50	48	52	54	29
Heavily Democratic †	50	52	49	45	70

* Omits 496 who could not be classified on both "father's vote" and "own vote."

** This category includes Cornell, Dartmouth, Harvard, Michigan, Wesleyan, Yale, where the number of students who said they usually align themselves with the Republicans exceeded the number reporting Democratic sympathies.

† This category includes UCLA, North Carolina, Texas, Wayne and Fisk where the number of students loyal to the Democrats exceeded the number loyal to the Republican party.

APPENDIX 15. PHILOSOPHY OF GOVERNMENT AND ATTITUDE TOWARD FREE
COLLEGE EDUCATION ACCORDING TO FATHER'S INCOME
(Eleven universities)

	Under *$3,000*	*$3,000-* *4,999*	*$5,000-* *7,499*	*$7,500-* *9,999*	*$10,000-* *19,999*	*$20,000-* *29,999*	*$30,000* *or more*
Total =	(267)	(799)	(620)	(418)	(417)	(165)	(162)
Philosophy of Government Scale **		(Percentage * in each group)					
Support laissez faire	30	31	29	31	31	41	47
Intermediate	27	26	26	27	26	24	22
Do not support laissez faire	43	43	45	41	43	35	31
College education should be free to everyone							
Agree	46	41	33	29	32	30	39
Disagree	44	48	57	61	58	61	45
Uncertain	10	11	11	10	10	9	16

Above the income columns, centered: *Father's annual income*

* Omits 127 students who did not provide information on father's income.
** For construction of this scale see footnote to Table 5-5.

APPENDIX 16. PHILOSOPHY OF GOVERNMENT * AMONG FRESHMEN,
SOPHOMORES, JUNIORS AND SENIORS
(Harvard and Yale)

		Year in College			
		First	*Second*	*Third*	*Fourth*
		(Percentage ** in each attitude group)			
Harvard	Total =	(120)	(110)	(111)	(109)
Support laissez faire		17	27	26	24
Intermediate		18	22	24	21
Do not support laissez faire		65	51	50	55
Yale	Total =	(86)	(70)	(75)	(65)
Support laissez faire		45	24	33	46
Intermediate		15	23	22	20
Do not support laissez faire		39	52	45	35

* For construction of this scale see footnote to Table 5-5.
** Fifth year students, special students, foreign students, and other non-matriculated students have been excluded from computations in the table.

APPENDIX 17. CONSTRUCTION OF SCALE OF FAITH-IN-HUMAN-NATURE

The scale of faith-in-human-nature included the items appearing below that are preceded by an asterisk.

(Eleven universities: Total = 2975)

(Percentage giving indicated response)

* Some people say that most people can be trusted. Others say you can't be too careful in your dealings with people. How do you feel about it?

Most people can be trusted	81
You can't be too careful	19

* Human nature is fundamentally cooperative.

Agree	68
Disagree	18
Uncertain	14
No answer	—

These days a person does not really know whom he can count on.

Agree	24
Disagree	67
Uncertain	8
No answer	1

* No one is going to care much what happens to you when you get right down to it.

Agree	31
Disagree	60
Uncertain	9
No answer	—

* If you don't watch yourself people will take advantage of you.

Agree	60
Disagree	28
Uncertain	11
No answer	1

* Would you say that most people are inclined to help others or to look out for themselves.

Help others	26
Look out for themselves	72
No answer	2

This scale—as indeed all scales in this volume—was constructed according to the Guttman technique.*

Actually, the selection of these five items represented the end product of several prior operations. In the 1950 study, a number of social and political questions which might be interpreted as reflecting faith-in-human-nature were found to form a scale pattern, using Guttman's criteria. This technique provided the unidimensionality of the measure, but the single dimension in this case was loaded by the political content of the items used.

The problem now became a theoretical rather than a methodological one. Granted that the questions were tapping the same dimension, was this dimension really "faith-in-human-nature?" Guttman's scaling method could rank people along both the manifest and the latent content of the dimension, but it could not define the dimension theoretically.

While we felt that the underlying dimension of these items actually was faith-in-human-nature, and internal validations substantiated this position, it seemed extremely difficult to separate the manifest social and political content of the items from their philosophical implications.

Consequently, when the 1952 study was planned, a series of new questions was inserted, directly tapping the manifest content of the dimension, faith-in-human-nature. The following steps were taken in selecting the items:

1. A total of thirty-six items in both questionnaires, which might in any fashion be related directly or indirectly to the dimension faith-in-human-nature were culled.

2. Five faculty members of the Department of Sociology and Anthropology at Cornell University were requested to sort these items into piles reflecting aspects of interpersonal relations. This method differed from the Thurstone item analysis, of course, in the sense (among others) that the experts were to determine the dimensions themselves rather than to rank each item with reference to a specified dimension.

3. Three or more of five judges agreed that nine of the thirty-six items dealt with faith-in-human-nature.

4. An attempt was made to scale these nine items, using the Guttman technique, and five of them showed sufficient freedom from error to indicate that they were actually on the same dimension. The coefficient of reproducibility for these five items is .92.

---

* Descriptions of that technique may be found in the following publications:

Louis Guttman, "A Basis for Scaling Qualitative Data," *American Sociological Review*, Vol. 9, 1944, pp. 139-150. "The Cornell Technique of Scale and Intensity Analysis," *Education and Psychological Measurement*, Vol. 7, 1947, pp. 247-280.

Chapters 3 and 6 in Samuel A. Stouffer *et al.*, *Measurement and Prediction* (Princeton: Princeton University Press, 1950).

Louis Guttman and Edward A. Suchman, "A Solution to the Problem of Question Bias," *Public Opinion Quar.*, Vol. 11, 1947, pp. 445-455.

Edward A. Suchman, "The Logic of Scale Construction," *Education and Psychological Measurement*, Vol. 10, 1950, pp. 79-92.

APPENDIX 18. DEVELOPMENT OF A SCALE TO MEASURE ATTITUDE TO
SERVING IN THE ARMED FORCES [1]

Attitudes to Serving in Armed Forces

Students' attitudes toward being called into military service are definitely unfavorable. The analysis of a series of seven questions designed to form a scale of student opinion concerning military service showed consistently negative responses. The items were:

Attitudes to Serving in Armed Forces   Reproducibility .94

(Eleven universities: Total 2975)

1. When you think of your own personal situation, would you say that the advantages of going into full time military service outweigh the disadvantages for you, or is it the other way around?

    Percentage who responded:
    ** 5 Advantages heavily outweigh disadvantages
    * 11 Advantages tend to outweigh disadvantages
    * 21 Advantages and disadvantages are about equal
    * 34 Disadvantages tend to outweigh advantages
    29 Disadvantages heavily outweigh advantages

2. Which of the following statements comes closest to describing your own feelings about going into full time military service?

    Percentage who responded:
    ** 11 I'd like to get in
    * 64 I'd just as soon stay out if possible
    25 I don't want to go in at all

3. If it were entirely up to your own choice, after you graduate from college, would you prefer to go into full time military service or to stay out?

    Percentage who responded:
    * 3 Strongly prefer to go in
    * 7 Mildly prefer to go in
    * 6 Doesn't matter
    24 Mildly prefer to stay out
    60 Strongly prefer to stay out

4. If I had the opportunity to stay out of military service, I would certainly take advantage of it.

    Percentage who responded:
    72 Agree
    * 10 ?
    * 18 Disagree

---

[1] From *Student to Soldier*, by Edward A. Suchman, Robin M. Williams, Jr., and Rose K. Goldsen, August 1952, Cornell University, Department of Sociology and Anthropology.
* Positive response.
** Highly positive response; i.e., responses to these questions have been trichotomized in scaling.

5. In general, do you like or dislike the idea of being called to full time military service?

Percentage who responded:
* 3 Like the idea very much
* 11 Like it somewhat
* 19 Feel neutral about it
  31 Dislike it somewhat
  36 Dislike the idea very much

6. If it were up to you, would you want to be deferred from military service as long as possible?

Percentage who responded:
  40 Yes, definitely
* 34 Yes, probably
* 26 No

7. As things stand now, do you think it's best for you, personally, to go into military service and get it over with, or to stay out as long as you can?

Percentage who responded:
* 19 Best to go in and get it over with
* 49 Best to stay out until you graduate, then go in and get it over with
  32 Best to stay out as long as you can

The distribution of responses to all these questions indicates that only a small minority would like to get into military service. Yet about twice that proportion—although still a minority—don't want to go in at all. The large majority of the students locate their feelings somewhere between these two extremes, but decidedly on the unfavorable side.

In order to arrive at a distribution which would take into account all seven questions asked, and which would not be subject to the arbitrary variations of responses to any single question, a scale of intensity of feeling was constructed which, when related to the willingness-to-serve scale itself, locates an invariant cutting point free from the bias of any particular question wording. According to this analysis the cutting point would fall between the 83rd and 88th percentiles. This means that, on the whole, 83 per cent of students can be described as having negative attitudes toward serving, with 12 per cent positive and 5 per cent indifferent. The shape of the curve itself, with its sharp cutting point, is clearly indicative of the definitiveness of student opinion about this particular issue. There can be little doubt that the topic has real meaning for them.[1]

---

[1] This method of determining an objective invariant cutting point along an attitude continuum is described in Chapter 7, "The Intensity Component in Attitude and Behavior Research," of Vol. IV, *Measurement and Prediction, Studies in Social Psychology in World War II* (Princeton University Press, 1950).

ATTITUDE TO SERVING IN THE ARMED FORCES: CONTENT SCORES
BY INTENSITY SCORES

Content rank

Intensity Rank	Neg. 1	2	3	4	5	6	7	8	9	Pos. 10	Total Freq.	Cum. %
High 4	155	97	39	12	4	1	2	1	2	21	334	100
3	61	79	82	60	31	7	2	8	5	14	349	85
2	26	62	97	95	67	40	19	6	10	23	445	69
1	12	33	66	119	131	94	45	26	23	33	582	49
Low 0	—	6	27	62	87	99	95	56	40	20	492	22
Total frequency	254	277	311	348	320	241	163	97	80	111	2202	
Cumulative per cent	11	24	38	54	68	79	86	90	94	100		
Midpoint of content percentiles	6	18	31	46	61	74	83	88	92	97		
Median of intensity percentiles	89	77	62	47	37	28	19	19	22	51		

ATTITUDE TO SERVING IN ARMED FORCES: CONTENT SCORES BY INTENSITY SCORES

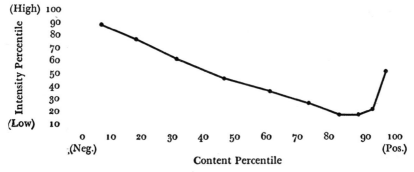

APPENDIX 19. PROPORTION OF STUDENTS WHO SAY CERTAIN GROUPS HAVE
THEIR OWN PERSONALITY *
(Eleven universities: Total 2975)

"This group has its own personality, something over and above the individual members in it." Does this statement above express the way you feel about any of the following groups? Check as many as apply.

	Percentage ** *who respond*
Your college	50
Your immediate family	46
Your church or religion	38
Your nationality	30
Your clique or a group of friends you go around with	25
Your fraternity	24
Your team (s)	16
Your club (s)	11
None	13

* See also Appendix 1 and Chapter 3 for additional analysis of responses to this question.

** The percentages should not be cumulated since each student could check more than one alternative.

APPENDIX 20. STRONG RELATIONSHIP BETWEEN RELIGIOUSNESS AND
ABSOLUTE APPROACH TO RELIGION
(Cornell 1952)

	Religiousness Scale				
	High				*Low*
	4	3	2	1	0
100% =	(133)	(266)	(427)	(467)	(278)
Score of Absolute Religious Belief		(Percentage in each scale-group)			
Orthodox 4	27	27	15	2	2
3	57	49	31	11	5
2	14	17	27	20	10
1	1	5	18	36	43
Unorthodox 0	1	3	9	32	41

APPENDIX 21. RESPONSES INDICATING ALIENATION AND ANOMIE

	Fisk (134)	No. Car. (414)	Texas (516)	Yale (297)	Wayne (519)	Harvard (453)	Cornell Men (655)	Cornell Women (245)	UCLA (467)	Dartmouth (365)	Michigan (488)	Wesleyan (277)
	(Percentage from each school giving indicated response)											
"There's little use in writing to public officials."												
Disagree	33	48	52	54	58	58	59	60	60	61	63	63
Agree	39	36	33	27	25	22	25	20	25	23	24	20
Uncertain	25	13	14	18	17	19	16	20	14	14	13	17
No answer	3	2	—	1	1	1	—	—	1	1	—	|
"It seems almost everything these days is a racket."												
Disagree	31	58	59	70	62	75	70	69	63	69	72	78
Agree	49	33	33	24	29	15	20	19	25	21	21	14
Uncertain	16	7	7	6	9	10	10	13	11	9	7	7
No answer	4	2	—	—	1	|	—	|	1	1	—	|
"Often when I'm with people I feel lonely."												
Disagree	78	81	83	81	84	78	86	82	86	87	85	88
Agree	15	13	12	14	12	15	9	9	9	7	9	6
Uncertain	3	4	5	5	3	6	5	9	4	5	6	6
No answer	4	2	—	|	1	1	|	|	1	1	—	|
"Since life is so short we might as well eat, drink, and be merry."												
Disagree	83	84	85	87	86	88	87	89	85	84	91	91
Agree	7	8	10	6	7	6	7	5	8	7	6	5
Uncertain	7	5	5	6	5	5	6	6	6	8	3	3
No answer	3	3	—	1	2	1	|	|	1	1	—	|
These days I often find myself giving up hope of amounting to anything (asked only at Cornell in 1952).												
Disagree							91	85				
Agree							4	10				
Uncertain							5	5				
No one is going to care much what happens to you when you get right down to it (asked only at Cornell in 1952).												
Disagree							64	60				
Agree							28	34				
Uncertain							8	6				

APPENDIX 22. NO RELATION BETWEEN CONFESSED CHEATING ON EXAMINA-
TIONS AND RELIGIOUSNESS OR BELIEF THAT ONE HAS AN ADEQUATE
GUIDE TO CONDUCT

(Eleven universities)

	Have you ever cheated or used crib notes on an examination . . . ?			
	No, Never	*Yes, Once* *	*Yes, More Than Once*	*Total*
Religiousness Scale	(Percentage** in each scale group)			
High 4	63	16	21	(297)
3	63	16	21	(639)
2	62	16	22	(935)
1	65	14	21	(679)
Low 0	63	14	23	(425)
Do you now feel that your present faith or personal philosophy is an adequate guide to conduct?	(Percentage† responding)			
Yes	63	15	22	(1769)
Don't know	60	18	22	(481)
No	63	14	23	(688)

* Includes 37 cases who admitted cheating but did not specify frequency.
** Percentages must be added horizontally.
† Omits 37 cases who gave no answer on conduct question.

APPENDIX 23. STUDENTS FROM POORER HOMES ARE MORE LIKELY TO
SCORE HIGH ON RELIGIOUSNESS SCALE

		Father's Annual Income			
(Eleven Universities)	*Under* *$5,000*	*$5,000-* *7,499*	*$7,500-* *9,999*	*$10,000-* *19,999*	*$20,000* *or More*
Total =	(1066)	(620)	(418)	(417)	(327)
Religiousness scale		(Percentage* in each position on Religiousness Scale)			
High 4	12	12	9	6	6
3	23	22	23	17	18
2	30	30	33	34	30
1	22	22	20	27	26
Low 0	13	13	15	15	19

Cornell 1952

If I found the person I was engaged to had had previous sex relations, I would break the engagement.	(Percentage** who agree or are uncertain)				
Men	37	27	34	26	22
Women	27	26	16	23	11

How often do you drink spirits?	(Percentage who say "never")				
Men	22	17	12	8	5
Women	22	14	13	7	4

* Omits 127 cases who did not provide information on father's income.
** The bases on which these per cents have been computed are:

Men	319	224	205	208	150
Women	82	96	89	84	45

Omitted are 35 men and 24 women who didn't know father's income or gave no answer.

APPENDIX 24. ANALYSES BASED ON THE CORNELL VALUES STUDY DATA

Blau, Peter M. "Orientation of College Students Toward International Relations," *American Journal of Sociology,* November 1953.

Fink, Raymond. "Some Social Psychological Factors in Stability or Response in Attitude Surveys." Ph.D. thesis on file at Cornell University. September 1956.

Goldsen, Rose K., with the assistance of Jessie L. Cohen. Report on the Cornell Student Body. June 1951. Social Science Research Center, Cornell University. Mimeographed.

Jacobs, Philip E. *Changing Values in College.* Harpers, 1958. (This book has drawn much of its primary material from the data of the Cornell Values Study.)

Miller, Norman. "Social Class and Value Differences Among American College Students." Ph.D. thesis on file at Columbia University. 1958.

Ram, Vangala J. "The Value Approach: A Framework for the Comparative Analysis of Cultures. Ph.D. thesis on file at Cornell University, June 1957.

Rosenberg, Morris. "Faith in People and Success Orientation," in *The Language of Social Research,* edited by Paul F. Lazarsfeld and Morris Rosenberg. The Free Press, Glencoe, Ill., 1955, pp. 158-161.

Rosenberg, Morris. "Psychological Depression and Educational Attitudes," *Student Medicine,* 5, 1, October 1956, pp. 5-14.

Rosenberg, Morris, with Edward A. Suchman and Rose K. Goldsen. *Occupations and Values.* Free Press, 1958.

Suchman, Edward A., Robin M. Williams, Jr., and Rose K. Goldsen. Student to Soldier. Social Science Research Center, Cornell University, August, 1952. Mimeographed.

Suchman, Edward A., Rose K. Goldsen and Robin M. Williams, Jr. "Attitudes Toward the Korean War," *The Public Opinion Quarterly,* 17, 2, September 1953, pp. 171-184.

Suchman, Edward A. "The Values of American College Students," in *Long Range Planning for Education,* of the American Council on Education, Washington, D. C., 1958, pp. 110-120.

Taietz, Philip, Bert Ellenbogen, and Charles E. Ramsey. "Occupational Choice—Some Implications for Recruitment of Social Workers," *Social Work,* April 1958, pp. 44-48.

Unger, Sanford. "The Sociology of Career-Oriented Women: in Exploratory Study." M.A. thesis on file at Cornell University, February 1955.

Williams, Robin M., Jr., Edward A. Suchman and Rose K. Goldsen. "Reactions of College Students to Manpower Policies and the Military Service Prospect," *The Educational Record,* April 1953, pp. 101-107.

Index

233

social class; *see* socio-economic status
social status, as occupational value, 27-28, 30-38, 43-44, 50, 56, 211, 212
social welfare, 43, 44
socio-economic factors and religious belief, 229
socio-economic status
  and attitude to economic issues, 113-115
  and drinking, 229
  and economic conservatism, 113-116
  and educational values, 14-16
  and fraternities, 69-74, 215
  and new middle class, 38-39
  and political philosophy, 113-116, 220
  and premarital sex, 229
Southern universities, 3, 159
Srole, Leo, 170n.
Stanton, F., 211
State Universities, 14
Stouffer, Samuel A., 181n., 222n.
success
  and educational values, 19-21, 208, 209
  as male role, 171
  as occupational value, 24, 211, 212
Suchman, Edward A., 140n., 222n., 223n.
Syracuse University students, 160

Tawney, R. H., 149, 149n.
Texas, University of, [introduction], 30, 84, 99, 123, 159, 204, 208, 210, 212, 216, 218, 227
Thielens, Wagner, 198n.

UCLA, [introduction], 65, 98, 112, 122, 123, 159, 204, 208, 210, 212, 216, 218, 227

values
  concept of, [introduction]
  role of university, 2-16
  selective function of, 13-14
  as standards, 21-22
  see also economic beliefs; educational values; goal values; occupational values; political philosophy; religiousness; reward values
voting; *see also* political party preference
  father's vote, 101
  qualifications for, 131, 137

Waller, Willard, 67n.
war
  disenchantment with measures to prevent war, 144-148
  and faith-in-human-nature, 150-152
  measures to prevent, 141-145, 147
  morality of, 140
  necessity for, 141
  opposition to, 140-152, 148
  free enterprise system a means to prevent, 147
Wayne University, [introduction], 60, 65, 83, 99, 112, 123, 204, 208, 210, 212, 216, 218, 227
Welfare state, 106-108, 110, 111, 128
Wesleyan University, [introduction], 6, 60, 64, 65, 84, 99, 123, 204, 208, 210, 212, 216, 218, 227
West, Patricia Salter, 34n.
Williams, Robin M., Jr., 223n.
work; *see* career
women and careers, 46-49
women's occupations, 49-52, 214

Yale University, [introduction], 6, 60, 65, 84, 99, 204, 208, 210, 212, 216, 218, 220, 227
  college system at, 76, 99, 159

Zeisel, Hans, 28n.

c.1.